THE LANGUAGE OF GOD
Hearing Heaven's Voice and Discerning the Counterfeit

Crystal Thomas

"My sheep hear My voice, and I know them, and they follow Me."
John 10:27 (NKJV)

Copyright Page

Copyright © 2025 by **Crystal Thomas**
All rights reserved.
No part of this publication may be reproduced, stored in a retrieval system, or transmitted in any form or by any means—electronic, mechanical, photocopying, recording, or otherwise—without prior written permission of the author, except for brief quotations used in reviews or articles.
All Scripture quotations are taken from the **New King James Version® (NKJV).**
Copyright © 1982 by Thomas Nelson.
Used by permission. All rights reserved.
Edited and formatted with professional assistance.
Cover design by Crystal Thomas
ISBN: 979-8-218-87037-9
Printed in the United States of America
First Edition

Dedication

To my husband, **Sean**,
and my two sons, **Garrett** and **Cameron**,
you are my greatest gifts on this side of Heaven.
Thank you for the countless hours you've spent listening
as I shared the deep revelations of God,
and for being truly captivated by every discovery along the way.

And above all, to **Jesus Christ**,
the One who still speaks,
may every word written here echo Your heart and glorify Your name.

Table Of Contents

Chapter 1: Dreams & Visions 1

Chapter 2: Spiritual Senses 31

Chapter 3: Discernment 59

Chapter 4: Signs and Wonders 75

*Appendix A: Signs and Wonders 93

Chapter 5: The Prophetic 101

*Appendix B: Understanding Prophetic Function 137

Chapter 6: Imagination 141

Chapter 7: Angels 169

*Appendix C: Angelic Encounters 189

Chapter 8: The Bride of Christ 195

Chapter 9: Witchcraft 211

Chapter 10: Exposing the New Age Movement 245

*Appendix D: Modern Expressions of Witchcraft 271

Chapter 11: Deliverance 281

Chapter 12: Study 327

About the Author 347

INTRODUCTION

Every believer carries within them the very DNA of Heaven. We were created to be conduits of God's presence: vessels through which His power, wisdom, and voice flow into the earth. We were never meant to study Him from a distance, but to walk as living expressions of His divine language.

When I first began preparing to teach on this topic, the Holy Spirit drew my attention back to the beginning of all things.

"Then God said, 'Let there be light'; and there was light."
Genesis 1:3 (NKJV)

Those words did not merely illuminate creation; they released the entire frequency of existence. God spoke, and energy, power, and light burst forth in perfect harmony. Every atom, every vibration, every living cell still carries the echo of that command: *"Let there be light."*

If all creation came into being through His words, then humanity—made in His image—was also spoken into existence by that same divine, creative language. We are not only recipients of God's speech; we are part of His language. Within us is a divine code, a living message written by the Creator Himself. This is why so many hearts instinctively search the supernatural for truth, because deep within, our spirit remembers the voice that first spoke us into being. Yet the very thing the world is searching for is not found in energy, mysticism, or hidden knowledge, but in God Himself, the true Source of all revelation and reality.

Our DNA is not random. It is the alphabet of Heaven inscribed into flesh. Just as we form words with letters, our cells form life with sequences of nucleotides: letters, words, sentences, and chapters written by the Author of existence. Scientists can map and study this genetic code, yet even they stand in awe of its design. We are walking testimonies that God's Word is still alive and active.

Heaven's Ladder Within

When Jacob dreamed of a ladder reaching from Earth to Heaven with angels ascending and descending (Genesis 28), he was seeing a spiritual reality that mirrors what God designed within us. The double helix of our DNA resembles that very ladder: a bridge of divine communication. One strand ascends; one descends; messages flow continually between realms. Just as angels carry heavenly instruction, the very molecules of life within us carry the command of God when we are submitted to his Lordship.

You were created to receive, perceive, and release His revelation. Through the indwelling Holy Spirit, you have access to the same communication Jacob witnessed, truth flowing between Heaven and earth, unseen yet alive within you.

"We do not look at the things which are seen, but at the things which are unseen. For the things which are seen are temporary, but the things which are unseen are eternal."
2 Corinthians 4:18 (NKJV)

There are two realms, the temporal and the eternal, and you were designed to function in both. You are a spirit being who possesses a soul and lives in a physical body. Though your feet walk the earth, your spirit belongs to another Kingdom. The more we understand the divine language written within us, the more we become bridges between realms—vessels through whom Heaven speaks, moves, and makes itself known on the earth.

The Invitation

This book is an invitation to awaken to that reality. To rediscover the language of Heaven woven into your being. To learn the ways God still speaks—through dreams and visions, through your spiritual senses, through discernment and prophecy—and to recognize how the enemy tries to counterfeit those same expressions.

As you read, may your spiritual senses sharpen, your understanding deepen, and your heart be set ablaze with wonder. May you see that the language of God is not distant—it is alive within you. And may your life become a continual conversation between Heaven and earth.

PART I
THE WAYS GOD SPEAKS
Revelation, Encounter, and Awakening

God has always desired communion with His creation. From the beginning, His voice shaped the world and still calls to the hearts of His people. He speaks through dreams and visions, through the whisper of the Spirit, through the written Word, and through the many subtle movements of His presence. This section explores the divine language of Heaven— how God communicates, how we perceive it, and how to respond with faith and purity. May your spirit be awakened to hear the sound of His voice, and may each chapter draw you closer to the One who still speaks.

- Chapter 1:　Dreams & Visions
- Chapter 2:　Supernatural Senses
- Chapter 3:　Discernment
- Chapter 4:　Signs & Wonders

Chapter 1: Dreams & Visions

Hearing the Voice of God in the Night and Seeing with the Eyes of the Spirit

---

THE LANGUAGE OF THE SPIRIT IN THE LAST DAYS

God has never been silent toward His people. From the moment He breathed life into Adam, His desire has been communication, heart to heart, spirit to spirit. Every movement of God throughout history begins with a word. When He created, He spoke. When He redeemed, He revealed. When He sent His Son, He called Him *the Word made flesh.* God's nature is to speak; His people's calling is to listen.

In every generation, God has chosen unique ways to express His voice. To Noah, He spoke through direct command; to Moses, face to face; to the prophets, in visions and symbols; and to Joseph, in dreams. Through Jesus, God's voice was embodied, and through the Holy Spirit, that same voice continues to echo within His people today. The same Spirit who hovered over the waters in Genesis now hovers over hearts, still speaking, still guiding, still revealing the mysteries of Heaven.

> *"And it shall come to pass in the last days, says God, that I will pour out My Spirit on all flesh; your sons and your daughters shall prophesy, your young men shall see visions, your old men shall dream dreams."*
> ***Acts 2:17 (NKJV)***

This was not poetic exaggeration; it was a prophetic announcement. The age of the Spirit, the era we now live in, would be marked by divine communication poured out on *all flesh.* God's voice would no longer be reserved for prophets, priests, or kings. Sons and daughters, young and old, men and women alike, would all become carriers of revelation.

Dreams and visions are not fringe experiences or mystical side effects; they are evidence that the Holy Spirit is actively working in the earth. To reject them is to close the door on one of God's most intimate languages.

In these final days, the voice of God is not diminishing; it is multiplying. Yet many believers remain spiritually deaf because they are listening on the wrong frequency. Like Nicodemus, they approach divine truth through natural reasoning and miss the spiritual reality right before them.

"Nicodemus said to Him, 'How can a man be born when he is old? Can he enter a second time into his mother's womb and be born?"
John 3:4 (NKJV)

Nicodemus had studied Scripture all his life, yet when the Word Himself stood before him, he could not comprehend. Jesus revealed the mystery: "Unless one is born of water and the Spirit, he cannot enter the kingdom of God." The kingdom operates by the Spirit, not the flesh. In the same way, the language of Heaven must be discerned spiritually.

If God's voice could be compared to radio waves, He is transmitting on a spiritual frequency, but many believers are still tuned to the natural band. The signal is there, but the receiver is out of sync. Faith becomes the antenna that connects the believer to that unseen realm. The call to live by faith is, in essence, the call to listen beyond the noise of earth, to tune into the whispers of Heaven.

When the Holy Spirit speaks, He does so through multiple expressions: Scripture, the inward witness, prophetic words, impressions, circumstances, and, yes, dreams and visions. These manifestations are not new methods but ancient pathways. God spoke to Pharaoh in a dream. He appeared to Solomon in a dream. He guided Joseph, the earthly father of Jesus, through dreams. He unveiled the book of Revelation to John through visions. Throughout history, dreams and visions have served as divine compasses, directing the hearts of men and women toward their appointed purpose.

To understand the voice of God in this hour, we must learn His language again. We must not reduce His speech to *only* the pages of a sermon or a Sunday encounter. The Holy Spirit is speaking daily, even nightly, breathing revelation into the lives of those willing to listen. Scripture has always taught that God speaks in the night seasons, and now modern science is simply catching up. Neuroscientists have discovered that the brain continues to process information, emotions, and even external stimuli during sleep, confirming what the Bible revealed thousands of years ago: that dreams are a meaningful interface between the natural and the spiritual, between our waking thoughts and the deeper places of the heart.

We are living in a prophetic generation, one called not merely to quote what God once said, but to hear what He is saying *now*. His Spirit still moves, His voice still echoes, and His people must again become fluent in the language of the Spirit.

DREAMS: THE NIGHT PARABLES OF GOD

When the noise of the day fades and the body grows still, the soul becomes a canvas for God's brushstrokes. In the hidden hours of the night, when the mind ceases its striving and the heart slips into rest, Heaven often chooses that silence to speak. Dreams are one of the most personal and poetic ways God communicates with His children. They are parables of the night, pictures, symbols, and narratives crafted by the Spirit to reveal the unseen.

From the earliest pages of Scripture, God has spoken through dreams. He warned Abimelech of sin, established Jacob's covenant, gave Joseph destiny, instructed Solomon, and protected the infant Jesus. God's nature has not changed; His voice is still creative, intimate, and intentional. Job declared:

"For God may speak in one way, or in another,
Yet man does not perceive it.
In a dream, in a vision of the night,
When deep sleep falls upon men,
While slumbering on their beds,

Then He opens the ears of men,
And seals their instruction."
Job 33:14–16 (NKJV)

Job understood something profound: God speaks, but we often fail to perceive. He chooses the night because that is when our defenses are down and our spirits are most receptive. Dreams bypass the filters of logic and reason. They pierce directly into the heart, sealing divine instruction that our waking minds might resist.

Dreams carry messages unique to each person. They can teach, warn, correct, comfort, or call us to intercession. They can reveal hidden fears or illuminate hidden faith. They can confirm a word, expose a lie, or unlock a new dimension of calling. Because dreams are symbolic, they invite us into a relationship with God to seek interpretation. They require humility, hunger, and discernment.

Jesus often taught in parables for the same reason God still gives dreams: to reveal truth to those who will seek Him, and to conceal it from those content with surface understanding. A parable demands pursuit. It requires leaning in to listen. Dreams do the same; they invite conversation, not mere observation.

"These things we also speak, not in words which man's wisdom teaches but which the Holy Spirit teaches, comparing spiritual things with spiritual."
1 Corinthians 2:13 (NKJV)

"And the disciples came and said to Him, 'Why do You speak to them in parables?'
He answered and said to them, 'Because it has been given to you to know the mysteries of the kingdom of heaven, but to them it has not been given... Therefore I speak to them in parables, because seeing they do not see, and hearing they do not hear, nor do they understand.'"
Matthew 13:10–13 (NKJV)

Spiritual revelation cannot be interpreted by natural intellect. Dreams operate in the same realm as prophecy; they originate from the Spirit, not the mind. They contain heavenly wisdom, wrapped in mystery, waiting to be discerned by those who walk with the Interpreter Himself.

There is also something deeply relational about the way God uses dreams. They are not impersonal decrees but intimate exchanges. The Creator of galaxies stoops low to whisper to His beloved in the stillness of the night. He speaks in pictures because images bypass arguments. They slip past our reasoning and root directly into our spirit. A dream can shift a destiny more powerfully than a thousand words could ever explain.

Throughout Scripture, God often used dreams to reveal His covenant plans long before they were fulfilled. Joseph dreamed of leadership long before he saw a throne. Jacob saw angels ascending and descending long before he returned to his homeland. The Magi were warned in a dream before they knew the danger of Herod's plan. Every dream carried divine timing. It arrived at the intersection of human vulnerability and divine sovereignty.

Dreams also expose what words conceal. They are mirrors of the soul, revealing what lies buried beneath daily busyness. Sometimes a dream confronts us with the truth about our heart, resentment we haven't faced, fear we've ignored, or faith we've let grow cold. When interpreted through the lens of the Holy Spirit, even these confronting dreams become gifts. They lead us to repentance and renewal.

God's Word and His Spirit always work together. A dream from God will never contradict Scripture, but it will often apply Scripture to one's personal life. For instance, the Word says, "Fear not." But in a dream, God might show you standing before a storm, handing Him your umbrella —a vivid picture of surrendering fear for trust. It's the same truth, just wrapped in personal imagery. This is what makes dreams so powerful: they take timeless truth and make it intimate.

Dreams are also part of how God fulfills His promise to pour out His Spirit on all flesh. They democratize the prophetic. You do not have to be a prophet to receive a dream from God. Young or old, new believer or seasoned minister, God speaks to anyone who will listen. His voice is not bound by education, position, or platform; it is bound only by relationship.

Sometimes God speaks through a series of dreams, layering revelation piece by piece. This progressive unfolding teaches us dependence. It trains us to listen repeatedly rather than rely on a single encounter. Like puzzle pieces, each dream fits with another, forming a larger picture of God's plan.

"For we know in part and we prophesy in part."
1 Corinthians 13:9 (NKJV)

Dreams remind us that revelation is progressive, not instantaneous. God gives us fragments so that we remain close enough to hear the rest. The wise believer learns to treasure these fragments, knowing that one night's dream may hold tomorrow's answer.

There is also a holy mystery in how dreams intersect both the natural and the supernatural. The human brain may process symbols, but the spirit perceives substance. The mind might forget the details, but the heart remembers the message. The Spirit of God can use the language of our memories, emotions, and imagination to paint divine truth. It is not the dream itself that carries power; it is the breath of God within it.

Every believer should approach dreams with reverence, not fear or fascination. They are sacred invitations, not curiosity. The moment we awaken from one, we should ask, *"Lord, what are You saying to me?"* That posture turns ordinary sleep into a prophetic encounter.

When received rightly, dreams build intimacy. When stewarded wisely, they build destiny. When interpreted by the Spirit, they build faith. They are God's night language, His whispers written in imagery across the canvas of our rest.

THE PURPOSE AND POWER OF DREAMS

Every dream has a purpose. Nothing Heaven does is random, and no word that proceeds from God's mouth returns void. When the Lord visits a believer in the night, it is not to entertain or mystify—it is to instruct, reveal, and prepare. Every divine dream carries intention.

Some dreams are revelatory, bringing insight into something we could never have known on our own. Others are corrective, confronting attitudes or actions that grieve the Spirit. Some are prophetic, revealing events yet to come, while others are confirmational, reaffirming a word God has already spoken through Scripture or prophecy. Still others are intercessory, awakening us in the night to pray for someone or something in danger. In every case, dreams are purposeful; they come to build, to warn, to heal, and to align.

Job declared that God "opens the ears of men and seals their instruction" while they sleep (Job 33:16). That means the instruction of Heaven is sometimes sealed not in a sermon, but in a symbol, written by the Spirit upon the heart while the mind rests.

A dream may arrive gentle as a whisper or vivid as a storm. It may seem confusing at first glance, but when interpreted by the Holy Spirit, it becomes a treasure chest of truth. God hides His wisdom in imagery not to frustrate us, but to invite us closer. He wants conversation, not just curiosity. Curiosity, alone, wants to *know about* God; conversation wants to *know God Himself.* He gives a revelation that provokes a relationship.

"Call to Me, and I will answer you, and show you great and mighty things, which you do not know."
Jeremiah 33:3 (NKJV)

Dreams that Build Faith

Dreams often come to strengthen faith. When our natural eyes can no longer see the promise, the Spirit paints it upon the canvas of the heart. Gideon, trembling in insecurity, was strengthened through a dream he overheard in the enemy's camp (Judges 7:13–15). God could have sent an angel to declare victory, but instead, He allowed Gideon to overhear a dream. It was God's way of saying, *"I am already working behind the scenes."*

Dreams have a way of enlarging faith because they bypass unbelief. A believer may doubt with the mind, but in a dream, the spirit recognizes truth instantly. Many have testified to waking from a God-given dream with renewed courage, peace, or conviction, emotions that could not have been produced by human willpower alone. When God speaks in a dream, His word carries the same creative power as when He said, "Let there be light." It plants faith where fear once lived.

Dreams that Warn and Protect

God also uses dreams to warn and protect. Before judgment or danger, He often gives forewarning to those who will listen. In Scripture, God warned Pharaoh through dreams about the coming famine. He warned Joseph, Mary's husband, to flee to Egypt to protect Jesus. He warned the Magi not to return to Herod.

If those dreams had been ignored, history would have unfolded very differently.

"Then, being divinely warned in a dream that they should not return to Herod, they departed for their own country another way."
Matthew 2:12 (NKJV)

"Now when they had departed, behold, an angel of the Lord appeared to Joseph in a dream, saying, 'Arise, take the young Child and His mother, flee to Egypt, and stay there until I bring you word; for Herod will seek the young Child to destroy Him.'"
Matthew 2:13 (NKJV)

Dreams can preserve lives, marriages, ministries, and nations. They are Heaven's early warning system. The Holy Spirit often reveals the enemy's plan before it manifests so that intercession can dismantle it. What may appear to be a strange or troubling dream is sometimes God sounding an alarm for prayer. When we wake unsettled, our first response should not be fear but discernment: *"Lord, what are You showing me?"*

Dreams that Reveal the Heart

Dreams also serve as mirrors of the soul. They can expose what lies hidden beneath layers of busyness or denial. A believer may say, "I've forgiven," but dream of the offense repeatedly until they surrender it at the cross. The Spirit uses dreams to surface unhealed wounds or unresolved fears so that He can bring healing. This is why not every disturbing dream is demonic; some are diagnostic. They reveal what the Great Physician desires to heal.

"For the word of God is living and powerful... and is a discerner of the thoughts and intents of the heart."
Hebrews 4:12 (NKJV)

The Word divides soul from spirit, and dreams often act as its scalpel. Through them, God distinguishes what is from the flesh and what is from His Spirit. They invite us into honest self-examination under the light of His love.

Dreams that Direct and Confirm

In moments of confusion or decision-making, dreams can serve as a compass. They point toward obedience. When Joseph of Nazareth doubted what to do about Mary's pregnancy, the Lord gave direction in a dream: "Do not be afraid to take to you Mary your wife" (Matthew 1:20). What appeared scandalous by sight was sacred by revelation.

Dreams do not replace Scripture, but they apply it personally. The Word says, *"Trust in the Lord with all your heart, and lean not on your own understanding."* Dreams give us pictures of what trusting looks like in our particular story. A dream might show a person at a crossroads, choosing between two paths—one narrow, one wide. That image, interpreted through Scripture, becomes divine direction.

Dreams can also confirm what God has already spoken. When the Spirit is leading you into a new season or decision, He may confirm it repeatedly through the Word, prophecy, and even dreams. This is not a coincidence; it is divine orchestration. God is establishing His word "by the mouth of two or three witnesses."

Dreams that Call to Intercession

Some dreams come not for you, but for others. God may show you a person, city, or situation that needs prayer. These dreams are invitations to partner with Heaven in intercession. When you awaken burdened from a dream, resist the temptation to overanalyze. Instead, take it immediately to prayer. Many believers have testified to waking in the night with a sense of urgency to pray, only to discover that God protected someone or intervened in a crisis at that very moment.

The Lord still searches for those willing to stand in the gap. Sometimes, His search reaches into your sleep.

"So I sought for a man among them who would make a wall, and stand in the gap before Me on behalf of the land."
Ezekiel 22:30 (NKJV)

When God finds such a person, He trusts them with secrets. To dream is to be entrusted with divine intelligence. What you see is not always for public declaration, it is often for private intercession.

Dreams that Unlock Destiny

Perhaps the most powerful function of dreams is their ability to align us with destiny. Dreams are not merely reflections of who we are, but revelations of who we are becoming. When Joseph dreamed as a young man, he saw sheaves bowing and stars giving homage. The imagery was symbolic, but the message was prophetic: God was revealing Joseph's future authority and calling. The dream preceded the journey; it was both promise and preparation.

Joseph's dream did not instantly elevate him; it sent him into a process. Dreams show us what will be, not necessarily what is. They give us glimpses of the destination so we can endure the detours. Between the dream and its fulfillment lies testing, misunderstanding, and time. But the dream remains a compass pointing toward destiny.

When God gives a dream, He provides the seed of the future. The wise believer treasures it, journals it, prays into it, and allows it to mature in the soil of obedience. The dream becomes an anchor of hope in seasons of delay.

Dreams are Heaven's classroom. They teach faith, humility, and discernment. They reveal God's care for the most minor details of our lives. They remind us that we are not alone, even while we sleep. And they testify to a truth that has never changed: the same God who spoke to Abraham, Jacob, and Joseph still speaks today. Dreams are not rare occurrences for the few; they are love letters for the listening.

DISCERNING THE SOURCE

Not every dream or vision is divine. The spirit world, much like the natural world, is full of activity and sound. Different voices speak; different forces seek attention. Just as there are heavenly frequencies that release truth, there are also counterfeit ones that distort it. Discernment, therefore, becomes the believer's safeguard and compass.

The apostle John warned the early Church:

"Beloved, do not believe every spirit, but test the spirits, whether they are of God; because many false prophets have gone out into the world."
1 John 4:1 (NKJV)

Testing the spirit behind a dream or vision is not skepticism; it is obedience. God never calls His people to blind acceptance but to spiritual discernment. God doesn't ask us to turn off our minds or accept things without question. Faith in scripture is not blind; the Spirit of Truth illuminates it. He calls us to see and trust His will spiritually. When Paul says we *"walk by faith, not by sight,"* he isn't saying we walk in ignorance. He means we walk by spiritual perception, not merely natural observation. Dreams and visions, like prophecy, must be weighed, examined, and measured by the Word and the witness of the Holy Spirit. Discernment of dreams and visions gives faith its focus.

Every dream and vision originates from one of three primary sources: the *Spirit of God*, the *human soul*, or the *kingdom of darkness*. Understanding these three streams equips us to discern the origin of what we see and hear.

1. Heavenly Revelation – The Voice of the Spirit

Dreams and visions from God carry a purity that the soul cannot manufacture. They bear the signature of peace, even when the message is sobering. They align perfectly with Scripture and reveal the character of Jesus Christ. Their purpose is always redemptive, to draw the heart nearer to God, to bring conviction without condemnation, to instruct without fear.

A heavenly dream will never flatter the flesh or contradict the Word. It may correct you, warn you, or challenge your perspective, but it will never lead you into rebellion or confusion. When interpreted rightly, it brings clarity and strength.

For example, when Joseph dreamed of his future leadership, the dream did not make him proud; it prepared him. Though his brothers misjudged him, the dream anchored him through betrayal, prison, and delay. True revelation stabilizes you in the storm; it does not inflate you in success.

Heavenly visions, likewise, manifest God's presence tangibly. They may leave you trembling, weeping, or filled with awe. Ezekiel fell on his face; Isaiah cried, "Woe is me, for I am undone"; John fell as though dead. These reactions are not fear of darkness, but reverence before holiness. Divine revelation produces humility.

"The testimony of Jesus is the spirit of prophecy."
Revelation 19:10 (NKJV)

Every authentic dream or vision ultimately points back to Jesus. If it magnifies man, self, or fear, it has missed its purpose. But if it magnifies Christ and aligns with His Word, it bears Heaven's seal.

2. The Human Soul – The Voice Within

Some dreams come not from Heaven or hell, but from within us. These are *soulish* dreams, reflections of our emotions, thoughts, or physical state. They are not inherently sinful, but they are natural rather than supernatural.

A weary mind may replay the day's anxieties in sleep. A person burdened by fear may dream of being chased or trapped. Someone deeply in love might dream of the person they're thinking about. These dreams are mirrors, not messages. They reveal what the heart is processing.

Ecclesiastes gives a simple but profound insight:
"For a dream comes through much activity."
Ecclesiastes 5:3 (NKJV)

In other words, the busyness of the mind can produce dreams just as surely as the breath of God can. Distinguishing between the two requires sensitivity to the Spirit.

Soulish dreams often fade quickly. They lack the lingering presence or conviction that accompanies divine revelation. When you awaken from a God-given dream, there is weight upon your spirit—peace, awe, conviction, or clarity. When you awaken from a soulish dream, there is often nothing but confusion or disinterest.

Yet even soulish dreams can be used by the Lord. They reveal the state of our inner life. They show what needs surrender, healing, or rest. When you notice recurring patterns in dreams that are emotional or anxious, it can be the Spirit showing you where your heart is weary. These dreams can act as mirrors, revealing what the Spirit desires to restore.

3. The Kingdom of Darkness – The Counterfeit Voice

The enemy also seeks to influence the realm of dreams and visions. Satan cannot create, but he can counterfeit. His goal is deception, to twist the supernatural and corrupt discernment. He will mix truth with distortion, fear with fascination, in hopes of luring the believer away from intimacy with God and into dependence on experiences.

Demonic dreams often carry specific marks. They produce fear, panic, or hopelessness. They may accuse, condemn, or pervert. They may replay trauma to reopen old wounds, or plant lies about God's nature. They aim to erode peace, not to bring revelation.

Jesus said of the devil:

> "He was a murderer from the beginning, and does not stand in the truth, because there is no truth in him. When he speaks a lie, he speaks from his own resources, for he is a liar and the father of it."
> ***John 8:44 (NKJV)***

Lies are his language. In dreams, he often imitates light but subtly twists its message. He may use Scripture out of context, just as he did with Jesus in the wilderness. The believer's defense is the same as the Master's: the written Word. When you measure every dream and vision by Scripture, deception is disarmed.

Some demonic dreams are meant to provoke fear because fear empowers the enemy the way faith empowers God. If you awaken from a nightmare or a dream of darkness, do not panic; pray. Speak the name of Jesus aloud. Renounce the spirit of fear and replace it with truth. Remember: the enemy can roar, but he cannot rule in your life unless you give him authority to do so. Your authority in Christ extends even to the realm of dreams.

Distinguishing the Source

Discerning which stream a dream or vision flows from requires both Word and Spirit. The Bible provides the plumb line of truth; the Holy Spirit provides the witness of peace. A simple test is this: *What fruit does it produce?*

- **Heavenly revelation** produces *peace, awe, humility, direction,* and *faith.*
- **Soulish dreams** produce *reflection,* often showing what is already in your heart.
- **Demonic dreams** produce *fear, shame, confusion,* or *spiritual heaviness.*

Jesus said,

> *"You will know them by their fruits."*
> ***Matthew 7:16 (NKJV)***

Revelation is the same; the source determines the fruit.

Some believers have opened doors to demonic influence unknowingly through occult practices, unforgiveness, fear, or exposure to darkness. When these doors are opened, the enemy can project counterfeit dreams. But the moment those doors are closed through repentance and the cleansing blood of Jesus, the atmosphere of the soul shifts. Dreams become clear again. Peace returns.

Purity of heart sharpens perception. A cluttered mind distorts it. This is why Jesus said,

"Blessed are the pure in heart, for they shall see God."
Matthew 5:8 (NKJV)

Purity does not earn revelation; it makes room for it.

The Spirit of truth longs to teach His people how to discern. He does not want us living afraid of deception; He wants us living anchored in discernment. The safest place to receive revelation is in intimacy with the Word and the presence of Jesus.

Guarding the Gates

The human mind has gates through which we see, hear, and meditate upon. What enters those gates influences the landscape of our dreams. When our eyes are fixed on worldly images, violence, or impurity, the soul becomes clouded, and spiritual sight dulls. But when our hearts are filled with worship, gratitude, and the Word, the atmosphere of our inner life becomes hospitable to Heaven's voice.

Guarding your gates is not about legalism; it's about stewardship. If you want God to trust you with divine communication, create an environment that honors His presence. The Spirit of God is gentle; He dwells where He is desired.

Psalm 16:7 declares,

"I will bless the Lord who has given me counsel;
My heart also instructs me in the night seasons."

When the Lord becomes the focus of your days, your nights will echo His counsel.

Discernment, then, is not suspicion; it is sensitivity to truth. It is the skill of recognizing Heaven's voice amid the noise of competing signals. When you train your spirit to test what you hear and see, dreams and visions become less confusing and more confirming. You will begin to notice the fragrance of God's presence in the revelation that comes from Him, and the staleness of anything that does not.

True discernment does not make you fearful of the supernatural; it makes you confident in Christ. The Holy Spirit does not silence revelation; He sanctifies it.

VISIONS: SEEING WITH THE EYES OF THE SPIRIT

If dreams are the language of the night, visions are the language of awakened sight.
A vision is when God opens the eyes of the heart to perceive what the natural eye cannot see. It may appear in the mind's eye, like a living picture, or it may unfold before the physical eyes in open manifestation. Both carry the same purpose: to reveal, to instruct, and to draw the believer deeper into the reality of Heaven.

When Paul prayed for the Ephesian Church, his request was not merely that they would know doctrine, but that they would see.

"The eyes of your understanding being enlightened; that you may know what is the hope of His calling, what are the riches of the glory of His inheritance in the saints."
Ephesians 1:18 (NKJV)

The word "understanding" can be translated as "heart" or "spirit." Paul was praying that the eyes of their spirit would be opened. Spiritual sight is not a rare gift reserved for the few; it is a natural result of walking closely with the Holy Spirit. Every believer can grow in perceiving what God is doing and seeing from Heaven's perspective.

The Nature of Visions

Visions are divine pictures given to awaken spiritual understanding. They can occur in various ways, through the imagination, in deep prayer, during worship, or in moments of supernatural encounter. Some happen while the eyes are closed; others unfold before open eyes.

Scripture uses several Hebrew and Greek words for vision, each revealing a nuance of how God communicates. Daniel's book mentions multiple types: *chazown* (revelation or prophetic insight), *chezev* (a night vision), *mar'ah* (appearance or mirror image), and *mar'eh* (sight or manifestation). Each suggests that visions can range from inward perception to outward revelation.

Throughout history, men and women of God have experienced these varying degrees of vision:

- **Abraham** saw a vision of covenant when God showed him the stars and promised descendants beyond number (Genesis 15).
- **Isaiah** saw the Lord high and lifted, His robe filling the temple with glory (Isaiah 6).
- **Ezekiel** saw the likeness of God's glory and the wheels of His throne (Ezekiel 1).
- **Daniel** saw kingdoms rising and falling, the Ancient of Days enthroned, and the Son of Man receiving dominion (Daniel 7).
- **Peter** saw a sheet lowered from Heaven filled with unclean animals—a vision that broke centuries of religious division and opened the Gospel to the Gentiles (Acts 10).
- **John** saw the throne of Heaven, the Lamb, and the revelation of the end of days (Revelation 4–22).

Every one of these visions carried transformation. A true vision changes perspective; it never leaves a person the same. Isaiah's vision purified his lips. Ezekiel's vision commissioned his calling. Daniel's visions unveiled the times and seasons of nations. Peter's vision destroyed prejudice. John's visions preserved the Church through the ages.

The Purpose of Visions

Visions come to do what words alone cannot: to impart spiritual understanding through sight. Where dreams speak in story, visions speak in symbol and light. They translate revelation into imagery so that the spirit may grasp what the mind cannot yet articulate.

Visions often come to:

- **Reveal God's nature and glory.**
  Many Old Testament prophets were shown the majesty of God so that they might carry reverence into their ministry. A single glimpse of His holiness changes how one speaks, prays, and lives.
- **Unveil divine strategy.**
  God gives visions to show what He is about to do or how we are to cooperate. In Acts 16, Paul saw a man of Macedonia pleading, "Come over and help us." The vision redirected his entire mission.
- **Release encouragement and strength.**
  Visions can infuse courage in moments of despair. When Stephen was being stoned, he saw Jesus standing at the right hand of the Father (Acts 7:55). That vision turned martyrdom into victory.
- **Expose sin and warn of judgment.**
  The prophets often saw visions of God's displeasure with injustice or idolatry. Yet even these came from mercy, to call the people back before destruction came.
- **Teach spiritual truth.**
  Some visions are allegorical, designed to illustrate principles of the Kingdom. The vision of dry bones in Ezekiel 37 was not literal; it was a divine lesson about restoration and hope.

In every case, the goal is transformation. A true vision will always produce spiritual fruit: humility, repentance, worship, obedience, or greater faith.

How Visions Differ from Dreams

While dreams come during sleep, visions often occur in a state of wakefulness. A dream requires rest; a vision frequently requires focus. Yet they are intertwined; both are channels of revelation.

Dreams tend to be symbolic, sometimes mysterious; visions are usually clearer, carrying revelation with immediate impact.

A dream may plant a seed of direction, while a vision may ignite the fire to act. A dream might reveal what's coming; a vision might show what's happening now, or vice versa. Both are expressions of God's heart, designed to align His people with His purpose.

Avenues of Vision

Visions can occur through various spiritual avenues; each suited to how God has designed the individual. Scripture and experience reveal several patterns:

- **The Mind's Eye (Inner Vision):**
  This is the most common form. It occurs within the imagination as a vivid mental picture or unfolding scene. The Spirit impresses images upon the heart much like Jesus painted word pictures through parables. Don't dismiss these as "just imagination"—the sanctified imagination is one of the Spirit's primary canvases.

- **Open Visions:**
  These are rare but powerful moments when a person sees a scene with their physical eyes while fully awake. Peter's vision in Acts 10 or John's in Revelation 1 are examples. These moments carry strong purpose—usually confirmation, commissioning, or revelation of divine authority. Open visions are not "more spiritual" than inner ones; they simply serve a different function.

- **Trances:**
  The book of Acts records that Peter "fell into a trance" (Acts 10:10). In this state, a person's body may be at rest while their spirit becomes fully alert. Trances often happen during prayer or worship when the presence of God becomes tangible. They allow a believer to perceive multiple layers of revelation simultaneously, much as Daniel or Ezekiel did.

- **Being Caught Up in the Spirit:**
  John described, "I was in the Spirit on the Lord's Day" (Revelation 1:10). Paul also spoke of being "caught up to the third heaven" (2 Corinthians 12:2). These are high-level encounters in which the believer's spirit is lifted into the heavenly realm for divine disclosure. They are not to be sought for thrill or status but received in humility and purpose.

Each of these expressions of vision is initiated by God, not manufactured by man. We cannot force a vision any more than we can summon the wind. Our part is to remain yielded and pure, creating an atmosphere where the Spirit delights to reveal.

When God Opens the Eyes

Visions often come suddenly. One moment you are praying, the next your spiritual eyes are opened. It may last seconds or minutes, but in those moments, time seems suspended. You are aware of Heaven's reality as greater than Earth's.

When Elisha's servant panicked at the sight of the Syrian army, the prophet prayed,

"Lord, I pray, open his eyes that he may see."
Then the Lord opened the eyes of the young man, and he saw. And behold, the mountain was full of horses and chariots of fire all around Elisha."
2 Kings 6:17 (NKJV)

That story defines the nature of spiritual sight. The enemy's forces were visible, but God's army was invisible until the eyes of the spirit were opened. The young man's fear vanished the moment he saw Heaven's perspective.

Visions change perception. They don't always change circumstances, but they change how we see them. When you see from God's viewpoint, fear loses its power. Vision transforms reaction into revelation.

The Seer Anointing

Throughout Scripture, those who regularly received visions were often called *seers*. The word means "one who sees." But in the New Covenant, this is not a title; it's an invitation. Every believer indwelt by the Holy Spirit carries the potential for prophetic sight.

The purpose of the seer anointing is not to multiply visions but to purify perception. It's not about quantity, it's about quality, through the lens of the Spirit rather than the eyes of the flesh. God isn't seeking spiritual spectators; He's raising up interpreters, those who will see and then act in obedience.

The seer anointing develops in the same way as hearing God's voice: through intimacy, purity, and practice. The more you fellowship with the Holy Spirit, the more sensitive your inner vision becomes. Worship clears the atmosphere of the heart; the Word sharpens discernment; obedience increases clarity.

Many believers dismiss their first impressions as imagination, yet that is often how the Spirit begins to train them. What seems faint at first grows clearer with trust. The more you write, pray over, and respond to what you see, the more Heaven entrusts you with revelation.

"Call to Me, and I will answer you, and show you great and mighty things, which you do not know."
Jeremiah 33:3 (NKJV)

That promise includes sight. God delights to "show" His people what they could not otherwise see.

Visions remind us that Christianity is not a religion of theory but of encounter. The God of the Bible has not grown distant or silent. He is still revealing Himself to those who watch, still showing His plans to those who will look.

As dreams unveil the voice of Heaven in the stillness of night, visions unveil Heaven's divine perspective in the brightness of day. Together, they form a whole language of divine revelation, one that calls the believer into partnership with the Living Word.

THE STEWARDSHIP OF REVELATION

Every revelation from God — whether dream, vision, or prophetic word — is a sacred trust. It is not a badge of spirituality, but a call to stewardship. When Heaven opens its voice to the human heart, it expects response, reverence, and responsibility. Revelation is not given to entertain curiosity but to cultivate maturity.

When Joseph interpreted Pharaoh's dreams, he said something profound:

"Do not interpretations belong to God?"
Genesis 40:8 (NKJV)

In that short statement lies one of the most essential truths about the prophetic life: the meaning of what God shows you belongs to Him. You can receive revelation, but only the Spirit can unlock interpretation. Without Him, even the most vivid dream remains a mystery.

Receiving with Humility

The first posture of stewardship is humility. We do not control when or how God speaks. Dreams and visions are divine gifts, not spiritual achievements. A humble heart recognizes that revelation does not make one superior; it makes one accountable. Every picture, impression, or insight must be held with open hands, surrendered to the Lord who gave it.

Humility also protects us from pride and error. Pride wants to interpret quickly, to speak before seeking, to declare before discerning. But humility waits for the witness of the Spirit. Joseph waited two years in prison before his gift opened a door to interpret Pharaoh's dream. That waiting refined his discernment and proved his character.

Revelation without humility leads to distortion. Humility without revelation leads to silence. True maturity lives in the balance of both, hearing clearly and responding reverently.

Recording What You Receive

One of the most practical yet powerful ways to steward revelation is to *record it.*

When God spoke to Habakkuk, He gave this instruction:
*"Write the vision and make it plain on tablets,
That he may run who reads it."*
Habakkuk 2:2 (NKJV)

Writing preserves revelation. It honors the Word of the Lord and trains your heart to value His voice. When you document dreams or visions, you are saying, "This matters. I intend to remember what You've said."

Keep a dedicated journal by your bedside. When you awaken from a dream — even if it seems fragmented — write it immediately. Details fade quickly, but the act of writing often brings clarity. Over time, patterns emerge. You may see that God has been speaking repeatedly about a theme: a call, a warning, or an area of growth.

Some dreams are puzzle pieces that fit together over months or years. Without a record, you lose the thread. With a record, you build a tapestry.

In seasons of silence, those journals become reminders that God *has* spoken and will speak again. They strengthen faith in the waiting.

Interpreting with the Spirit

Interpretation is not about decoding symbols like solving a riddle; it's about the relationship. The same Spirit who gives revelation is the only One qualified to explain it. Jesus said the Holy Spirit "will guide you into all truth" (John 16:13).

That means the Spirit not only shows us mysteries; He walks us through understanding them. Interpretation is learned by intimacy, not intellect.

To interpret rightly:
- Begin in prayer. Ask the Holy Spirit, *"What are You saying through this?"*
- Return to the Word. All divine revelation will harmonize with Scripture.

- Pay attention to recurring imagery or themes in your life. God often personalizes His symbols.
- Seek counsel from mature believers if needed, especially for weighty or directional dreams. God uses community to confirm His voice.

But never run to people before you run to God. Human wisdom can confirm what He's saying, but should never replace His Spirit's leading.

Testing by the Word

Every dream or vision must bow to Scripture. The written Word is the anchor that holds prophetic experience steady. The Holy Spirit never contradicts Himself; what He reveals will always align with what He has already written.

If a dream contradicts the Word of God, it is not from God, no matter how powerful it feels. If a vision leads you away from Christ or into fear, it must be rejected. But if it deepens love, awakens holiness, or brings peace that agrees with the Word, it can be trusted.

"The entirety of Your word is truth,
And every one of Your righteous judgments endures forever."
Psalm 119:160 (NKJV)

The Bible is not the enemy of revelation — it is the measuring line. It is how we discern authenticity. The same Spirit who breathed Scripture is the One who breathes dreams. The two will always agree.

Responding in Obedience

Revelation demands a response. The purpose of hearing God is not information but transformation. A dream may reveal a hidden sin, will you repent? A vision may call you to a new assignment, will you obey? A warning may urge you to intercede, will you pray?

God never reveals without reason. What He shows, He expects you to steward. The revelation you act on becomes the foundation for more. Jesus said, "To him who has, more will be given." This means that when you are faithful with one word, He entrusts you with greater ones.

Sometimes obedience is simple: pray, forgive, rest, worship. Other times, it is costly: speak the truth, leave comfort, step into the calling. But obedience is the currency of revelation. The more we obey, the more clearly we hear.

Handling the Weight of Revelation

Some dreams or visions carry significant weight. They may concern nations, leaders, or prophetic warnings. Such a revelation requires discernment and restraint. Not everything God shows is meant to be shared publicly. Some things are revealed only in prayer.

Daniel saw visions that he was commanded to seal. Mary treasured and pondered her revelations in her heart. Mature believers know when to speak and when to stay silent. Revelation is not permission; it is responsibility.

Always ask the Holy Spirit: *"Why are You showing me this?"* The answer will determine how you steward it. Sometimes He reveals so you can declare. Other times, so that you can intercede. Occasionally, simply so you can understand His heart.

The more deeply you know Him, the more wisely you will handle His mysteries.

Protecting Revelation from Contamination

The enemy cannot create Godly revelation, but he can corrupt it through pride, fear, or self-focus. When a person begins to seek experiences more than they seek the Giver, purity fades. Revelation without intimacy becomes empty. Experiences without humility become idolatry.

Stay grounded in the Word. Stay accountable in the community of believers. Keep your heart anchored in love. Never chase manifestations; chase the Presence. Revelation will follow those who pursue the Lord Himself.

> *"But seek first the kingdom of God and His righteousness,*
> *And all these things shall be added to you."*
> **Matthew 6:33 (NKJV)**

When your focus is His kingdom, revelation remains pure. When your pursuit is His righteousness, discernment remains sharp.

Maturity and Mystery

God rarely gives complete understanding at once. He reveals in measured steps so we continue walking by faith. The mature believer learns to hold mystery with peace. Not every dream must be immediately interpreted. Some words must rest like seeds until the appointed time.

Joseph's dreams took years to unfold. John's visions still echo through history. God's timeline is not our own. When revelation tarries, wait in trust. The One who gave it will also bring it to pass.

> *"For the vision is yet for an appointed time;*
> *But in the end, it will speak, and it will not lie.*
> *Though it tarries, wait for it;*
> *Because it will surely come,*
> *It will not tarry."*
> **Habakkuk 2:3 (NKJV)**

Stewardship, then, is not about possessing revelation — it is about partnering with it. To steward revelation well is to walk humbly with God, guarding His voice in your heart until His purpose is fulfilled.

APPLICATION, ACTIVATION, AND CLOSING PRAYER

Revelation is not only to be admired; it is to be *applied*. Dreams and visions are invitations into partnership with God. The Father reveals not to overwhelm us, but to involve us. When He speaks, He is entrusting us with a portion of His heart, a fragment of His perspective, a spark of His plan.

To walk faithfully with the language of Heaven, we must become both listeners and doers, contemplative in presence yet courageous in response.

Living with Open Eyes and Ears

Every believer can cultivate sensitivity to the Spirit's voice. This begins not with striving but with stillness. The Holy Spirit's voice is most clearly heard by those who live in rest — whose hearts are not cluttered by hurry, noise, or fear. The Psalmist wrote:

"Be still, and know that I am God."
Psalm 46:10 (NKJV)

Stillness is not inactivity; it is an attentive posture. It means living aware of His nearness, listening as much as speaking, observing as much as asking. When you slow down enough to listen, you begin to notice how often He's been speaking all along.

Train your heart to recognize His language. Often, God will begin speaking through impressions, faint images, or subtle senses long before open visions appear. When you learn to acknowledge those gentle whispers, you prepare yourself for deeper revelation.

Practical Habits that Nurture Revelation

If you desire to grow in hearing and seeing, nurture the environment of your inner life. Revelation flourishes where reverence dwells.

Here are some practices that help cultivate a heart ready for dreams and visions:

- **Invite the Presence of God before Sleep**
  Play worship quietly, pray in the Spirit, or read a passage of Scripture before bed.
  Ask the Lord to sanctify your imagination and fill the atmosphere of your rest with His peace. Many believers find that when they fall asleep in His presence, their nights become classrooms of revelation.

- **Keep a Night Journal**
  Write down every dream or impression you remember, even if it feels small or strange.
  Date it, include key emotions, colors, and symbols.
  Over time, you'll see threads of divine consistency, recurring themes that reveal what God is developing in you.
- **Pray Over What You See**
  Don't rush to interpret. Begin in prayer. Ask, "Lord, what are You saying to me? What do You want me to do?" Dreams and visions are conversation starters, not conclusions. Let interpretation unfold through dialogue with Him.
- **Test Everything by Scripture**
  The Word is your foundation. If any dream or vision contradicts the nature or truth of Jesus, discard it. God's voice and God's Word never compete; they confirm one another.
- **Guard Your Gates**
  What you watch, hear, and dwell upon shapes your inner world. If your waking hours are filled with darkness, your nights will echo it. But if your mind is set on things above, your sleep becomes fertile ground for the Spirit's voice.
- **Respond in Obedience**
  Revelation without response becomes stagnation. Act on what God shows you, pray for the person He highlights, shift the habit He corrects, pursue the calling He confirms. Every act of obedience polishes the lens of your spirit, making His voice clearer the next time.
- **Stay in Accountability and Community**
  Share revelation with trusted, mature believers who walk in discernment. Counsel protects purity and anchors you in humility. Revelation grows best in the soil of community, not isolation.

A Lifestyle of Seeing and Hearing

Dreams and visions are not random supernatural moments; they are part of the ongoing conversation between Creator and creation. To walk with God is to live alert: ears tuned to His whisper, eyes open to His wonders. The believer who learns to see through Heaven's lens walks in peace when others panic, because they perceive from a higher realm.

When you live by revelation, you no longer interpret life by circumstance, but by covenant. You begin to understand that Heaven's activity often hides beneath Earth's appearance. You see beyond what is visible into what is eternal.

> *"While we do not look at the things which are seen, but at the things which are not seen.*
> *For the things which are seen are temporary, but the things which are not seen are eternal."*
> **2 Corinthians 4:18 (NKJV)**

This is what it means to see with the eyes of the Spirit. To walk by faith is to perceive what the world calls invisible and to live accordingly.

A Prophetic Generation

In this final hour, the Lord is raising a prophetic generation, not limited to a few pulpit voices, but a company of sons and daughters who know His voice intimately. They will dream His dreams and see His visions. They will discern truth in a world drunk on deception. They will carry revelation not as spectacle, but as stewardship.

Through them, the wisdom of God will be made known in workplaces, families, schools, and nations. Through them, the knowledge of the Lord will cover the earth as the waters cover the sea.

These are the ones who have learned to listen. They will walk in both the power and purity of revelation, lovers first, interpreters second. They will see not just the supernatural, but the heart of the Father behind it.

Closing Exhortation

Beloved, the same Spirit who hovered over the waters in Genesis now hovers over your life, waiting for your agreement. He longs to reveal what the Father is doing.

He longs to teach you the rhythms of Heaven, when to speak, when to rest, when to look, when to listen.

He still gives dreams to direct, visions to confirm, and revelation to empower.

He still opens the eyes of the blind and the ears of the deaf.

And He still whispers in the night to those who love His voice more than their sleep.

Value what He shows you. Guard what He entrusts to you. And remember: the most significant revelation is not a picture or a prophecy, it is the Person of Jesus Christ.

Every dream, every vision, every word should lead you closer to Him.

Prayer of Consecration and Activation
Father,

I thank You that You are still speaking. You are not silent, and You have not changed.

You spoke through prophets, through parables, through visions of the night, and You still speak through Your Spirit today.

Open the eyes of my heart to see You rightly.

Sanctify my imagination and fill it with Your light.

Teach me to discern Your voice amid the noise of this world.

Let my dreams become altars of encounter.

Let my visions reveal Your heart.

Guard me from deception, fear, and distraction.

I surrender every part of my life, my nights, my days, my thoughts, my senses, to the leading of Your Spirit.

Make me trustworthy with revelation.

Please help me to listen with humility, to interpret with wisdom, and to obey with courage.

I ask You for fresh outpouring, that Your sons and daughters would prophesy,

That young and old alike would dream Your dreams and see Your visions.

Let the language of Heaven fill the earth again.

In Jesus' name, Amen.

Chapter 2: Spiritual Senses
Living Beyond the Veil
Developing sight, hearing, taste, touch, and smell in the Spirit

---

There is a realm beyond what the human eye can perceive, a world unseen yet more real than what we can naturally touch or taste. The Apostle Paul writes,
> *"For the things which are seen are temporary, but the things which are not seen are eternal."*
> **2 Corinthians 4:18 (NKJV)**

Every believer is invited into this realm, not to escape the natural world, but to perceive it through Heaven's perspective. This spiritual dimension is not reserved for prophets or mystics; it is the inheritance of every born-again believer. God designed humanity to walk in communion with Him, to discern His presence and His will. From the beginning, Adam and Eve were created with spiritual sensitivity; they walked with God in the cool of the day (Genesis 3:8). When sin entered, those senses were dulled, and the awareness of His presence was veiled. But through Christ, the veil has been torn (Matthew 27:51), and the believer can once again live in fellowship with the unseen God.

When we were born again, the Spirit of God entered our human spirit and made us a new creation (2 Corinthians 5:17). Along with that new life came new senses, spiritual faculties designed to discern God's movement, hear His voice, feel His presence, and perceive both good and evil. The Word of God becomes not only our foundation but the training ground for these senses.
> *"But solid food belongs to those who are of full age, that is, those who by reason of use have their senses exercised to discern both good and evil."*
> **Hebrews 5:14 (NKJV)**

Just as an athlete disciplines the body through repetition and endurance, the believer must discipline the inner man through prayer, obedience, and the Word. Spiritual maturity is not the product of time alone; it is the result of use. Every step of obedience, every moment of worship, every encounter with Scripture sharpens our spiritual awareness.

These spiritual senses must be exercised. Just as physical muscles grow through use, our spiritual discernment sharpens through intimacy, obedience, and practice. This chapter will walk you through the five spiritual senses — sight, hearing, taste, touch, and smell — and how to awaken them to experience God more deeply.

THE CALL TO MATURITY

Spiritual maturity is not determined by how long we have attended church but by how well our spiritual senses have developed. Many believers remain spiritual infants, living on milk rather than solid food (Hebrews 5:12-13). Yet, the Father desires that His children grow into maturity, able to discern truth from error, to know His voice, and to walk in His wisdom.
Babies in Christ depend on others to feed them, but mature believers discern truth for themselves through fellowship with the Spirit. As we grow, we move beyond hearing about God to experiencing Him. His Word becomes alive, no longer letters on a page but a living encounter with the Living Word, Jesus Christ (John 1:14).

> *"But solid food belongs to those who are of full age, that is, those who by reason of use have their senses exercised to discern both good and evil."*
> **Hebrews 5:14 (NKJV)**

When the Holy Spirit takes the Word and reveals Christ to you, He's training your inner man to see, hear, feel, and discern.

This training is not always comfortable; it requires surrender, correction, and persistence. But as your senses are exercised, you begin to discern the difference between what feels right and what is right, between what is good and what is God.

To "exercise" your senses means to practice using them regularly. A musician becomes skilled not by owning an instrument but by playing it daily; so too, a believer becomes sensitive to God's voice by engaging with Him daily. It's not enough to have the Holy Spirit; we must be led by Him (Romans 8:14).

Spiritual maturity is the gateway to divine partnership. The Lord does not reveal His secrets to the casual observer, but to those who have proven faithful in fellowship. Jesus said,

"No longer do I call you servants... but I have called you friends, for all things that I heard from My Father I have made known to you."
John 15:15 (NKJV)

Friendship with God is developed through spiritual maturity, which involves consistently using our spiritual faculties to understand His will and His ways. As you move forward, keep in mind this vital truth: spiritual growth is not about seeking experiences but about deepening your relationship with God. The more you come to know Him, the more your senses become attuned to His reality. Maturity is not a goal to be achieved; rather, it is the result of ongoing surrender.

Two Realms: The Natural and the Eternal
"For we walk by faith, not by sight."
2 Corinthians 5:7 (NKJV)

"Since you were raised with Christ, seek those things which are above, where Christ is, sitting at the right hand of God."
Colossians 3:1 (NKJV)

There are two realms constantly at work: the natural realm, which is limited by time and space, and the spiritual realm, which is eternal and governed by the Word of God. These two realities coexist, though only one will endure forever. The natural realm is visible, temporary, and subject to decay; the spiritual realm is invisible, everlasting, and sustained by the presence of God Himself.

Every believer lives simultaneously in both realms. The natural realm allows us to function in the physical world, to build, work, and interact with creation. But the spiritual realm is where our true identity exists. The Apostle Paul declared that believers are already "seated with Christ in heavenly places" (Ephesians 2:6), meaning that our authority, perspective, and inheritance originate not from earth but from Heaven.

Understanding these realms is essential for spiritual maturity. When a believer is unaware of the spiritual dimension, they become ruled by natural circumstances. Fear, offense, and doubt dominate when we interpret life only through what is visible. But when we awaken to the eternal realm, we begin to respond rather than react—to live from faith, not sight.

Walking by faith means aligning your decisions, emotions, and worldview with the unseen promises of God. It is the conscious choice to view everything through Heaven's lens. Just as a radio picks up frequencies that are already present but unheard until tuned, the spirit of a believer must be tuned to the frequency of the Kingdom.

Jesus lived perfectly aware of both realms. Though He walked among men, He continually operated from His heavenly awareness. When He healed the sick, multiplied bread, or calmed storms, He was not performing as a magician; He was revealing the authority of the eternal realm over the natural. This same awareness is the inheritance of every Spirit-filled believer.

The Bible says,
> "While we do not look at the things which are seen, but at the things which are not seen."
> **2 Corinthians 4:18 (NKJV)**

This is not a denial of reality; it is the practice of viewing reality from Heaven's standpoint. The eyes of faith do not ignore pain or difficulty; they discern the presence of purpose behind it. Faith perceives beyond limitation into the eternal truth of God's nature.

Application

Every day, we are confronted with the tension between what we see and what we believe. The natural realm says, "You are sick," but the eternal realm declares,
> "By His stripes you are healed"
> **1 Peter 2:24 (NKJV)**

The natural realm says, "There is no way out," but Heaven says,
> "With God all things are possible"
> **Matthew 19:26 (NKJV)**

The natural says, "I'm alone," but the eternal truth is,
> "I will never leave you nor forsake you"
> **Hebrews 13:5 (NKJV)**

Faith bridges these realms. It is the hand that reaches into eternity and brings Heaven's reality into the present. Every act of obedience, every prayer of faith, and every declaration of the Word is an expression of that unseen Kingdom breaking into the seen world.

When we live with this awareness, we stop striving for God's presence and start realizing we already dwell in it. The veil between natural and supernatural grows thinner as we fix our hearts on the eternal. Like Jacob in Genesis 28:16, many believers live unaware that "Surely the Lord is in this place, and I did not know it." But once awakened, they learn to walk consciously in His abiding presence.

Keys To Operating Between Realms
- Acknowledge both realities. We are in the world but not of it (John 17:14, 16).
- Renew your mind. Transformation begins by replacing natural thinking with Kingdom truth (Romans 12:2).
- Feed your spirit. Spiritual strength grows as you meditate on the Word (Joshua 1:8).
- Speak faith. Words align the natural realm with spiritual truth (Proverbs 18:21).
- Stay aware of His presence. Continual communion cultivates eternal perspective (1 Thessalonians 5:17).

As we progress, we will explore how each spiritual sense functions within these two realms. The same God who created physical sight, sound, and touch has also given His children spiritual faculties to discern His movement and presence. To walk in the Spirit is to live as one who constantly interprets the natural world through the lens of eternity.

SPIRITUAL SIGHT – THE EYES OF THE HEART

"Open my eyes, that I may see wondrous things from Your law."
Psalm 119:18 (NKJV)

"The eyes of your understanding being enlightened; that you may know what is the hope of His calling."
Ephesians 1:18 (NKJV)

"Then Elisha prayed, and said, 'Lord, I pray, open his eyes that he may see.' Then the Lord opened the eyes of the young man, and he saw."
2 Kings 6:17 (NKJV)

Spiritual sight is one of the most vital faculties of the believer. It is the ability to perceive what God is revealing in the unseen realm, to view life, people, and circumstances through the lens of divine revelation. It is not just *"imagination,"* but an illumination of an avenue of dialogue;

not fantasy but faith becoming sight.

When Jesus said, "The Son can do nothing of Himself, but what He sees the Father do" (John 5:19), He unveiled the pattern of perfect spiritual sight. Christ did not operate by guesswork or human logic; He acted according to revelation. His physical eyes beheld people, but His spiritual eyes discerned purpose. Where others saw brokenness, He saw destiny.

Spiritual blindness is one of the enemy's greatest tactics. Paul wrote,
"Whose minds the god of this age has blinded, who do not believe, lest the light of the gospel… should shine on them."
2 Corinthians 4:4 (NKJV)
Blindness here refers not to physical sight but to perception, the inability to recognize God's truth even when it stands in front of us. But when the Holy Spirit comes, He removes the veil and floods the heart with light (2 Corinthians 3:16-18).

For the believer, developing spiritual vision is learning to interpret life through revelation, not reaction. The same light that revealed God to Moses in the burning bush is the same Spirit that illuminates Scripture in our hearts today. When the Spirit enlightens the "eyes of your understanding," you begin to perceive hope, calling, and inheritance, the three things Paul prayed every believer would grasp (Ephesians 1:18).
True sight begins in the heart. The psalmist prayed,
"In Your light we see light"
Psalm 36:9 (NKJV)
Only by His illumination can we discern truth from deception. The more our hearts are purified, the more precise our vision becomes. This is why Jesus declared,
"Blessed are the pure in heart, for they shall see God."
Matthew 5:8

Biblical Example
In 2 Kings 6, Elisha's servant was terrified when a Syrian army surrounded them. Fear clouded his natural vision. But Elisha prayed, "Open his eyes, Lord," and suddenly the servant saw chariots of fire and heavenly hosts encamped around them. The physical situation had not changed; the perspective had.

The revelation of that invisible army transformed despair into confidence. That is the power of spiritual sight — to see from Heaven's vantage point. Where others see opposition, those with unveiled eyes see opportunity. Where the world sees defeat, the believer sees destiny.
Jesus often asked His disciples, "Having eyes, do you not see?" (Mark 8:18). He was not speaking of physical blindness but spiritual dullness. Even though they had witnessed miracles, their hearts struggled to perceive His meaning. Many today still face this struggle, the inability to see what God is doing, even in the midst of divine activity.

Application
You may or may not see chariots of fire in your living room, but spiritual sight manifests in countless everyday ways.
When you look at a problematic person and, instead of reacting with frustration, you sense the Holy Spirit stirring compassion — that is seeing as God sees. When you recognize divine purpose in adversity, you are perceiving beyond the surface. When you feel led to pray for someone and later discover they were in crisis, you are discerning Heaven's promptings.
Sometimes, spiritual sight comes through flashes of color, pictures, or mental images during prayer or worship. These impressions are often the Spirit's way of speaking through the imagination He designed. The imagination becomes sanctified when it is surrendered to the Spirit. God frequently paints revelation upon that inner canvas, revealing prophetic glimpses, encouragements, or warnings.
The prophet Habakkuk was told,

"Write the vision and make it plain"
Habakkuk 2:2 (NKJV)

The more you record and steward what God shows you, the more precise your sight becomes. Vision grows with use. When we honor revelation, God entrusts us with more (Luke 8:18).

Everyday Illustration

Imagine driving through fog on a familiar road. You know the path, but visibility is low. You slow down, relying on headlights to cut through the mist. That's how many believers live; they have knowledge but lack vision. The headlights represent revelation, and without them, even the most familiar ground becomes uncertain.

But when the sun rises — symbolic of the Light of Christ — clarity returns. The obstacles were always there; they simply weren't visible. Likewise, when the Holy Spirit illuminates our hearts, we see what was previously hidden: motives, opportunities, and the nearness of God's hand.

Keys To Activation

- Pray daily for revelation: Ask, "Lord, open my eyes." (Psalm 119:18)
- Meditate on Scripture: The Word is spiritual light; it trains your perception.
- Journal what you see: Record dreams, impressions, and pictures. Revelation preserved becomes revelation multiplied.
- Guard your eyes: What you watch, read, and meditate on shapes your vision. If you bring garbage in, then there will be blindness out.
- Walk in purity: Matthew 5:8 says, "Blessed are the pure in heart, for they shall see God." Holiness sharpens perception.

Reflection

To "see" spiritually is to live aware of eternity in every moment. It is to recognize that what surrounds you in the natural world is not the whole story. The unseen world, both angelic and demonic, is real, and God calls His people to walk in discernment, not fear.

This is why Paul prayed not that believers would gain new eyes, but that the eyes of their hearts would be enlightened (Ephesians 1:18). The eyes are already present; they need illumination. The more time spent in His presence, the more the veil lifts, and the more you will begin to see life as He sees it: full of promise, purpose, and divine order.

SPIRITUAL HEARING – VOICE OF THE SHEPHERD

"My sheep hear My voice, and I know them, and they follow Me."
John 10:27 (NKJV)

"He who has ears to hear, let him hear!"
Matthew 11:15 (NKJV)

"Your ears shall hear a word behind you, saying, 'This is the way, walk in it,' whenever you turn to the right hand or whenever you turn to the left."
Isaiah 30:21 (NKJV)

Spiritual hearing is the ability to recognize and respond to God's communication. It is more than the occasional whisper in prayer; it is the cultivated awareness of His voice speaking through Scripture, circumstance, peace, conviction, and revelation.

Every believer is wired to hear God; the problem is not that God has stopped speaking, but that many hearts have stopped listening.

Jesus compared Himself to a Shepherd whose sheep "know His voice." The relationship between shepherd and sheep is one of intimacy and trust. Shepherds in the ancient Near East would sing a distinct melody so their flock could identify them even among other shepherds. Likewise, the Holy Spirit speaks in a tone recognizable to those who continually dwell in His presence.

The voice of the Lord is never random. It always aligns with His written Word and with His character. It may bring correction, but it never brings condemnation (Romans 8:1). Instead, it invites repentance rather than despair. The enemy's voice accuses; the Spirit's voice convicts with hope. Learning to distinguish the difference is part of spiritual maturity.

When Scripture says "Faith comes by hearing, and hearing by the word of God" (Romans 10:17), it implies a continual process: the more we hear, the deeper our faith grows. Hearing God transforms information into revelation, truth that moves from the head to the heart.

Biblical Example

Young Samuel learned this pattern as a child. Three times he heard his name in the night, assuming it was Eli. Only after instruction did he answer correctly: "Speak, Lord, for Your servant hears." (1 Samuel 3:10). That one response positioned him for a lifetime of prophetic ministry. Samuel's story reminds us that divine dialogue matures through mentorship, humility, and repetition.

Elijah, too, discovered that God's voice is not always dramatic. On Mount Horeb, he experienced wind, earthquake, and fire, but the Lord was in none of them. Then came "a still small voice" (1 Kings 19:12). The Lord teaches His people to recognize His whisper amid chaos. He doesn't compete with noise; He invites stillness.

In the New Testament, believers heard the Spirit speak in diverse ways:
• Philip heard an angelic instruction to approach the Ethiopian eunuch (Acts 8:26–29).
• The Holy Spirit directed Paul and Barnabas to separate for ministry (Acts 13:2).
• John heard the voice of Christ "like a trumpet" in Revelation 1:10.

God's communication is not limited to one method; His tone is always consistent, holy, loving, and purposeful.

Application

In daily life, spiritual hearing often manifests as subtle impressions:

- A thought arises—Call this person—and you later learn they needed prayer.
- You sense, don't take that path today, and discover later it would have led to trouble.
- During worship, a Scripture surfaces in your heart with unusual clarity.

These are moments of divine dialogue. The believer learns by testing and obedience. As Jesus said, "If anyone wills to do His will, he shall know concerning the doctrine" (John 7:17). Obedience increases clarity; disobedience dulls it.

Learning God's voice is like learning to recognize a loved one's tone in a crowded room; you know it instantly because of time spent together. The same intimacy develops through prayer, worship, and consistent time in the Word. Over time, the noise of fear and doubt fades, and the Shepherd's voice becomes unmistakable.

Everyday Illustration

Imagine tuning a radio dial. Countless stations are broadcasting, but only the one properly tuned comes through clearly. Spiritual hearing functions the same way. Heaven is constantly transmitting; our responsibility is to adjust our spiritual frequency and focus to receive it. Distraction and sin create static. Worship, Scripture, and obedience fine-tune the signal.

Keys To Activation
- Quiet your mind: Cultivate silence daily; He often speaks when we are still (Psalm 46:10).

- Stay in Scripture: The written Word is the foundation for recognizing the spoken Word.
- Test the spirits: Measure every impression against the character of Christ (1 John 4:1–3).
- Be a doer: Obedience sharpens perception; revelation unused fades quickly (James 1:22).
- Practice gratitude: Thank Him for each moment of guidance, which increases awareness.
- Guard your ears: Refuse to entertain gossip, fear, or negativity; what you feed on shapes what you hear.

Reflection

Spiritual hearing is the cornerstone of guidance. Without it, believers drift, led by emotion or circumstance rather than revelation. Yet God's intent has always been relational conversation, not mechanical religion. He spoke to Adam in the garden, to Noah about the ark, to Moses from the bush, and to Mary through an angel. Today, He speaks through the indwelling Spirit. The form has changed; the desire for fellowship has not.

Every time you pause to listen, you affirm His Lordship. To ignore His voice is to live as if He were silent; to obey His voice is to prove He is near. Jesus promised, "The Helper, the Holy Spirit... will teach you all things, and bring to your remembrance all things that I said to you." (John 14:26). The voice of the Shepherd still guides His flock, sometimes through a whisper, sometimes through the Word, always through love.

SPIRITUAL TASTE – THE GOODNESS OF GOD

> *"Oh, taste and see that the Lord is good; Blessed is the man who trusts in Him!"*
> ***Psalm 34:8 (NKJV)***

> *"How sweet are Your words to my taste, sweeter than honey to my mouth!"*
> ***Psalm 119:103 (NKJV)***

"Your words were found, and I ate them, and Your word was to me the joy and rejoicing of my heart."
Jeremiah 15:16 (NKJV)

"He said to me, 'Son of man, eat what you find; eat this scroll, and go, speak to the house of Israel.'"
Ezekiel 3:1 (NKJV)

Taste is one of the most intimate of the five senses because it requires contact and participation. You cannot taste from a distance; you must partake. Spiritually, tasting represents experience. It is one thing to hear that honey is sweet; it is another to let it melt on your tongue. The psalmist invites believers not simply to acknowledge God's goodness intellectually but to experience it personally.

Many people study God but have not yet tasted Him. Knowledge about God feeds the mind, but experiencing His goodness satisfies the soul. This sense of "taste" speaks of divine intimacy, of taking in the Word until it becomes part of you. Jesus said,

"If anyone eats of this bread, he will live forever; and the bread that I shall give is My flesh." **John 6:51 (NKJV)**

He was teaching us that true life is sustained by communion with Him.

The sense of taste is also tied to discernment. Just as your tongue distinguishes sweet from bitter, your spirit discerns truth from error. Job declared,

"Does not the ear test words and the mouth taste its food?"
Job 12:11 (NKJV)

Mature believers develop a spiritual palate that quickly recognizes when something is off, whether it's a false teaching, an unhealthy relationship, or an unclean motive.

A refined spiritual taste grows as we feed on purity. What we consume spiritually shapes our appetites. If we feast on negativity, fear, and compromise, we will crave what is unhealthy. But if we continually feed on the Word, prayer, and worship, we develop a hunger for holiness.

Biblical Example

The Israelites literally tasted the provision of Heaven through manna (Exodus 16:31). Scripture describes it as "white like coriander seed, and the taste of it was like wafers made with honey." Every morning, they gathered supernatural food that sustained them physically, a picture of how the Word of God spiritually sustains believers. Ezekiel and John both encountered divine "scrolls" containing God's Word. When they ate them, they reported that the taste was sweet like honey (Ezekiel 3:3; Revelation 10:9–10). Yet John added that afterward, it turned bitter in his stomach — showing that revelation carries responsibility. God's Word is delightful to receive but heavy to carry; truth brings joy but also accountability.

Jesus used this same picture when He instituted the Lord's Supper. To "eat" His body and "drink" His blood symbolized internalizing His covenant, not merely observing it. He was calling His followers beyond ritual into relationship, to taste His nature and live by His life.

Application

Spiritual taste manifests daily. Have you ever been reading Scripture and felt something within you come alive, as though a verse suddenly leapt off the page? That is the sweetness of revelation. The Holy Spirit is feeding your inner man.

Or perhaps you've experienced spiritual "bitterness," a discomfort when hearing something that doesn't align with truth. That inner unease is discernment at work, your spiritual palate signaling that something isn't pure. The more you grow in the Word, the quicker you recognize these contrasts.

When you worship and sense a refreshing washing over you like cool water, that is also a taste. You are drinking from the "rivers of living water" Jesus promised (John 7:38). Every encounter with God, every answered prayer, every moment of His nearness, adds depth to your spiritual appetite.

Just as the body can lose its sense of taste when sick, the soul can lose its appetite for spiritual things when malnourished by sin, busyness, or distraction.

"As the deer pants for the water brooks, so pants my soul for You, O God."
Psalm 42:1 (NKJV)

This verse reminds us that a healthy spirit longs for continual communion with Him.

Everyday Illustration

Think of a child trying something sweet for the first time, eyes widen, joy bursts, and there's a desire for more. In the same way, when believers truly encounter God's goodness, they are forever marked by hunger for more of Him. That hunger is holy. The Kingdom operates on a paradox: those who are full still hunger, and those who hunger are constantly satisfied (Matthew 5:6).

Keys To Activation
- Feast on Scripture daily: God's Word is spiritual nourishment (Matthew 4:4). Make time to read slowly, tasting every word.
- Guard your spiritual diet: Avoid content that dulls your appetite for holiness (Philippians 4:8).
- Cultivate gratitude: Thanksgiving enhances sensitivity to God's goodness.
- Fast occasionally: Physical fasting sharpens spiritual appetite and heightens awareness.
- Ask God for deeper hunger: Pray Psalm 63:1 — "O God, You are my God; early will I seek You; My soul thirsts for You."

Reflection

Spiritual taste draws us into deeper satisfaction in Christ. David's invitation to "taste and see" is both an experience and a command. It means, Try Him. Experience Him for yourself. When you do, you realize that His presence satisfies more than success, His Word nourishes more than worldly wisdom, and His peace fills voids that earthly pleasure cannot reach.

The more you taste of Him, the more you lose appetite for anything that is not of Him. The psalmist said,

"Whom have I in heaven but You? And there is none upon earth that I desire besides You"
Psalm 73:25 (NKJV)

When the Lord becomes your portion, every other craving bows.

SPIRITUAL TOUCH – FEELING GOD'S PRESENCE

"Then He touched their eyes, saying, 'According to your faith let it be to you.'"
*Matthew 9:29 **(NKJV)***

"Then the Lord put forth His hand and touched my mouth, and the Lord said to me, 'Behold, I have put My words in your mouth.'"
Jeremiah 1:9 (NKJV)

"And Jesus, moved with compassion, put out His hand and touched him, and said to him, 'I am willing; be cleansed.'"
Mark 1:41 (NKJV)

"Then one having the likeness of a man touched me again and strengthened me."
Daniel 10:18 (NKJV)

Touch is the sense of connection, transfer, and impartation. It represents closeness, the bridging of two realities. In the natural, touch allows us to feel texture, temperature, and presence. In the spirit, touch is the awareness of God's nearness and power moving through us.

Jesus frequently touched those He healed. He could have spoken the word from afar, but His physical contact communicated compassion and divine intimacy. When He touched the leper in Mark 1:41, He broke cultural boundaries and transmitted Heaven's wholeness into human brokenness. His touch said, "You are not untouchable."

The woman with the issue of blood (Luke 8:43–48) didn't just reach for His garment; she reached through faith. Her physical action mirrored her spiritual conviction, and power flowed. Jesus perceived the transfer instantly, saying, "Someone touched Me, for I perceived power going out from Me." This shows us that faith is the spiritual hand that draws virtue from God.

Spiritual touch goes both ways: God touches us to strengthen, purify, and heal, and through us, He touches others. The believer becomes a conduit of divine presence, carrying the life of Christ into the world through simple acts of obedience and compassion.

Touch also represents sensitivity to atmosphere. Many believers experience the tangible presence of God through physical sensations such as warmth, peace, chills, or gentle pressure. These sensations are not emotions but indicators of nearness. They train us to recognize when the Spirit is moving.

However, discernment is crucial. The enemy can mimic sensation to create confusion or fear, but God's presence always aligns with peace. Colossians 3:15 reminds us, "Let the peace of God rule in your hearts." Peace is the ultimate test for spiritual authenticity.

Biblical Example

Isaiah was touched by a live coal from Heaven's altar. The seraphim said, "Behold, this has touched your lips; your iniquity is taken away" (Isaiah 6:7). The touch of Heaven purified and commissioned him.

Jeremiah's lips were touched when God placed His words within him (Jeremiah 1:9). Daniel received strength through the touch of an angel (Daniel 10:18). Each encounter shows that when Heaven touches earth, transformation follows.

When Jesus was transfigured, His disciples fell in fear until He "touched them and said, 'Arise, and do not be afraid'" (Matthew 17:7). His touch replaced terror with peace. Every touch from God carries purpose — healing, comfort, empowerment, or sanctification.

Application

Have you ever entered a room and instantly felt the atmosphere —tension, peace, or heaviness —before anyone spoke? That's your spirit, feeling the unseen realm. When you sense a burden for someone, a pull to intercede, or a sense of warmth when praying, you are responding to the Spirit's touch.

During worship, you might feel a gentle weight on your shoulders or tears welling up unexpectedly. That's the nearness of God drawing you deeper into communion. These sensations should never be sought for their own sake but recognized as evidence of His closeness.

Sometimes, God allows you to feel what another person feels so that you can intercede for them. This is a gift of compassion, not to overwhelm you, but to connect your heart to His.,

"Bear one another's burdens and so fulfill the law of Christ."
Galatians 6:2 (NKJV)

Always remember feelings are indicators, not dictators. The Spirit's touch leads to peace, not confusion. If what you sense draws you to prayer, repentance, or worship, it is likely the Lord's invitation. If it leads to fear or condemnation, reject it and rest in His presence.

Everyday Illustration

Think of a musician tuning a delicate instrument. The strings must be sensitive enough to respond to the lightest touch of the bow. In the same way, our spirits must remain tender, responsive to the Spirit's slightest movement. Hardness of heart deadens sensitivity, but humility and worship keep us pliable.

Like freshly molded clay on the Potter's wheel, the believer's spirit is shaped by divine hands. When the Potter's fingers press, it is not to crush but to form. When He touches, He is molding us into vessels that can carry His glory.

Keys To Activation
- Cultivate compassion: God's power flows through love, not performance. (1 Corinthians 13:2)
- Lay hands in faith: Healing and impartation come through physical obedience (Mark 16:17–18).
- Pay attention to peace: The Spirit's touch always aligns with rest and order (Philippians 4:7).
- Intercede when burdened: Turn emotional weight into prayer (Romans 8:26).
- Invite the Spirit's nearness: Whisper, "Holy Spirit, make me aware of You."
- Remain sensitive: Keep your heart soft before God. Sensitivity requires stillness and purity (Ezekiel 36:26).

Reflection
Spiritual touch is the language of divine intimacy. Through it, God reassures His people that He is not distant or abstract but personal and present. Every time the Spirit's presence brushes your heart in prayer, He reminds you that you are known and loved.
When you minister healing or comfort to others, you become His hands extended. You are the vessel through which Heaven touches earth. This is why Jesus said,
"As the Father has sent Me, I also send you.'
John 20:21 (NKJV)
His touch continues through the surrendered believer.

SPIRITUAL SMELL – THE FRAGRANCE OF CHRIST

"Now thanks be to God who always leads us in triumph in Christ, and through us diffuses the fragrance of His knowledge in every place."

2 Corinthians 2:14 (NKJV)

"Your name is ointment poured forth; therefore the virgins love You."
Song of Solomon 1:3 (NKJV)

"Your lips, O my spouse, drip as the honeycomb; honey and milk are under your tongue; and the fragrance of your garments is like the fragrance of Lebanon."
Song of Solomon 4:11 (NKJV)

"While the king is at his table, my spikenard sends forth its fragrance."
Song of Solomon 1:12 (NKJV)

Of all the senses, smell is perhaps the most mysterious. Fragrance is invisible, yet powerful; it fills an entire space, lingers in memory, and can change an atmosphere instantly. Spiritually, smell represents discernment and atmosphere. It's the awareness of what's present in a space before anything is said or seen.

The Bible repeatedly connects aroma and worship. When Noah built an altar after the flood, "the Lord smelled a soothing aroma" (Genesis 8:21). In Exodus, God gave precise instructions for the sacred incense to be burned continually in the tabernacle, symbolizing the prayers of the saints (Exodus 30:7–8; Psalm 141:2). In Revelation, John saw golden bowls of incense representing "the prayers of the saints" (Revelation 5:8). Worship and intercession release a spiritual fragrance that ascends before God.

Jesus' obedience was called "a sweet-smelling aroma" to the Father (Ephesians 5:2). When we walk in love and obedience, our lives emit the same fragrance of Christ. Conversely, sin and rebellion carry a stench in the spiritual realm. Ecclesiastes 10:1 warns, "Dead flies putrefy the perfumer's ointment, and cause it to give off a foul odor." In other words, compromise contaminates the beauty of our devotion.

You carry His fragrance when you abide in Him. The more time you spend in His presence, the more His aroma clings to you. Like clothing infused with perfume, those who dwell close to God carry a scent of Heaven wherever they go. People may not know why, but they sense peace, holiness, or conviction when you enter the room. That is the fragrance of Christ testifying through you.

Biblical Example

Mary of Bethany demonstrated this reality in John 12. She broke an alabaster flask of costly perfume and poured it on Jesus' feet. The Scripture says,

"And the house was filled with the fragrance of the oil."
John 12:3 (NKJV)

Her act of worship released both a physical and spiritual aroma that lingered long after she left. Even as Jesus went to the cross, the fragrance of her devotion likely remained upon Him.

The same oil that cost Mary everything became a memorial that outlived her. Jesus said,

"Wherever this gospel is preached in the whole world, what this woman has done will also be told as a memorial to her."
Mark 14:9 (NKJV)

Worship, when poured out in love, leaves an eternal fragrance.

Just as the presence of God carries a fragrance, the presence of darkness carries a stench. Throughout scripture, judgment, corruption, and rebellion are repeatedly linked with the odor of sulfur, decay, and rot. The Bible describes the destruction of Sodom with *fire and brimstone*, depicts wickedness as producing a *stench instead of a sweet aroma*, and portrays the final dwelling place of Satan as a lake burning with *fire and sulfur*. These images are not random; they reveal the spiritual nature of the demonic realm. Heaven releases the fragrance of Christ; hell releases the odor of corruption. This is why, throughout church history and even in modern deliverance ministry, believers have often reported foul or sulfur-like smells during moments of demonic manifestation.

"Upon the wicked He will rain coals;
Fire and brimstone and a burning wind
Shall be the portion of their cup."
Psalm 11:6 (NKJV)

"And so it shall be:
Instead of a sweet smell, there will be a stench…"
Isaiah 3:24 (NKJV)

These demonic smells are not to inspire fear but to heighten discernment. Just as a foul odor warns of corruption in the natural, unpleasant spiritual smells can alert you to unclean influences. In such moments, respond not with panic but authority, cleansing the atmosphere with worship, the Word, and the name of Jesus.

Application

Have you ever smelled something familiar during prayer or worship, a floral fragrance, the scent of oil, or a refreshing sweetness, even though no natural source was present? Many believers testify that such moments accompany the presence of the Holy Spirit or angelic activity.

Or perhaps you've walked into a place and felt an immediate heaviness without knowing why. Your spirit may have been discerning an atmosphere of fear, pride, or oppression — the spiritual equivalent of an unpleasant odor. As a carrier of Christ's presence, you have the authority to shift that environment.

Our lives should "smell" like Heaven. In the workplace, at home, in ministry, we release a spiritual aroma through our words, actions, and attitudes. When we choose forgiveness over bitterness, we diffuse the fragrance of grace. When we worship through trials, we fill the air with the scent of faith.

Everyday Illustration

Incense, when first lit, produces smoke that rises slowly but fills a room. This is a picture of persistent prayer. The believer's prayers may seem small or unnoticed at first, but they are saturating the atmosphere of Heaven. Over time, that fragrance changes the environment both in the spiritual and natural realms.

The early church was known for this kind of fragrance. Their love, humility, and unity carried a scent distinct from the world. Paul wrote, "We are to God the fragrance of Christ among those who are being saved and among those who are perishing" (2 Corinthians 2:15). To some, the fragrance of the Gospel is life; to others, it is conviction. But to God, it is always pleasing.

Keys To Activation
- Live as a living sacrifice: Worship is a pleasing aroma to God (Romans 12:1).
- Keep your spirit pure: Bitterness, offense, and sin produce spiritual decay (Hebrews 12:15).
- Practice gratitude and praise: Thanksgiving releases Heaven's fragrance into your atmosphere.
- Use prayer and worship as incense: Fill your home with the sweet aroma of His presence (Psalm 141:2).
- Declare Christ's lordship: His fragrance overpowers every foul spirit and restores purity.
- Anoint with oil in faith: Like Mary, acts of worship and devotion leave lingering spiritual residue.

Reflection
The sense of smell teaches us how powerfully unseen forces shape visible outcomes. A room filled with worship feels different than one filled with anger; a believer walking in forgiveness carries peace that others can "sense." This is why the Holy Spirit emphasizes inner purity — what's within you will always become the fragrance around you.

The church is called to be the perfume of Heaven in a world that reeks of corruption. When believers walk in holiness and love, their lives release a witness far more potent than words. This is evangelism by aroma, the fragrance of Christ diffusing through daily faithfulness, compassion, and truth.

The more time spent at His feet, the stronger the scent becomes. Just as Mary's perfume filled the house, time in God's presence fills our lives with a fragrance that can't be manufactured, only imparted.

Training for Glory

Beloved, God designed your spiritual senses not for entertainment but for intimacy and discernment. These gifts are not given to satisfy curiosity, but to deepen communion. When you train them, you begin to walk as Jesus walked, fully aware of the Father's presence in every moment, guided not by emotion but by revelation.

The more you exercise your spiritual senses, the less easily you'll be deceived. The world dulls sensitivity with noise, distraction, and sin. The enemy thrives in confusion, numbing hearts through constant stimulation and busyness. But the Spirit of God sharpens sensitivity through quietness, prayer, and the Word. It is in stillness that the whisper of Heaven becomes clear (Psalm 46:10).

Just as our natural senses define how we navigate the physical world, our spiritual senses guide us through the unseen one. Without sight, hearing, touch, taste, and smell in the Spirit, believers stumble in darkness, unable to discern between what is divine and what is counterfeit. But when these senses are awakened, we begin to walk in spiritual confidence, able to perceive both the beauty of Heaven and the schemes of Hell, not to fear the latter, but to triumph over it.

Paul wrote,
> *"Set your mind on things above, not on things on the earth."*
> ***Colossians 3:2 (NKJV)***

To set your mind above is to train your perception, to tune your spiritual senses heavenward. It means living with the awareness that every situation, no matter how ordinary, carries eternal weight. Every conversation becomes a potential encounter; every obstacle a disguised opportunity for the Kingdom to manifest.

The Holy Spirit is the divine trainer of our inner senses. He takes what belongs to Jesus and reveals it to us (John 16:14). Through His instruction, we learn to see with spiritual eyes, hear with clarity, taste of divine goodness, feel the weight of His glory, and carry the fragrance of His presence. These faculties do not develop overnight; they mature through fellowship. The more we yield, the sharper they become.

To train for glory means to live intentionally aware of the unseen. Like Moses, who "endured as seeing Him who is invisible" (Hebrews 11:27), we are called to act from revelation, not reaction. We grow through practice, through daily surrender, consistent obedience, and the steady pursuit of His voice.

Remember, you were made to live beyond the veil, to discern the invisible with clarity and peace. This is the maturing of the sons and daughters of God. This is where authority flows from intimacy. It is where discernment is born, and where revelation becomes transformation. You were never meant to believe in God from afar; you were created to perceive, experience, and partner with Him in the advancing of His Kingdom.

Personal Prayer And Declaration Of Activation
Father, in the name of Jesus,
I thank You that You have made me a new creation and filled me with Your Holy Spirit. I desire to know You more deeply — not only through words, but through experience.
Lord, open the eyes of my heart to see what You are doing. Remove every veil that blinds my perception. Let me behold Your beauty in the ordinary moments of my day.
Train my ears to recognize Your voice above every other sound. Teach me to pause and listen for Your whisper. Let Your Word dwell richly in my heart so I may discern truth from error.

Let me taste and see Your goodness. Feed me daily with Your living Word. Make Your presence my greatest delight and satisfaction.

Let me feel Your touch, Holy Spirit — Your comfort when I am weary, Your strength when I am weak. Use my hands to heal, my heart to intercede, and my life to carry Your compassion.

And, Lord, let me carry the fragrance of Christ wherever I go. May my words, actions, and attitudes spread the aroma of Your love. Cleanse every place I walk with Your presence and peace.

Today, I yield my spiritual senses to You.
Train them, refine them, and awaken them for Your glory.
May I walk in discernment, see beyond the natural, and live in constant awareness of You.
In Jesus' mighty name,
Amen.

Reflection

"But we all, with unveiled face, beholding as in a mirror the glory of the Lord, are being transformed into the same image from glory to glory."
2 Corinthians 3:18

The invitation to exercise your spiritual senses is an invitation to transformation. Every glimpse of His glory changes you; every sound of His voice refines you; every touch of His presence renews you. You were born again to perceive what natural eyes cannot see.

Lift your eyes, beloved.
You were made to live beyond the veil.

Chapter 3: Discernment
Perceiving What the Natural Eye Cannot

"I am Your servant; give me understanding, that I may know Your testimonies."
Psalm 119:125 (NKJV)
True sight begins where self-reliance ends.

THE EYES OF THE SPIRIT

There is a kind of sight that goes far beyond the natural eye, a vision of the spirit, born out of intimacy with God and refined through the wisdom of His Word. The Psalmist's prayer echoes the cry of every heart that longs for clarity amid the noise of the world: *"I am Your servant; give me understanding."* True discernment begins here, in humility, not in expertise.

Discernment is more than a cautious instinct or a mental skill. It is a divine faculty, a spiritual perception that allows the believer to separate what *appears* from what *is*. The Apostle Paul wrote,

"The natural man does not receive the things of the Spirit of God, for they are foolishness to him; nor can he know them, because they are spiritually discerned."
1 Corinthians 2:14 (NKJV)

To the carnal mind, the things of the Spirit seem intangible or irrational, but to the spiritual mind, they are life and peace. Discernment, therefore, is not learned by intellect but by revelation; it is the Spirit granting us Heaven's perspective.

"For the word of God is living and powerful, and sharper than any two-edged sword, piercing even to the division of soul and spirit... and is a discerner of the thoughts and intents of the heart."
Hebrews 4:12 (NKJV)

The Word of God doesn't simply inform, it unveils. It cuts through motives, illusions, and pretense, revealing what lies hidden within. When the Spirit dwells richly in a believer, He gives the power to see beyond surface appearances, to discern what is true, pure, and aligned with the heart of God.

Everyday Illustration

Imagine driving late at night through thick fog. You can barely see the road ahead, but in the distance, a faint light from a lighthouse cuts through the haze. Though your natural vision is limited, that light becomes your guide.

Discernment functions just like that. When confusion surrounds us, the Holy Spirit becomes the light that pierces through uncertainty, guiding us safely toward truth.

The Nature of Spiritual Discernment

In Scripture, the Greek word for discern—*anakrino*—means *to examine closely, to separate, to investigate.* Spiritual discernment is the divine ability to separate light from darkness, truth from distortion, and the voice of God from the noise of emotion.

Discernment is not suspicion. Suspicion judges; discernment prays. Suspicion is rooted in fear; discernment is birthed in love. Suspicion isolates, but discernment intercedes.

A discerning heart does not expose to shame but exposes to heal; it sees what is wrong in order to make room for what is right.

"All the words of my mouth are with righteousness; nothing crooked or perverse is in them. They are all plain to him who understands, and right to those who find knowledge."
Proverbs 8:8–9 (NKJV)

To discern is to see as God sees, to weigh with divine balance, to sense with holy sensitivity. Discernment and wisdom are inseparable; wisdom governs *action,* discernment governs *perception.* One reveals what to do, the other reveals what is true.

When discernment is active, the believer walks in safety. The Prophet Hosea wrote,

> *"Who is wise? Let him understand these things. Who is prudent? Let him know them. For the ways of the Lord are right; the righteous walk in them, but transgressors stumble in them."*
> ***Hosea 14:9 (NKJV)***

The one who walks in discernment does not stumble, because they no longer rely on sight; they rely on light.

Everyday Illustration

A young woman meets someone who speaks eloquently about faith and godliness, yet something in her spirit feels uneasy. Months later, the person's motives are exposed as manipulative. That "check" she felt wasn't suspicion; it was discernment. The Holy Spirit was whispering beneath the noise, showing her what the natural eye could not see.

THE SPIRIT-GIVEN GIFT OF DISCERNMENT

While every believer is called to grow in wisdom and understanding, there exists a distinct spiritual gift called the *discernment of spirits*, a supernatural empowerment of the Holy Spirit that allows one to distinguish the source behind words, actions, or atmospheres.

> *"But the manifestation of the Spirit is given to each one for the profit of all: for to one is given the word of wisdom through the Spirit, to another the word of knowledge through the same Spirit... to another discerning of spirits."*
> ***1 Corinthians 12:7–10 (NKJV)***

This gift cannot be taught in a classroom. It is imparted by the Spirit Himself and developed through intimacy with Him. It enables the believer to perceive whether something originates from God's Spirit, the human spirit, or demonic spirits.

A discerning believer doesn't merely hear words; they perceive the heart and the spiritual influence beneath them. They can sense when the Holy Spirit is present, when human emotion is driving something, or when the enemy is attempting to mimic God's voice. This is why discernment is vital; it guards the believer from being misled by the counterfeit.

A Gift of Protection and Direction

Discernment is both **protective** and **directive**. It shields the believer from deception and helps guide them in the will of God.

The story of Paul and the slave girl in Philippi is a powerful example:

> *"Now it happened, as we went to prayer, that a certain slave girl possessed with a spirit of divination met us, who brought her masters much profit by fortune-telling. This girl followed Paul and us, and cried out, saying, 'These men are the servants of the Most High God, who proclaim to us the way of salvation.' And this she did for many days. But Paul, greatly annoyed, turned and said to the spirit, 'I command you in the name of Jesus Christ to come out of her.' And he came out that very hour."*
> *Acts 16:16–18 (NKJV)*

Outwardly, the girl's words sounded true, but the spirit behind them was not. Paul discerned that her source was demonic and confronted it in the authority of Christ. This moment teaches us that discernment goes beyond identifying *what is* being said; it reveals *who is* speaking through it.

Everyday Illustration: The Counterfeit Currency

Bank tellers are not trained by studying fake bills; they are trained by handling real currency until the genuine texture becomes unmistakable. When a counterfeit bill crosses their hand, they feel it immediately.

So, it is with spiritual discernment. The more we handle the authentic presence of God, the more easily we recognize what is false. We do not study deception; we study truth until deception becomes obvious.

Discerning Atmospheres and Encounters

Those who carry this gift often notice subtle spiritual shifts in their surroundings. They might sense heaviness where others sense nothing, or peace where others feel chaos. This sensitivity is not strange; it's spiritual awareness.

Elisha's servant experienced this when his natural eyes saw only danger, while Elisha discerned Heaven's protection.

"And Elisha prayed, and said, 'Lord, I pray, open his eyes that he may see.' Then the Lord opened the eyes of the young man, and he saw. And behold, the mountain was full of horses and chariots of fire all around Elisha."
2 Kings 6:17 (NKJV)

Discernment does not just expose darkness; it reveals divine activity. It helps us recognize when angels are present, when the Spirit is prompting prayer, or when an atmosphere is ready for a breakthrough.

For the Common Good

Discernment is never meant to make one superior. It is a **stewardship** that protects and strengthens the Body of Christ. Paul wrote that every spiritual manifestation is given "for the profit of all." Therefore, discernment must continuously operate in humility, love, and accountability.

The one who discerns rightly does not criticize; they intercede. They do not expose to bring shame or condemnation; they expose to heal. They function like spiritual watchmen, standing at the gate of the Church to guard the purity of what enters.

When motivated by love, the discerner becomes a shield for others. They sense danger before it strikes, deception before it spreads, and divine opportunity before it fades. This is not suspicion; it is spiritual sensitivity guided by compassion.

THE POWER AND PURPOSE OF DISCERNMENT

The gift of discernment is not a spiritual luxury; it is a necessity for every believer who desires to walk in truth.

Without it, even sincere Christians can mistake emotion for revelation or charisma for anointing. Discernment is the guardrail that keeps our pursuit of the supernatural anchored in Scripture and purity. It ensures that spiritual hunger is not hijacked by deception.

The Apostle Paul prayed that the Church in Philippi would develop this kind of clarity:

"That you may approve the things that are excellent, that you may be sincere and without offense till the day of Christ."
Philippians 1:10 (NKJV)

To "approve what is excellent" means to test and evaluate what is truly of God. Discernment refines our moral compass and our spiritual perception so that we can see the difference between what is good and what only *appears* good.

Seeing Beneath the Surface

Discernment gives us the wisdom to see beyond the surface of situations, people, and opportunities. It teaches us that not every open door is divine and not every closed door is demonic. Discernment asks not, "Is this convenient?" but, "Does this carry the fragrance of Heaven?"

"Abhor what is evil. Cling to what is good."
Romans 12:9 (NKJV)

But how can we cling to what is good if we cannot recognize it? Discernment is the ability to tell the difference between what flatters the flesh and what feeds the spirit.

Everyday Illustration

A young believer receives advice that sounds wise but doesn't sit right in their spirit. Their friend's words seem caring, yet something feels misaligned. When they take time to pray and open Scripture, the Holy Spirit confirms that the counsel, though well-meaning, wasn't rooted in truth. Discernment helped them choose obedience over opinion.

The Safety of the Discerning

Discernment brings stability and protection. It anchors the believer in peace, even when the path seems uncertain. The book of Proverbs promises this to those who walk in wisdom:

"My son, let them not depart from your eyes—keep sound wisdom and discretion; so, they will be life to your soul and grace to your neck. Then you will walk safely in your way, and your foot will not stumble. When you lie down, you will not be afraid; yes, you will lie down, and your sleep will be sweet."
Proverbs 3:21–24 (NKJV)

Discernment gives rest to the soul. When you know you are following the peace of God, anxiety loses its grip.

Discernment and the Renewed Mind

Paul taught that transformation begins in the mind:

"Do not be conformed to this world, but be transformed by the renewing of your mind, that you may prove what is that good and acceptable and perfect will of God."
Romans 12:2 (NKJV)

Renewing the mind is an act of discernment; it's learning to filter every thought through the truth of God's Word. As the believer grows in this, discernment becomes instinctive. They don't have to pause and question every impulse; their spirit has been trained by Scripture to recognize what is of God.

When discernment governs thought, emotion no longer dictates obedience. The believer no longer needs constant signs; they walk by the inward witness of peace. Isaiah described this beautifully:

"Your ears shall hear a word behind you, saying, 'This is the way, walk in it,' whenever you turn to the right hand or whenever you turn to the left."
Isaiah 30:21 (NKJV)

Discernment is that quiet voice behind the noise of life that says, *"This is the way."*

Light in the Age of Deception

We live in an age where deception often masquerades as wisdom, and darkness wears the mask of light. Jesus warned,

> *"Take heed that no one deceives you."*
> **Matthew 24:4 (NKJV)**

False prophets and counterfeit voices often speak in the name of God but carry no resemblance to His nature. The only defense is a discerning spirit anchored in truth.

A believer who knows the voice of the Shepherd cannot be easily fooled by imitation. Discernment does not come from studying darkness; it comes from gazing at the Light until all that isn't Him becomes obvious.

Everyday Illustration

A Christian conference features two speakers, both charismatic, both moving in signs. Yet one leaves the room peacefully, and the other leaves it heavy and confused. The discerning believer doesn't judge outwardly; they know which voice carried Heaven's fragrance. The difference isn't style, it's spirit.

Discernment allows us to walk in purity, even amid spiritual noise. It helps us remain unmoved by emotional extremes and grounded in the stillness of truth.

KEYS TO GROWING IN DISCERNMENT

Spiritual discernment is not something granted once for all, it deepens over time as we walk with God. It is cultivated through intimacy, obedience, and practice. Just as physical senses sharpen with use, spiritual senses mature through continual fellowship with the Holy Spirit and submission to His voice.

> *"But solid food belongs to those who are of full age, that is, those who by reason of use have their senses exercised to discern both good and evil."*
> **Hebrews 5:14 (NKJV)**

The more we respond to the Spirit's inner promptings, the sharper our perception becomes. Discernment is not gained through striving, but through surrender, yielding our instincts and emotions to the light of God's truth until our hearts beat in rhythm with His.

Surrender: The Foundation of Spiritual Clarity

The starting point of discernment is surrender. A self-willed heart cannot see clearly. Jesus modeled perfect discernment because He lived in perfect surrender. In the Garden of Gethsemane, He prayed,

> *"O My Father, if it is possible, let this cup pass from Me; nevertheless, not as I will, but as You will."*
> ***Matthew 26:39 (NKJV)***

At that moment of surrender, Heaven's will became clear. Discernment thrives when "I" is dethroned and Christ is enthroned. When we insist on our own way, our vision becomes clouded; when we yield, our sight becomes sharp.

Pride is the great enemy of discernment because pride assumes it already knows. But humility listens. James wrote,

> *"God resists the proud, but gives grace to the humble."*
> *— **James 4:6 (NKJV)***

Those who walk humbly receive insights others miss because they have laid down the need to be right to remain aligned with truth.

Peace: The Compass of the Spirit

Peace is the Holy Spirit's built-in navigation system. Paul reminded the church that "God is not the author of confusion but of peace" (1 Corinthians 14:33). When the Spirit speaks, He brings clarity and calm, not turmoil.

> *"And let the peace of God rule in your hearts, to which also you were called in one body; and be thankful."*
> ***Colossians 3:15 (NKJV)***

The word *rule* means *to act as an umpire*. Peace makes the call. If peace lifts, pause. If peace remains, proceed.

The Word: The Eternal Standard

True discernment always aligns with Scripture. The Bible is the measure of all revelation and experience.

"The entrance of Your words gives light; it gives understanding to the simple."
Psalm 119:130 (NKJV)

Light exposes what darkness conceals. Any impression, dream, or prophetic word must be weighed against the Word of God. The Spirit who speaks never contradicts the Scriptures He inspired.

The discerning believer is therefore a student of the Word. The more we know the written truth, the more accurately we perceive the living truth when He speaks. Scripture calibrates our inner compass; it teaches us how God thinks, what He values, and what He will never endorse.

Everyday Illustration

A believer hears someone teach that "grace means we no longer need repentance." The message sounds liberating, but something feels wrong. They search the Scriptures and read Jesus' words to the church in Revelation, *"Be zealous and repent."* Immediately, clarity comes. The Spirit's discernment, anchored in the Word, exposes the lie wrapped in flattery.

Intimacy: The Wellspring of Discernment

Discernment grows strongest in the soil of intimacy with God. The closer we walk with the Holy Spirit, the more we recognize His movement. Jesus said,

"My sheep hear My voice, and I know them, and they follow Me."
John 10:27 (NKJV)

Intimacy creates familiarity with the Shepherd's tone just as a child knows a parent's voice in a crowded room, so a believer attuned to God recognizes His whisper amid the noise of the world.

Discernment is not about just detecting evil; it is about knowing God. It is not only to be alert to the devil's schemes, but the main goal is to be aligned with the Spirit's heart. As our fellowship with Him deepens, discernment becomes natural; it flows from love.

Discernment, then, matures through **surrender, peace, Scripture, and intimacy**. It is not a gift to boast about, but a grace to steward. The more we yield, the clearer we see.

DISCERNMENT AND SPIRITUAL WARFARE

Every believer lives within two realms, the seen and the unseen. What we perceive with our eyes is temporary, but the spiritual realm is eternal. Discernment allows us to navigate both without confusion or fear. The Apostle Paul reminds us:
"For we do not wrestle against flesh and blood, but against principalities, against powers, against the rulers of the darkness of this age, against spiritual hosts of wickedness in the heavenly places."
Ephesians 6:12 (NKJV)
Our battles are not with people, but with unseen powers that influence the visible world. Discernment gives the believer the ability to recognize where the true conflict lies and to respond with spiritual authority instead of emotional reaction.

Discerning the Holy Spirit
The highest function of discernment is not to detect darkness, but to recognize **the movement of the Holy Spirit**. It begins not with identifying deception, but with recognizing truth. Jesus said,
"When He, the Spirit of truth, has come, He will guide you into all truth."
John 16:13 (NKJV)
The Spirit of God never confuses; He clarifies. His voice produces peace, conviction, and life. To discern Him requires a quieted heart, for His whisper is often drowned out by the noise of emotion and anxiety.

A mature believer can sense when the Spirit's presence increases or withdraws. Like Moses, they know when to move because the cloud has lifted, and when to stay because His glory remains.

Discerning Demonic Spirits

The gift of discernment also exposes **demonic influence**, not to stir fear, but to bring freedom. Jesus declared,

> *"These signs will follow those who believe: In My name they will cast out demons."*
> ***Mark 16:17 (NKJV)***

Evil spirits often operate subtly, through manipulation, deception, or emotional distortion. A spirit of fear may masquerade as anxiety; a spirit of pride may disguise itself as confidence. Discernment recognizes the unseen source without condemning the person.

When Jesus rebuked Peter, saying, *"Get behind Me, Satan!"* (Matthew 16:23), He wasn't attacking Peter's heart; He was confronting the spirit speaking through him. This is the nature of discernment; it separates the person from the influence.

Demonic activity reveals itself through its *fruit*. Jesus said,

> *"You will know them by their fruits."*
> ***Matthew 7:16 (NKJV)***

If an atmosphere carries confusion, fear, or accusation, it's not the Holy Spirit. By contrast, the fruit of the Spirit, love, joy, peace, and self-control (Galatians 5:22–23), reveals God's presence. Discernment teaches us to judge not by emotion, but by fruit.

When darkness is exposed, we don't panic; we proclaim victory. Discernment doesn't magnify the devil; it magnifies Jesus' triumph.

Discerning Angelic Activity

God's angels are also active in the unseen realm, serving those who belong to Him.

> *"Are they not all ministering spirits sent forth to minister for those who will inherit salvation?"*
> ***Hebrews 1:14 (NKJV)***

Throughout Scripture, angels deliver messages, offer protection, and carry out God's commands. Yet discernment is needed here as well, for Satan "transforms himself into an angel of light" (2 Corinthians 11:14).

When angels truly come from God, their presence aligns with Scripture, glorifies Jesus, and produces clarity, along with a holy fear of the Lord — not pride or arrogance. Every authentic angelic encounter in Scripture carries the same pattern: the angel's message agrees with God's Word, the angel refuses to accept worship, and the encounter draws the person closer to obedience, humility, and reverence before God.

Mary's encounter with Gabriel led her to surrender to God's will (Luke 1:26–38). John's vision in Revelation reveals the true posture of angelic beings: they refuse worship and direct all glory to God alone (Revelation 22:8-9).

False Light and Counterfeit Revelation

From Eden to today, deception remains the enemy's favorite weapon. The serpent's words to Eve mixed truth with lies, and mankind's discernment failed. Modern deception often looks spiritual; it quotes Scripture, uses the language of revelation, and mimics the supernatural.

"Many false prophets will rise up and deceive many."
Matthew 24:11 (NKJV)

Discernment equips believers to test everything by the Word and the witness of the Spirit. It teaches us that not every dream, voice, or "angelic encounter" originates from Heaven. The question is simple: Does it glorify Jesus? Does it align with Scripture? Does it produce peace and holiness?

Discernment is protection from deception, even when cloaked in brilliance.

Discerning in Love, Not Fear

True discernment always operates from love, never suspicion. Fear distorts perception; love purifies it. Jesus discerned sin and hypocrisy yet moved with compassion toward those bound by it.

When love governs discernment, our goal is not to expose but to restore. The discerner who sees clearly but loves poorly is still blind. Discernment that flows from love sees through deception while still believing for redemption.

"Perfect love casts out fear."
1 John 4:18 (NKJV)

When love leads, even warfare becomes worship. We discern not to fight in panic, but to enforce Christ's victory with peace and authority.

"He who is in you is greater than he who is in the world."
1 John 4:4 (NKJV)

Application: Living as a Discerning Believer

Discernment is not a mystical ability for a select few; it is the birthright of every believer who walks with the Holy Spirit. It is the quiet wisdom that steadies us in an unstable world. To live a discerning life is to live alert, to walk with open eyes, tuned ears, and a yielded heart that listens for Heaven's rhythm amid earthly noise.

Paul exhorted,

"Test all things; hold fast what is good. Abstain from every form of evil."
1 Thessalonians 5:21–22 (NKJV)

Testing all things doesn't mean living in suspicion; it means living in submission to the Spirit who reveals truth. The discerning believer pauses before reacting, prays before deciding, and measures every voice by the peace of Christ.

Discernment is the inward knowing that not every opportunity is divine, not every delay is demonic, and not every door that closes is punishment. Sometimes discernment reveals that God's "no" is His mercy in disguise.

Discernment in Daily Life

The gift of discernment is not confined to the church; it guides every aspect of life. In relationships, it teaches us to love wisely, to see beyond charm, and to discern character over charisma. In decisions, it helps us recognize timing, when to move, when to wait, when to speak, and when to be silent. In prayer, it sharpens our focus, so we war effectively, targeting roots instead of branches.

"Your ears shall hear a word behind you, saying, 'This is the way, walk in it.'"
Isaiah 30:21 (NKJV)

When we learn to live by this inner voice of the Spirit, life becomes less about guessing and more about guiding. The Holy Spirit becomes our Counselor in every detail, our unseen Guide who reveals what the natural mind could never perceive.

Discernment also protects the believer in a digital world where countless "voices" compete for spiritual influence. The discerning Christian listens carefully to online teachings, prophetic messages, or movements, always asking: *Does this reflect the heart of Jesus? Does it align with the Word of God? Does it produce love, holiness, and peace?*

Discernment also opens the door for compassion-led action. Sometimes God reveals what others cannot see, not so we can judge incorrectly, but so we can pray.

Living with discernment means walking in continual dependence on the Holy Spirit. It means refusing to be moved by emotion or opinion, but instead by the peace that confirms God's will. The discerning believer carries authority with gentleness and clarity with humility.

Discernment does not make us untrusting; it makes us unshakable. It is the eye of the spirit that keeps us steady when the world around us loses focus.

Closing Prayer
Heavenly Father,
I thank You for the precious gift of discernment. You are the God who sees all things, and You have invited me to see through Your eyes. I ask You to sharpen my spiritual senses—to know truth from error, light from darkness, and Your voice above every other sound.

Lord, I surrender my heart and mind to You. Where my understanding falls short, let Your Spirit lead me into all truth.

Teach me to walk in wisdom, to listen for Your peace, and to anchor every decision in Your Word. Let discernment guard my steps and guide my speech.

Holy Spirit, fill me with Your presence. Deliver me from confusion, pride, and fear. Make me sensitive to Your leading and let my discernment always flow from love. Help me to see people through Your compassion, to pray with accuracy, and to act with grace.

Father, keep me anchored in truth in a world that trades it for emotion. Let my sight be pure, my motives clean, and my heart steadfast. May my discernment glorify Jesus, protect the Body of Christ, and reveal Your Kingdom wherever I go.

In Jesus' name,
Amen.

Chapter 4: Signs and Wonders
The Manifest Power of God Revealed

THE GOD WHO STILL MOVES

From Genesis to Revelation, the Bible reveals a God who continually demonstrates His power among His people. He is not a silent observer in heaven, but an active participant in the story of humanity. Every miracle, healing, and divine encounter throughout Scripture speaks of His heart to make Himself known.

Signs and wonders are heaven's way of saying, *"God is here."* They are not random acts of supernatural display, but expressions of His covenant love and divine nature. Each one reveals who He is: merciful, mighty, faithful, and near.

"My speech and my preaching were not with persuasive words of human wisdom, but in demonstration of the Spirit and of power."
1 Corinthians 2:4 (NKJV)

The Kingdom of God is not a theory to be studied; it is a reality to be lived. When God moves in signs and wonders, He confirms that His Word is truth, His presence is real, and His purposes are unstoppable.

God has always been a God of manifestation. He revealed Himself to Adam in the garden by walking with him in the cool of the day.
Genesis 3:8 (NKJV)

He revealed Himself to Abraham through covenant and promise, to Moses through fire and voice, and to the prophets through visions and divine encounters. Every time God revealed Himself, He did so through both *Word and Power.*

It has never been His desire for His people to know Him merely through information, but through encounter.

> *"Oh, taste and see that the Lord is good; Blessed is the man who trusts in Him."*
> ***Psalm 34:8 (NKJV)***

This is not a passive invitation; it is a call to experience the living God. His nature has not changed. What He did in the lives of His people thousands of years ago, He still delights to do today.

When Jesus walked the earth, He did not only teach doctrine; He demonstrated dominion. He healed the sick, opened blind eyes, cleansed lepers, multiplied bread, calmed storms, and raised the dead. Every act of power was a mirror of the Father's heart, revealing what heaven looks like when it invades earth.

> *"He who has seen Me has seen the Father."*
> ***John 14:9 (NKJV)***

And after His ascension, He sent the Holy Spirit to continue this same work through the Church.

> *"Jesus Christ is the same yesterday, today, and forever."*
> ***Hebrews 13:8 (NKJV)***

The same power that raised Him from the dead now abides in every believer.

> *"But if the Spirit of Him who raised Jesus from the dead dwells in you, He who raised Christ from the dead will also give life to your mortal bodies through His Spirit who dwells in you."*
> ***Romans 8:11 (NKJV)***

God still heals. He still speaks. He still performs wonders among His people.

Too many have reduced the miraculous to the pages of history, as though the book of Acts ended with the apostles. But the story of Acts was never a conclusion; it was a beginning. It is the unfolding of a Kingdom that continues to manifest itself through yielded hearts. God still delights to reveal His glory in ways that both confound the intellect and awaken the spirit.

> *"The heavens declare the glory of God; And the firmament shows His handiwork."*
> ***Psalm 19:1 (NKJV)***

The earth still bears witness to His hand. The lives of His people are still the canvas on which He paints His wonders. The same God who spoke light into darkness now shines His light into human hearts through the gospel of Jesus Christ.

"For it is the God who commanded light to shine out of darkness, who has shone in our hearts to give the light of the knowledge of the glory of God in the face of Jesus Christ."
2 Corinthians 4:6 (NKJV)

When we talk about miracles, we are not speaking of ancient myths or poetic legends. We are speaking of the living reality of God's involvement with His creation. His power was never meant to be confined to sacred texts or ancient memories; it was meant to be the rhythm of life for His people.

Every breath of a believer is sustained by the miraculous. The sunrise, the heartbeat, the peace that passes understanding, all are daily reminders that God still moves. Miracles are not interruptions in the natural order; they are the reintroduction of divine order into a fallen world. They are the fingerprints of a Father reclaiming what belongs to Him.

When the Church becomes aware of this truth, faith awakens, and the miraculous becomes possible again. Fear gives way to boldness, and passivity gives way to partnership, for we were never meant to be spectators of God's power but participants in it.

"For the kingdom of God is not in word but in power."
1 Corinthians 4:20 (NKJV)

When His people hunger once more for His presence, they will see His power revealed. And the world will know, just as the early Church knew, that our God is not an idea to be discussed but a Person to be encountered. He is still Emmanuel—*God with us*—the same God who moves mountains, opens prison doors, heals hearts, and changes lives.

SIGNS AND WONDERS DEFINED

Throughout Scripture, miraculous acts are described with words such as signs, wonders, mighty works, and power. These are not interchangeable, but together they reveal the fullness of God's activity among His people.

In the Old Testament, two primary Hebrew words are used to describe miracles. *Oth* refers to a *sign*—a visible marker or event that points beyond itself to a greater divine reality. It is a supernatural indicator meant to reveal God's presence or confirm His word. The second term, *mopheth*, means *wonder*—something extraordinary that evokes awe, reverence, and holy fear. Together, these words show that biblical miracles were never mere spectacles; they were signs that pointed to God and wonders that stirred the heart to worship. These two often appear together, such as in Exodus 7:3:

"And I will harden Pharaoh's heart, and multiply My signs and My wonders in the land of Egypt."
Exodus 7:3 (NKJV)

A sign is a divine marker. It may be astonishing or straightforward, like the rainbow that marked God's covenant with Noah, or the blood on the doorposts that protected Israel in Egypt.

"I set My rainbow in the cloud, and it shall be for the sign of the covenant between Me and the earth."
Genesis 9:13 (NKJV)

"Now the blood shall be a sign for you on the houses where you are. And when I see the blood, I will pass over you."
Exodus 12:13 (NKJV)

Signs reveal purpose and direction; they point people back to God. They are not meant to glorify the event itself but to draw attention to the One behind it. When God gives a sign, He invites us into revelation, saying in essence, *"Look at Me; I am near."*

A wonder overwhelms the human heart with awe. It moves beyond explanation, stirring reverence and worship.

"I will meditate on all Your work, and talk of Your deeds."
Psalm 77:12 (NKJV)

Wonders are divine interruptions of natural order, moments when Heaven touches earth and creation bends to the will of its Creator. They stretch the human mind to its limits and awaken the soul to the reality that God is greater than comprehension. When God performs wonders, He invites us not only to witness His power but to adore His presence.

In the New Testament, the Greek words *semeion (sign)* and *teras (wonder)* are often used together, as in Acts 2:43:
"Then fear came upon every soul, and many wonders and signs were done through the apostles."
Acts 2:43 (NKJV)

A sign appeals to the understanding; it communicates that something divine is taking place. A wonder appeals to the imagination; it causes hearts to marvel at the greatness of God. Together, they reveal both the message and the majesty of Heaven.

The Gospel of John uniquely refers to Jesus' miracles as *signs*. Each miracle was a visible revelation of who He was, the Word made flesh. Turning water into wine signified transformation. Feeding the five thousand signified divine sufficiency. Raising Lazarus signified victory over death. John writes:

"And truly Jesus did many other signs in the presence of His disciples, which are not written in this book; but these are written that you may believe that Jesus is the Christ, the Son of God, and that believing you may have life in His name."
John 20:30–31 (NKJV)

Signs and wonders are therefore not random acts of divine power; they are expressions of divine purpose. They reveal that God is both transcendent and immanent —above all yet intimately involved in His creation.

Even creation itself stands as an ongoing sign of His majesty.

"For since the creation of the world His invisible attributes are clearly seen, being understood by the things that are made, even His eternal power and Godhead, so that they are without excuse."
Romans 1:20 (NKJV)

When we recognize the language of signs and wonders, we begin to perceive God not only in extraordinary events but in the ordinary rhythms of life. Every sunrise, every answered prayer, every moment of peace in chaos is a whisper of His miraculous hand.

In this way, signs and wonders are not simply supernatural events; they are Heaven's vocabulary. They remind us that God is still speaking, still moving, and still revealing His glory on the earth.

PURPOSE OF SIGNS AND WONDERS

God's miraculous works are never without meaning. Each sign and wonder carries divine purpose. When God performs a miracle, He is not merely displaying might; He is communicating meaning. Every act of power becomes a *language*, a visible word from Heaven that speaks directly to the heart of humanity.

- **To Reveal His Nature and Glory**
  Every miracle displays a facet of His character. Healing reveals His compassion; provision reveals His generosity; deliverance reveals His mercy.
  "That they may know that You, whose name alone is the Lord, are the Most High over all the earth."
  Psalm 83:18 (NKJV)

- **To Confirm His Word**
  God confirms what He says through supernatural evidence. Signs are not substitutes for truth; they are its validation.
  "And they went out and preached everywhere, the Lord working with them and confirming the word through the accompanying signs."
  Mark 16:20 (NKJV)

- **To Lead People to Salvation**
  Miracles are invitations to encounter Jesus. They are the open doors through which hearts perceive His love and believe.

"Now when He was in Jerusalem at the Passover, during the feast, many believed in His name when they saw the signs which He did."
John 2:23 (NKJV)

- **To Strengthen Believers' Faith**
Signs and wonders remind us that God is active and faithful. They renew hope and anchor us in His presence.
"You are the God who does wonders; You have declared Your strength among the peoples."
Psalm 77:14 (NKJV)

SIGNS AND WONDERS IN THE OLD TESTAMENT

From the first chapter of Genesis to the final prophecies of Daniel, God's power was displayed in the lives of His people:

- **Deliverance**
God parted the Red Sea for Israel's escape.
"Then Moses stretched out his hand over the sea; and the Lord caused the sea to go back by a strong east wind all that night, and made the sea into dry land, and the waters were divided."
Exodus 14:21 (NKJV)

He shut the mouths of lions to protect Daniel and stood with the three Hebrew men in the fiery furnace.
"My God sent His angel and shut the lions' mouths, so that they have not hurt me, because I was found innocent before Him."
Daniel 6:22 (NKJV)

"Look! I see four men loose, walking in the midst of the fire; and they are not hurt, and the form of the fourth is like the Son of God."
Daniel 3:25 (NKJV)

- **Provision**
He sent manna from heaven and caused water to flow from a rock.
"So when the children of Israel saw it, they said to one another, 'What is it?' For they did not know what it was. And

Moses said to them, 'This is the bread which the Lord has given you to eat.'"
Exodus 16:15 (NKJV)
"Then Moses lifted his hand and struck the rock twice with his rod; and water came out abundantly, and the congregation and their animals drank."
Numbers 20:11 (NKJV)

- **Revelation**
  Moses encountered the burning bush, and Isaiah saw the Lord high and lifted up.
  "And the Angel of the Lord appeared to him in a flame of fire from the midst of a bush. So he looked, and behold, the bush was burning with fire, but the bush was not consumed."
  Exodus 3:2 (NKJV)
  "I saw the Lord sitting on a throne, high and lifted up, and the train of His robe filled the temple."
  Isaiah 6:1 (NKJV)

- **Victory**
  The walls of Jericho fell at the sound of praise.
  "So the people shouted when the priests blew the trumpets. And it happened when the people heard the sound of the trumpet, and the people shouted with a great shout, that the wall fell down flat."
  Joshua 6:20 (NKJV)

Every act of divine power revealed that God was not only the Creator but also the Covenant Keeper, faithful to guide, protect, and dwell among His people.

THE MINISTRY OF JESUS: THE MIRACLE WORKER

In the New Testament, Jesus Christ revealed the Kingdom through a continuous flow of supernatural works. His miracles were not separate from His message; they were the message in motion.

"Jesus of Nazareth, a Man attested by God to you by miracles, wonders, and signs which God did through Him in

your midst."
Acts 2:22 (NKJV)

- He turned water into wine to show His transforming power.

  "This beginning of signs Jesus did in Cana of Galilee, and manifested His glory; and His disciples believed in Him."
  John 2:11 (NKJV)

- He fed the multitudes to reveal Himself as the Bread of Life.

  "And Jesus said to them, 'I am the bread of life. He who comes to Me shall never hunger, and he who believes in Me shall never thirst.'"
  John 6:35 (NKJV)

- He healed the blind and the leper to display the mercy of the Father.

  "Then Jesus put out His hand and touched him, saying, 'I am willing; be cleansed.' Immediately, his leprosy was cleansed."
  Matthew 8:3 (NKJV)

  "He answered and said, 'Whether He is a sinner or not I do not know. One thing I know: that though I was blind, now I see.'"
  John 9:25 (NKJV)

- He raised Lazarus from the dead to demonstrate His authority over death.

  "Now when He had said these things, He cried with a loud voice, 'Lazarus, come forth!' And he who had died came out bound hand and foot with graveclothes."
  John 11:43–44 (NKJV)

Every miracle was a visible expression of invisible truth: the Kingdom of Heaven had come near.

THE EARLY CHURCH: CARRIERS OF THE MIRACULOUS

After Jesus ascended, the outpouring of the Holy Spirit empowered believers to walk in the same miraculous power.

"And through the hands of the apostles, many signs and wonders were done among the people."
Acts 5:12 (NKJV)

- Peter's shadow healed the sick.

"So that they brought the sick out into the streets and laid them on beds and couches, that at least the shadow of Peter passing by might fall on some of them."
Acts 5:15 (NKJV)

- Paul's handkerchiefs carried healing virtue.

"Now God worked unusual miracles by the hands of Paul, so that even handkerchiefs or aprons were brought from his body to the sick, and the diseases left them and the evil spirits went out of them."
Acts 19:11–12 (NKJV)

- Prison doors opened by angelic intervention.

"Now behold, an angel of the Lord stood by him, and a light shone in the prison; and he struck Peter on the side and raised him up, saying, 'Arise quickly!' And his chains fell off his hands."
Acts 12:7 (NKJV)

- Earthquakes broke chains in worship.

"Suddenly there was a great earthquake, so that the foundations of the prison were shaken; and immediately all the doors were opened and everyone's chains were loosed."
Acts 16:26 (NKJV)

The supernatural was not occasional; it was normal. It confirmed that the same Jesus who walked in Galilee was still walking with His people by His Spirit.

"And they went out and preached everywhere, the Lord working with them and confirming the word through the accompanying signs."
Mark 16:20 (NKJV)

TRUE AND FALSE WONDERS: THE NEED FOR DISCERNMENT

Scripture also warns that not all supernatural manifestations are from God. Satan imitates the miraculous to deceive hearts.

"The coming of the lawless one is according to the working of Satan, with all power, signs, and lying wonders."
2 Thessalonians 2:9 (NKJV)

Even Pharaoh's magicians could replicate some of Moses' miracles, but their power was limited and counterfeit.

"But Pharaoh also called the wise men and the sorcerers; so the magicians of Egypt, they also did in like manner with their enchantments. For every man threw down his rod, and they became serpents. But Aaron's rod swallowed up their rods."
Exodus 7:11–12 (NKJV)

True miracles bring glory to Christ, produce righteousness, and lead to life. False ones exalt man, stir pride, and bring confusion.

Jesus cautioned,

"For false christs and false prophets will rise and show great signs and wonders to deceive, if possible, even the elect."
Matthew 24:24 (NKJV)

Discernment, guided by the Holy Spirit, is vital for the believer. The Spirit of truth reveals what is genuine, protecting the church from deception.

"Beloved, do not believe every spirit, but test the spirits, whether they are of God; because many false prophets have gone out into the world."
1 John 4:1 (NKJV)

WALKING NATURALLY SUPERNATURAL

The miraculous is not meant to be rare; it is intended to be *normal* for the believer. The supernatural life is not reserved for prophets or apostles alone, but for every son and daughter of God who walks in faith and intimacy with Him. Jesus did not perform miracles to prove divinity; He performed them to model partnership with the Father.

> *"Most assuredly, I say to you, he who believes in Me, the works that I do he will do also; and greater works than these he will do, because I go to My Father."*
>
> **John 14:12 (NKJV)**

This is the inheritance of every follower of Christ. The same Spirit that empowered Jesus' ministry has been given to us. The same power that raised Him from the grave now lives within every believer.

> *"But if the Spirit of Him who raised Jesus from the dead dwells in you, He who raised Christ from the dead will also give life to your mortal bodies through His Spirit who dwells in you."*
>
> **Romans 8:11 (NKJV)**

When we live surrendered to the Holy Spirit, Heaven's resources flow naturally through our lives. Miracles cease to be rare interruptions and instead become the natural overflow of communion with God. As we walk in faith and obedience, Heaven touches earth through our words, prayers, and actions.

When we pray for healing, declare God's promises, or step out in faith, we are not trying to convince God to move; we are simply agreeing with what He already desires to do. We partner with His will to bring His Kingdom into visible expression.

> *"And these signs will follow those who believe: In My name they will cast out demons; they will speak with new tongues; they will take up serpents; and if they drink anything deadly, it will by no means hurt them; they will lay hands on the sick, and they will recover."*
>
> **Mark 16:17–18 (NKJV)**

Living naturally supernatural does not mean we will always experience dramatic demonstrations of power. More often, God's hand moves quietly in the details of daily life.

A mother's prayer heals her child. A bill is paid unexpectedly. A word of encouragement restores a weary soul. These are all *signs*, reminders that the God of Scripture is still moving today.

> *"Jesus Christ is the same yesterday, today, and forever."*
>
> **Hebrews 13:8 (NKJV)**

The Kingdom of God is both majestic and personal. It meets us in our ordinary moments, revealing His care in the small as well as the great. Every answered prayer, every moment of divine peace, and every gentle whisper of the Spirit is a wonder within reach—a testimony that Heaven is near.

"Be anxious for nothing, but in everything by prayer and supplication, with thanksgiving, let your requests be made known to God; and the peace of God, which surpasses all understanding, will guard your hearts and minds through Christ Jesus."
Philippians 4:6–7 (NKJV)

When the people of God learn to see Him in both the grand and the subtle, the miraculous becomes a rhythm of life. For the believer who walks in awareness of His presence, every moment holds the potential for a divine encounter. The natural becomes the dwelling place of the supernatural, Heaven revealed through yielded hearts.

The more we walk with God in the ordinary, the more He invites us into the extraordinary. Every answered prayer and quiet wonder becomes a stepping stone into a deeper encounter. The Father never meant for us to live content on the shores of faith; He calls us to launch into the deep, to explore the vastness of His power and presence.

THE CALL TO GO DEEPER

Many believers remain content standing at the shorelines of faith, watching from a safe distance as others step into the waters of the miraculous. But the invitation of the Spirit is clear:

"Deep calls unto deep at the noise of Your waterfalls; all Your waves and billows have gone over me."
Psalm 42:7 (NKJV)

God is calling His people to move beyond comfort, into deeper realms of faith and encounter. The Spirit still whispers the same invitation He gave Peter: *"Come."* It was not until

Peter stepped out of the boat that he learned the reality of walking on water. Faith only matures when it is tested in the deep.

There is always more in God, more to know, more to trust, more to see. Every answered prayer is a door to greater intimacy, every miracle a reminder that we have only begun to taste the fullness of His Kingdom.

To go deeper means surrender. It means trading the safety of shallow waters for the wonder of the unknown. It means allowing God to stretch our belief beyond reason, to lead us where dependence becomes our only confidence.

"Come, and let us go up to the mountain of the Lord, to the house of the God of Jacob; He will teach us His ways, and we shall walk in His paths."
Isaiah 2:3 (NKJV)

Those who go deeper learn that the miraculous life is not built on striving, but on *abiding*. It is in the secret place, where we listen, wait, and yield, that the greatest manifestations of His presence unfold. The surface may feel safer, but it's in the depths where transformation happens.

"The secret of the Lord is with those who fear Him, and He will show them His covenant."
Psalm 25:14 (NKJV)

God longs to reveal Himself to those who are willing to dive below the surface of routine religion and into the living waters of His Spirit. There, the waves of His glory carry us into encounters that change everything.

The call to go deeper is not for the few; it is for all who hunger to know Him as He truly is. For it is in the depths that the mysteries of His Kingdom are unveiled, and the ordinary becomes holy ground.

THE GOD OF WONDERS STILL REIGNS

The greatest wonder of all is not in the splitting of seas or the shaking of mountains; it is the transformation of a human heart by the love of God. The same power that raised Christ from the dead now restores souls, revives hope, and renews lives.

> *"Blessed be the Lord God, the God of Israel, who only does wondrous things!"*
> ***Psalm 72:18 (NKJV)***

Signs and wonders are the fruit of a divine relationship. They are love made visible and faith made tangible. When we seek the God of wonders more than the wonders of God, His glory is revealed in and through us. The world will see His power and know that Jesus lives.

> *"Behold, I and the children whom the Lord has given me are for signs and wonders in Israel."*
> ***Isaiah 8:18 (NKJV)***

WALKING IN THE REALITY OF SIGNS AND WONDERS

The study of signs and wonders calls us not merely to observe God's miracles but to *partner* with them. Every believer is called to be a living demonstration of God's Kingdom on earth.

- **Cultivate Expectancy**
  Believe that God still moves in power today. Miracles often begin with a heart that expects.
  > *"Then He touched their eyes, saying, 'According to your faith let it be to you.'"*
  > ***Matthew 9:29 (NKJV)***

- **Walk in Sensitivity to the Holy Spirit**
  Signs follow those whom he leads. Spend time listening for His voice; obedience is often the doorway to the miraculous.
  > *"For as many as are led by the Spirit of God, these are sons of God."*
  > ***Romans 8:14 (NKJV)***

- **Pray with Bold Faith**
  Don't hesitate to pray for the impossible. Heaven is not intimidated by human limitation.
  "For with God nothing will be impossible."
  Luke 1:37 (NKJV)
- **Keep Jesus as the Focus**
  Miracles are never about human fame, they are about divine glory. Always point back to Him.
  "For of Him and through Him and to Him are all things, to whom be glory forever. Amen."
  Romans 11:36 (NKJV)
- **Share What God Has Done**
  Testimonies build faith and invite His power to move again. What you celebrate, you cultivate.
  "Oh, give thanks to the Lord! Call upon His name; Make known His deeds among the peoples!"
  Psalm 105:1 (NKJV)

As you apply these principles, remember that the greatest miracle is transformation, a life surrendered to the presence and purposes of God. Signs and wonders will follow naturally when our hearts are anchored in Him.

PRAYER: A CRY FOR THE GOD OF WONDERS

"Please, show me Your glory."
Exodus 33:18 (NKJV)

Heavenly Father,

We thank You that You are the same yesterday, today, and forever. You are still the God who works wonders among Your people. Today, we open our hearts and invite You to move again—in our homes, our churches, and our generation.

Lord, stir our faith to believe for the impossible. Let signs and wonders follow our obedience as we carry Your presence into the world. Teach us to live with sensitivity to Your Spirit, and to walk in purity, humility, and power.

Give us discernment to recognize what is truly of You. Let Your miracles always lead us closer to Jesus, not merely to amazement but to transformation.

We ask for fresh fire, Lord—manifest Your glory in and through us, so that nations may see Your light and turn to You.

We declare today: *You alone do wondrous things.* Let our lives become testimonies of Your greatness.

In the mighty name of Jesus,
Amen.

Appendix A: Signs and Wonders
A Biblical Reference Guide (NKJV)

Introduction

Throughout the Word of God, divine power is displayed in visible, awe-inspiring ways that reveal His nature and confirm His Word. From the first light of creation to the visions of Revelation, every sign and wonder testifies that *"the Lord, He is God."*

"Now when all the people saw it, they fell on their faces; and they said, 'The Lord, He is God! The Lord, He is God!'"
1 Kings 18:39 (NKJV)

This appendix serves as a scriptural resource — a reference for study, teaching, or personal devotion — listing the major signs, wonders, and miracles throughout both the Old and New Testaments.

Each event reveals a facet of God's glory, reminding believers that the same power still moves today through the Holy Spirit.

I. Old Testament Signs and Wonders
A. Creation and Covenant Beginnings
- Creation of Heaven and Earth – *Genesis 1–2*
- Formation of Adam and Eve – *Genesis 2:7, 21–22*
- The Flood and the Ark – *Genesis 6–8*
- The Rainbow as a Sign of Covenant – *Genesis 9:13–17*
- Confusion of Languages at Babel – *Genesis 11:7–9*

B. Patriarchal Miracles
- God's appearances to Abraham – *Genesis 12:7; 15:17–18; 18:1–14*
- Destruction of Sodom and Gomorrah – *Genesis 19:24–25*
- Birth of Isaac to barren Sarah – *Genesis 21:1–2*
- Provision of a ram in place of Isaac – *Genesis 22:13–14*
- Jacob's ladder dream – *Genesis 28:12–17*

- God changes Jacob's name to Israel – *Genesis 32:24–30*
- Joseph's prophetic dreams and interpretations – *Genesis 37–41*

C. Wonders of the Exodus
1. The Burning Bush – *Exodus 3:2–5*
2. Rod turned to serpent – *Exodus 4:2–4*
3. Moses' hand made leprous and healed – *Exodus 4:6–7*
4. Ten Plagues of Egypt – *Exodus 7–12*
   • Water to blood • Frogs • Lice • Flies • Pestilence • Boils • Hail • Locusts • Darkness • Death of the firstborn
5. The Passover and blood as protection – *Exodus 12:13*
6. The Red Sea divided – *Exodus 14:21–31*
7. Pillar of Cloud and Fire – *Exodus 13:21–22*
8. Manna from Heaven – *Exodus 16:14–35*
9. Water from the Rock – *Exodus 17:6*
10. Glory of God on Mount Sinai – *Exodus 19:16–20*
11. Tablets written by God's finger – *Exodus 31:18*
12. Moses' face shining with glory – *Exodus 34:29–35*

D. Miracles in the Wilderness
- The earth swallows Korah's rebellion – *Numbers 16:31–33*
- Aaron's rod buds – *Numbers 17:8*
- Fiery serpents and the bronze serpent – *Numbers 21:6–9*
- Balaam's donkey speaks – *Numbers 22:28–31*

E. Miracles in the Conquest
- Jordan River parted – *Joshua 3:14–17*
- Walls of Jericho fall – *Joshua 6:20*
- Sun and moon stand still – *Joshua 10:12–14*
- Hailstones destroy Israel's enemies – *Joshua 10:11*

F. Wonders in the Time of the Judges

- Gideon's fleece (wet and dry) – *Judges 6:36–40*
- Samson's supernatural strength – *Judges 14–16*

G. Miracles in the Prophets' Era
- Hannah's barren womb opened – *1 Samuel 1:19–20*
- Dagon's idol falls before the Ark – *1 Samuel 5:2–4*
- Fire from heaven on Elijah's altar – *1 Kings 18:36–38*
- Widow's oil and flour multiplied – *1 Kings 17:8–16*
- Widow's son raised to life – *1 Kings 17:17–24*
- Elijah taken up to heaven – *2 Kings 2:11*
- Elisha parts the Jordan – *2 Kings 2:14*
- Healing of Naaman's leprosy – *2 Kings 5:14*
- The floating axe head – *2 Kings 6:6*
- 185,000 Assyrian soldiers destroyed by an angel – *2 Kings 19:35*
- The shadow moves backward (sign to Hezekiah) – *2 Kings 20:9–11*

H. Exilic and Prophetic Wonders
- Three men delivered from the fiery furnace – *Daniel 3:25–27*
- Daniel preserved in the lions' den – *Daniel 6:22*
- Handwriting on the wall at Belshazzar's feast – *Daniel 5:5–31*
- Ezekiel's visions of God's glory and the wheel within a wheel – *Ezekiel 1:4–28*
- The valley of dry bones vision – *Ezekiel 37:1–10*
- Jonah swallowed and preserved by a great fish – *Jonah 1:17*

II. New Testament Signs and Wonders
A. Miraculous Birth and Early Life of Jesus
- Angelic announcements to Mary and Joseph – *Luke 1:26–38; Matthew 1:20–21*
- Elizabeth's barren womb opened – *Luke 1:24–25*
- The virgin birth of Christ – *Matthew 1:18–25*
- The star guiding the wise men – *Matthew 2:1–2*

- Angelic appearances to shepherds – *Luke 2:8–14*
- Divine warning to Joseph to flee – *Matthew 2:13–15*

B. Miracles in Jesus' Ministry

A comprehensive list of His miracles may be found throughout the Gospels: turning water into wine (John 2:1–11), calming storms (Mark 4:35–41), healing the blind, deaf, and lame (Mark 7:31–37), feeding multitudes (Matthew 14–15), raising the dead (John 11:43–44), and countless others revealing His compassion and authority.

C. Miracles in the Early Church
- Pentecost: tongues of fire and rushing wind – *Acts 2:1–4*
- Healing of the lame man at the temple – *Acts 3:1–8*
- Ananias and Sapphira's deaths – *Acts 5:1–11*
- Angelic release from prison – *Acts 5:19–20*
- Philip's miracles in Samaria – *Acts 8:6–7*
- Philip transported by the Spirit after baptizing the Ethiopian eunuch – *Acts 8:39–40*
- Saul's conversion – *Acts 9:3–9*
- Peter raises Tabitha (Dorcas) – *Acts 9:36–41*
- Elymas struck blind – *Acts 13:11*
- Paul and Silas freed by an earthquake – *Acts 16:25–26*
- Paul heals the sick with handkerchiefs – *Acts 19:11–12*
- Eutychus raised from the dead – *Acts 20:9–10*
- Paul unharmed by a viper bite – *Acts 28:3–6*
- Healings on Malta – *Acts 28:8–9*

D. Prophetic and Cosmic Signs
- The veil torn at Christ's death – *Matthew 27:51*
- Earthquake and resurrection of saints – *Matthew 27:52–53*
- Angelic appearances at the empty tomb – *Matthew 28:2–6*
- Visions to Peter, Paul, and John – *Acts 10; 2 Corinthians 12; Revelation 1–22*

- End-time cosmic wonders – *Matthew 24:29–30; Revelation 6–19*

Closing Reflection

From the dawn of creation to the final revelation of Jesus Christ, God's power has been displayed through signs and wonders that reveal His glory and authority. Every miracle is a message, every wonder a witness.

Though the forms may change, the same Spirit who moved upon the waters in Genesis is still moving upon hearts today. His signs still point to salvation, His wonders still reveal His glory, and His power still confirms His Word.

"You are the God who does wonders; You have declared Your strength among the peoples." **Psalm 77:14 (NKJV)**

PART II
THE VOICE OF THE SPIRIT
Understanding, Partnership, and Prophetic Flow

God doesn't only speak *to* His people; He speaks *through* them. The same Spirit that hovered over the waters in Genesis now abides within us, revealing mysteries, releasing revelation, and empowering believers to carry His heart. This section explores the partnership between Heaven and Earth, how the Holy Spirit teaches, guides, and communicates through dreams, prophecies, and sanctified imagination. It is here that hearing becomes speaking, and revelation becomes transformation. May you learn to yield your voice to His voice and become a vessel through which Heaven's words find their expression on earth.

- Chapter 5:   The Prophetic
- Chapter 6:   Imagination
- Chapter 7:   Angels
- Chapter 8:   The Bride

Chapter 5: The Prophetic
Heaven's Voice Through Human Vessels
Exploring the Nature, Culture, and Calling of the Prophetic Life

---

THE CALL TO HEAR THE VOICE OF GOD

Every generation carries a longing to hear God's voice. Since the Garden of Eden, humanity has desired to walk in fellowship with its Creator, not only to worship Him, but to *know His heart*. When Adam walked with God in the cool of the day (Genesis 3:8), there was no barrier, no distance, no confusion. God's voice was the rhythm of daily life.

That same desire burns in the heart of every believer today. Deep within our spirit, there is a cry to discern the sound of Heaven once again, to recognize what the Spirit of the Lord is saying in our time. This is the foundation of the prophetic life: communion.

The prophetic is not an optional gift or mysterious phenomenon reserved for a few select ministers. It is the continuation of a divine conversation that began before time itself. Through Jesus Christ, the veil was torn; through the Holy Spirit, Heaven's voice was released into human hearts.

"My sheep hear My voice, and I know them, and they follow Me."
John 10:27 (NKJV)

This verse doesn't describe an elite spiritual class; it describes every follower of Christ. The ability to hear God's voice is not a talent; it is part of your inheritance as a child of God. Every believer is designed to live prophetically, to hear, discern, and respond to the living voice of the Holy Spirit.

The prophetic is simply this: God speaking through human vessels who are surrendered to His will. The purpose is never to exalt the messenger, but to reveal the message, Jesus Christ.

"For the testimony of Jesus is the spirit of prophecy."
Revelation 19:10 (NKJV)

When a believer begins to walk prophetically, something powerful happens: Heaven's perspective starts to shape earthly reality. Fear gives way to faith. Confusion yields to clarity. Lives are changed not because we've spoken, but because God has.

This is why the prophetic is vital in the Church today. We live in a time of countless voices, yet the greatest need of our generation is to hear *one voice*, the voice of the Lord. The prophetic ministry trains the believer to discern that voice amid the noise, to speak with precision, and to carry the heart of Heaven into the world.

To walk in the prophetic is to live as a conduit between realms, standing on earth while echoing the sound of Heaven.

Understanding the Distinction: The Office and the Spirit of Prophecy

Before we continue, it's essential to understand that the *office of a prophet* and the *spirit or gift of prophecy* are not the same. Scripture distinguishes between the two. The **office of a prophet** (Ephesians 4:11) is a leadership mantle given by Christ to specific individuals who are called to govern, equip, and mature the Body of Christ. These prophets carry a long-term ministry assignment and a higher level of accountability to steward revelation for the Church at large.

The spirit of prophecy, however, is the anointing released by the Holy Spirit that allows any Spirit-filled believer to hear and communicate the heart of God for edification, exhortation, and comfort (1 Corinthians 12:10; 14:3). Every believer can move in this prophetic grace, but not all are called to the governmental office.

The Weight of the Office

Those called to the office of a prophet carry a unique weight that extends beyond the basic function of prophecy. While all believers may prophesy for edification, exhortation, and comfort (1 Corinthians 14:3), prophets are entrusted with direction, correction, confirmation, and governmental alignment within the Body of Christ. Their words often carry the burden of intercession and strategy for regions, leaders, and nations. Through divine insight, they call the Church back to covenant faithfulness and establish order among the gifts.

Because their influence can shape doctrine and destiny, prophets are held to a higher level of accountability before God. Their authority is not self-assumed but appointed by Christ (Ephesians 4:11). They are not only hearers but also builders, laying foundations, raising standard-bearers, and protecting the purity of the Church's prophetic flow.

The prophetic gift blesses the individual believer, but the prophetic office safeguards the direction of the Church. Both are vital, yet their purposes and responsibilities differ. Understanding this distinction helps us honor the gift in every believer while properly recognizing and submitting to the governing voice of the prophetic office.

This chapter focuses on the spirit and culture of prophecy, the lifestyle of hearing God's voice and releasing His heart that every son and daughter is invited to walk in.

UNDERSTANDING THE PROPHETIC GIFT

Prophecy is not human intuition or spiritual guesswork. It is the divine flow of revelation from the Holy Spirit through a yielded vessel. The Apostle Paul gives us a foundational understanding in **1 Corinthians 12:4–11 (NKJV):**

"There are diversities of gifts, but the same Spirit.
There are differences of ministries, but the same Lord.
And there are diversities of activities, but it is the same God who works all in all.
But the manifestation of the Spirit is given to each one for the profit of all:
for to one is given the word of wisdom through the Spirit, to another the word of knowledge through the same Spirit,

> *to another faith by the same Spirit, to another gifts of healings by the same Spirit,*
> *to another the working of miracles, to another prophecy, to another discerning of spirits,*
> *to another different kinds of tongues, to another the interpretation of tongues.*
> *But one and the same Spirit works all these things, distributing to each one individually as He wills."* ***1 Corinthians 12:4-11 (NKJV)***

Within this passage, prophecy is listed among the gifts, alongside wisdom, knowledge, faith, healing, miracles, tongues, and discernment. Yet all these gifts are expressions of the same Spirit, functioning in different ways for the edification of the Body of Christ.

The prophetic gift, therefore, is not self-generated; it originates from God Himself, not human thought or effort. True prophecy is birthed from the mind and heart of God, spoken through His Spirit, and carried by willing vessels.

A Gift Freely Given, Not Earned

The gifts of the Spirit are acts of divine generosity. They are not rewards for holiness or proof of spiritual superiority; they are grace in motion.

> *"But one and the same Spirit works all these things, distributing to each one individually as He wills."* ***1 Corinthians 12:11 (NKJV)***

No one can earn or purchase prophetic ability. Jesus already paid for it through His death and resurrection. When He ascended, He poured out the Holy Spirit so that His people could carry His voice.

> *"And it shall come to pass in the last days, says God, That I will pour out of My Spirit on all flesh; Your sons and your daughters shall prophesy, Your young men shall see visions, Your old men shall dream dreams. And on My menservants and on My maidservants*

> *I will pour out My Spirit in those days;*
> *And they shall prophesy."* ***Acts 2:17-18 (NKJV)***

This passage from Acts is not a poetic ideal; it is a prophetic reality. Every believer has the privilege and calling to hear and declare the words of God.

The Function and Purpose of Prophecy

Prophecy is not merely about predicting the future; it is about revealing God's perspective in the present. While prophetic revelation can include insight into what is to come, its highest goal is to bring transformation and to reveal the heart of the Father.

> *"But he who prophesies speaks edification and exhortation and comfort to men."*
> ***1 Corinthians 14:3 (NKJV)***

- **Edification**
  Builds faith and strengthens spiritual foundations.
- **Exhortation**
  Calls people nearer to God's will and encourages obedience.
- **Comfort**
  Reminds the weary and wounded of God's nearness and compassion.

The prophetic gift, when functioning correctly, never humiliates or manipulates. Instead, it uplifts and restores, pointing hearts back to the Father.

Prophecy and the Character of God

God's nature determines how prophecy operates. Since *"God is love"* (1 John 4:8), prophecy must also flow from love.
The prophetic is the extension of His heart, revealing His goodness, mercy, and redemptive purpose.

> *"Pursue love, and desire spiritual gifts, but especially that you may prophesy."*
> ***1 Corinthians 14:1 (NKJV)***

Prophecy without love becomes performance. Prophecy born from love carries healing and life. True prophetic ministry reveals the heart of the Father to His children, not to showcase human gifting, but to communicate divine affection.

When the Holy Spirit speaks through a believer, He doesn't merely convey information; He releases **impartation, transformation, and invitation.** Each prophetic word says, *"I see you, I know you, and I still have a plan for you."*

The Testimony of Jesus: The Ultimate Aim

At its core, prophetic ministry exists to glorify one Person: Jesus Christ.

"For the testimony of Jesus is the spirit of prophecy."
Revelation 19:10 (NKJV)

Every authentic prophetic word must ultimately lead people to a deeper revelation of Jesus, His nature, His truth, His kingdom.

Whenever prophecy draws attention to the messenger instead of the Messiah, it has missed its purpose. The prophetic should always magnify Christ above personality.

Prophetic Partnership

The believer's role is to become a willing **partner** with the Holy Spirit. Prophecy does not require perfection; it requires surrender. A heart aligned with the Spirit becomes a vessel through which divine wisdom flows.

"Abide in Me, and I in you. As the branch cannot bear fruit of itself, unless it abides in the vine, neither can you, unless you abide in Me."
John 15:4 (NKJV)

Prophecy is one of the fruits that grows from intimacy. The deeper the believer abides in Christ, the stronger and purer the prophetic flow becomes.

Summary for Study
- Prophecy is a gift of the Holy Spirit.
- It operates for the profit of all, not personal glory.

- Its purpose is edification, exhortation, and comfort.
- It reveals the heart of God's love.
- Its ultimate aim is to exalt Jesus Christ.

When believers understand these truths, prophecy ceases to be mysterious and becomes a joyful partnership with the Spirit of God.

THE CULTURE OF HEAVEN

The prophetic is far more than a single moment of inspiration or a powerful word spoken in a church service. It is a way of living and seeing. It is not confined to a platform; it's cultivated in everyday communion with God.

Every kingdom, every nation, every people has a culture, a distinctive way of thinking, behaving, and expressing itself. Heaven is no different. Heaven's culture flows directly from the nature of its King, and that nature is love.

When Jesus walked the earth, He perfectly modeled Heaven's prophetic culture. Every word He spoke, every action He took, every miracle He performed reflected the Father's heart.

To live prophetically means to live as Jesus lived — in constant alignment with Heaven's heartbeat. The prophetic believer doesn't wait for special moments to hear God's voice. They walk in continual sensitivity to His presence, ready to respond to His prompting at any time.

"For as many as are led by the Spirit of God, these are sons of God."
Romans 8:14 (NKJV)

Being led by the Spirit is the essence of prophetic living. It means we respond to God's movement in every aspect of life —not just in ministry, but also in work, relationships, and daily decisions. The prophetic believer's life becomes a conversation between Heaven and earth.

Prophetic Culture vs. Religious Culture

Religion focuses on performance, image, and routine. Prophetic culture focuses on relationship, transformation, and authenticity.

Religion says, *"I must do to please God."*
Prophetic culture says, *"I listen and obey because I love God."*

Religious mindsets often limit the prophetic to occasional spiritual experiences. Heaven's perspective sees it as an ongoing conversation between a Father and His children.

When you understand the prophetic as a culture, you realize that every part of life can carry divine purpose. Every conversation, every prayer, every act of service becomes a potential moment of revelation.

"Therefore, from now on, we regard no one according to the flesh."
2 Corinthians 5:16 (NKJV)

In prophetic culture, we see others not as they are in the natural, but as God sees them in the Spirit. This transforms relationships, perspectives, and communities.

Translating Heaven's Heart

Prophetic ministry isn't only about relaying information; it's about translating God's heart. Every prophetic word must carry the tone and compassion of Heaven.

When a person receives a prophetic word, they are not just hearing facts about their life; they are encountering the love of God for them personally. Prophecy says, *"I've asked the Father what He thinks of you, and this is what He shared."*

Humility is essential in prophetic culture. We are not the authors of revelation, only the stewards. Every word we release must reflect His nature: gentle, truthful, and redemptive.

"Now then, we are ambassadors for Christ, as though God were pleading through us."
2 Corinthians 5:20 (NKJV)

Prophecy is Heaven's plea of love spoken through earthly voices. The prophetic person becomes a translator of divine emotion, communicating not just what God says, but how He feels.

Heaven's Perspective: Finding the Gold

An authentic prophetic culture trains people to look for potential rather than fault, to find gold in the dirt. It takes no prophetic gift to see sin or weakness; we live in a fallen world. But it takes the Spirit of God to see destiny where others see failure.

"Then God said, 'Let there be light'; and there was light."
Genesis 1:3 (NKJV)

When darkness covered the earth, God didn't describe it; He changed it. Faithful prophetic ministry does the same. It speaks to what *should be*, not just to what *is*.

Jesus demonstrated this beautifully. When He looked at Peter, He didn't define him by his impulsive failures. He declared, *"You are Peter, and on this rock I will build My church."* Prophecy calls out identity from the midst of imperfection.

Prophetic believers learn to do likewise. They don't expose the darkness in others; they speak to the light inside them.

"The Spirit of the Lord God is upon Me,
Because the Lord has anointed Me
To preach good tidings to the poor;
He has sent Me to heal the brokenhearted,
To proclaim liberty to the captives,
And the opening of the prison to those who are bound."
Isaiah 61:1 (NKJV)

Prophecy always carries this anointing to heal, restore, and proclaim freedom. It reveals how God sees a person, not how the world labels them.

Prophetic Culture Builds Community

The prophetic should never isolate people; it unites them. A healthy prophetic culture strengthens the Church and cultivates trust among believers.

In such a community:
- Words are spoken in love, not judgment.
- People are quick to forgive because they view others through God's eyes.

- Spiritual gifts flow freely, but in order and humility.
- Encouragement replaces gossip.

Prophetic culture is meant to reflect Heaven's family, filled with grace, accountability, and authenticity.

"Let all things be done for edification."
1 Corinthians 14:26 (NKJV)

Every prophetic expression — whether words, art, music, prayer, or counsel — should build up, not tear down. In a prophetic culture, people encounter God's presence through how we love and communicate.

Summary for Study
- Prophetic culture is a lifestyle, not a moment.
- It reflects Heaven's nature — love, mercy, and truth.
- Prophecy translates the heart of God, not merely His thoughts.
- It looks for redemption, not accusation.
- It builds community and unity, not isolation.

To live prophetically is to carry Heaven's culture wherever you go, in your home, your workplace, your friendships, and your worship. When believers walk in prophetic love and discernment, the world encounters the King through them.

THE PRACTICE OF PROPHECY

The Posture of Hearing

Every prophetic journey begins not with speaking, but with listening. Hearing the voice of God depends more on posture than on performance. God is always speaking; the question is whether we are still enough to listen.

"Be still, and know that I am God."
Psalm 46:10 (NKJV)

Stillness is not silence; it is alignment. It is the inward quieting of the soul so that the spirit becomes attentive. Prophetic hearing is birthed from intimacy, not activity. Those who learn to dwell in the secret place of prayer and worship will always discern what God is saying.

> *"He who dwells in the secret place of the Most High*
> *Shall abide under the shadow of the Almighty."*
> ***Psalm 91:1 (NKJV)***

Prophetic people must learn to guard their atmosphere. Constant noise, whether emotional, digital, or relational, can drown out the whisper of the Spirit. God often speaks softly because He wants to draw us near.

Recognizing the Voice of the Shepherd

How do we know it is God speaking? Jesus gives the clearest answer:

> *"My sheep hear My voice, and I know them, and they follow Me."*
> ***John 10:27 (NKJV)***

This means His voice is recognizable to those in a relationship with Him. Over time, as you grow closer to the Lord, you begin to discern His tone, rhythm, and heart.

God speaks in many ways:
- A gentle inward impression that brings peace and clarity.
- A scripture quickened to your spirit with new life.
- A vision, dream, or picture that carries divine symbolism.
- A prophetic word from another believer confirming what He already told you.

However, all true revelation must align with Scripture. The Spirit of God will never contradict the Word He inspired.

> *"However, when He, the Spirit of truth, has come, He will guide you into all truth; for He will not speak on His own authority, but whatever He hears He will speak; and He will tell you things to come."*
> ***John 16:13 (NKJV)***

When God speaks, His voice brings conviction, not condemnation; peace, not fear; clarity, not confusion. His voice always draws us closer, never drives us away.

Discerning the Source

A mature prophetic believer learns to **discern the source** of what they hear. Not every spiritual voice originates from the Holy Spirit.

There are three possible sources of inspiration:
1. **The Spirit of God**
   Pure revelation that reflects His nature and truth.
2. **The human soul**
   Thoughts and desires influenced by emotion, memory, or bias.
3. **Demonic deception**
   False inspiration meant to imitate or distort God's voice.

This is why the gift of discerning of spirits (1 Corinthians 12:10) is essential. Discernment protects revelation. It separates what is divine from what is human or deceptive.

"Beloved, do not believe every spirit, but test the spirits, whether they are of God."
1 John 4:1 (NKJV)

Discerning rightly requires humility. Even seasoned believers must admit, *"I might be wrong."* Prophetic maturity grows through testing, accountability, and submission to others.

Delivering the Word of the Lord

Once a word has been received and discerned, the next step is to deliver it. How a word is communicated is just as important as what is said.

"Let two or three prophets speak, and let the others judge."
1 Corinthians 14:29 (NKJV)

This shows us that prophecy should continuously operate with humility, order, and accountability. Words released outside of love or timing can cause damage, even if they are true.

Principles for delivery:
- **Timing matters.**
  An accurate word at the wrong time can wound instead of heal.

- **Tone matters.**
  Speak with compassion; your voice should reveal the Father's heart, not harsh judgment.
- **Permission matters.**
  Always honor authority and the setting. Prophetic words should strengthen and unify, not disrupt or control.

The mature prophetic voice is more concerned with God's heart than human recognition. The goal is transformation, not attention.

Prophetic Responsibility and Accountability

Prophetic ministry carries weight because it carries influence. When we speak "Thus says the Lord," we are declaring Heaven's intent. This is why accountability is vital.

"Do not despise prophecies. Test all things; hold fast what is good."
1 Thessalonians 5:20–21 (NKJV)

Healthy prophetic culture invites testing and feedback. A teachable spirit welcomes correction because it values truth more than ego. Submitting words to trusted leaders ensures purity and keeps pride from distorting revelation.

Accountability doesn't limit the prophetic; it **protects** it. Prophets in both the Old and New Testaments operated in community, not isolation. God's design for prophetic ministry has always been relational, not independent.

When God Reveals Secrets

Sometimes the Lord entrusts His people with private or sensitive information. He does this not for exposure, but for intercession and redemption.

"It is the glory of God to conceal a matter,
But the glory of kings is to search out a matter."
Proverbs 25:2 (NKJV)

When God reveals secrets, they are to be handled with holiness. If He shows you someone's struggle, it's usually an invitation to pray, not to speak. Only when He clearly directs should you share what He reveals, and even then, it must be done in love.

God never exposes to shame; He reveals to heal. Prophetic integrity means knowing when to speak and when to stay silent.

> *"Surely the Lord God does nothing,*
> *Unless He reveals His secret to His servants the prophets."*
> ***Amos 3:7 (NKJV)***

Those secrets are sacred. The Lord shares His heart only with those He can trust to guard it.

Summary for Study
- The prophetic begins with listening before speaking.
- The voice of God is known through a relationship.
- Every revelation must be tested and aligned with Scripture.
- Prophetic words should be delivered with timing, tone, and permission.
- Accountability keeps prophetic ministry pure.
- When God reveals secrets, handle them with reverence and discretion.

The prophetic life is a holy partnership, an ongoing dialogue between Heaven and earth. Those who handle His voice with humility and purity will carry His authority with power.

THE POWER AND PURPOSE OF PROPHETIC WORDS

Prophecy Opens the Heavens

When the Word of the Lord is released, it doesn't simply inform, it transforms. Prophetic words are not lightweight phrases; they are spiritual keys that open heavenly doors and alter environments.

One way miracles are birthed is through prophecy. Many have thought that prophecy is limited to someone coming up and giving a personal word of encouragement or foretelling the future. But in truth, prophecy carries much greater power.

Prophecy is the divine partnership between Heaven and earth. When the prophetic flows, it opens the spirit realm for the glory of God to manifest in our midst. Supernatural occurrences begin to happen in the atmosphere through prophetic utterance. The Word of the Lord, when spoken in faith, creates a spiritual pathway for the miraculous.

"So shall My word be that goes forth from My mouth;
It shall not return to Me void,
But it shall accomplish what I please,
And it shall prosper in the thing for which I sent it."
Isaiah 55:11 (NKJV)

Prophecy joins with the Holy Spirit to establish God's will on earth. It's not only a declaration but a demonstration, Heaven touching earth through the agreement of faith and word.

The Prophetic Word as a Carrier of Glory

Prophetic words are carriers of presence and power. When released by the Spirit, they transport the atmosphere of Heaven into earthly realities.

Throughout Scripture, we see that when God spoke through His prophets, His glory followed:
- Elijah's declaration called down fire from Heaven (1 Kings 18:36–38).
- Elisha's prophetic command brought healing and provision (2 Kings 4:1–7).
- Ezekiel's obedience in prophecy caused dead bones to come to life (Ezekiel 37:1–10).

In each case, the spoken word opened the way for divine manifestation. Prophecy changes what exists by introducing what God desires.

"He sent His word and healed them,
And delivered them from their destructions."
Psalm 107:20 (NKJV)

When believers release prophetic words under the anointing of the Spirit, they are literally partnering with Heaven's creative power. The same Spirit who hovered over the waters in Genesis 1 still moves upon our words today when we speak under His direction.

Prophecy as Warfare

The prophetic is also a weapon in spiritual warfare. The Apostle Paul exhorted Timothy:

"This charge I commit to you, son Timothy, according to the prophecies previously made concerning you, that by them you may wage the good warfare."
1 Timothy 1:18 (NKJV)

Prophecies are not passive predictions; they are divine strategies. When God gives a prophetic word, it becomes both a promise and a battle plan. Believers are called to war with the word, to pray it, declare it, and align their actions with what God has spoken.

Every prophetic promise will face resistance because the enemy fears its fulfillment. Yet the Word of God is unbreakable. Prophecy anchors believers in seasons of uncertainty and strengthens faith when opposition arises.

"Heaven and earth will pass away, but My words will by no means pass away."
Matthew 24:35 (NKJV)

To war with prophecy means to let every word God has spoken become your confession, your prayer, and your standard. When you stand on the Word, Heaven backs you with power.

When the Prophetic Brings Alignment

Prophecy doesn't only reveal — it realigns.
When God speaks, He reorders lives, ministries, and even nations in accordance with His divine purpose. An accurate prophetic word will not only inspire but also position people for their destiny.

Through prophecy, wrong mindsets are challenged, divine timing is revealed, and spiritual direction is restored. This alignment is vital for the Body of Christ to walk in unity and purpose.

When individuals and churches align with the voice of God, they begin to operate in Heaven's rhythm rather than in earthly reactions. Prophecy brings clarity where confusion once ruled, replacing striving with strategy.

The prophetic word functions as divine ordering, guiding us into alignment with what God already foreknew and predestined for our lives.

The Corporate Impact of Prophecy
Prophecy is not only personal; it is corporate. When released in a community of faith, it builds unity, direction, and collective anointing.

"But he who prophesies speaks edification and exhortation and comfort to men."
1 Corinthians 14:3 (NKJV)

In Acts 13:2, the Holy Spirit spoke during a prophetic gathering, saying, *"Separate to Me Barnabas and Saul for the work to which I have called them."* That one moment of prophetic instruction birthed a movement that transformed the world.

Corporate prophecy opens the Church to divine strategy. It prevents stagnation and ensures that the people of God move forward in step with the Spirit. When a body of believers learns to listen and respond together, the Church becomes unstoppable.

The prophetic ministry builds the Church not through control, but through collaboration with the Holy Spirit.

Prophecy Changes Atmospheres
The spoken Word of the Lord shifts spiritual climates. Prophecy is more than communication; it is *creation*.
- In worship, prophecy opens the heavens.
- In prayer, it breaks barriers.
- In intercession, it releases a breakthrough.
- In evangelism, it reveals Jesus.

When prophetic utterance goes forth, faith rises, demonic resistance weakens, and God's glory manifests. The spiritual realm responds to the sound of His voice spoken through His people.

Every prophetic decree carries the DNA of Heaven: light, life, and authority.

When believers speak what Heaven is saying, they release the atmosphere of Heaven into earth's reality.

Summary for Study
- Prophecy opens the heavens for God's glory to manifest.
- Prophetic words carry healing, deliverance, and power.
- Prophecies are weapons of warfare to fight with faith.
- Prophecy brings alignment and divine order.
- Corporate prophecy unites and directs the Church.
- Every prophetic word carries the creative power of Heaven to transform the earth.

Prophecy is not merely a ministry; it's a movement of Heaven. When the Church learns to hear and release the Word of the Lord in purity and faith, nothing remains impossible.

GUARDING THE GIFT

The Need for Purity in the Prophetic

The prophetic anointing is a sacred trust. Every time the Lord allows His word to flow through a person, Heaven entrusts that vessel with divine communication. Such a privilege demands purity.

Prophetic purity is not about perfection of speech but about the posture of the heart. God looks for vessels who will carry His words with reverence and humility.

"Blessed are the pure in heart, for they shall see God."
Matthew 5:8 (NKJV)

To "see God" also means to perceive Him rightly. Purity of heart sharpens spiritual perception, enabling prophetic clarity. The purer the vessel, the more precise the sound.

When the heart becomes cluttered with pride, offense, ambition, or bitterness, the prophetic flow becomes polluted.

Instead of revelation, mixture takes its place. What once carried Heaven's fragrance begins to echo the flesh's emotions.

Purity protects revelation. It ensures that what is released is not just partially inspired but entirely aligned with the heart of the Father.

The Dangers of Mixture

Mixture happens when the voice of God is blended with human emotion, desire, or offense. It's not always intentional; sometimes it occurs subtly when we speak too quickly or let our own perspectives overshadow His.

Even genuine prophetic voices can miss the mark if they fail to keep the soul surrendered. The soul, consisting of mind, will, and emotions, is powerful and expressive, but it must be disciplined under the Spirit.

When prophetic words become influenced by hurt, fear, or self-promotion, they cease to reflect Heaven's sound. Mixture leads to confusion and weakens trust in prophetic integrity.

Humility is the safeguard against mixture. Those who remain teachable and willing to repent quickly will always find the prophetic flow cleansed and renewed.

"If we confess our sins, He is faithful and just to forgive us our sins and to cleanse us from all unrighteousness."
1 John 1:9 (NKJV)

Counterfeit Prophetic Anointing

Wherever the true prophetic exists, the counterfeit will attempt to imitate it. The enemy is not a creator; he is a corrupter. Anything valuable in the Kingdom will be targeted by deception.

A counterfeit prophetic anointing mimics divine revelation but originates from a corrupted source. In Scripture, Paul encountered a slave girl with a spirit of divination who accurately described him as a servant of God. Yet Paul discerned the deception and cast out the spirit (Acts 16:16–18). Accuracy does not equal authenticity.

Satan seeks to distort prophetic purity through two main influences:
1. **The Religious Spirit** – This spirit replaces revelation with rules, suppressing prophetic flow with fear and control. It criticizes genuine expressions of the Spirit and exalts tradition over truth.
2. **The Political Spirit** – This spirit manipulates influence for personal or social advantage. It replaces compassion with agenda and corrupts discernment with suspicion.

Together, these spirits attempt to impart false discernment that masquerades as prophetic wisdom but is, in fact, suspicion and offense. When someone operates under this influence, they begin to "discern" from woundedness rather than from the Spirit of truth.

It feels like a revelation, but it is rooted in reaction. It carries the weight of irritation, not intercession.

Whatever is misdiagnosed will be mistreated. When we interpret from offense, we prophesy from distortion. That's why guarding the heart is essential for those who steward God's voice.

> *"Keep your heart with all diligence,*
> *For out of it spring the issues of life."*
> **Proverbs 4:23 (NKJV)**

Speaking from Heaven, Not Hurt

Prophecy is powerful because it carries authority, but that authority must always flow from love, not offense. When we speak from unresolved pain, our words echo our wounds rather than His will. The prophetic then becomes opinionated instead of inspired.

To remain in the Spirit, prophetic voices must continually yield emotions, perspectives, and motives to the Lord. Before speaking, ask, *"Is this God's heart or mine?"*

When we let God heal our personal pain, our prophetic vision becomes clear again. Love reclaims the throne of the heart, and revelation regains its purity.

> *"Let all bitterness, wrath, anger, clamor, and evil speaking be put away from you, with all malice. And be kind to one another, tenderhearted, forgiving one another, even as God in Christ forgave you."*
> **Ephesians 4:31–32 (NKJV)**

Forgiveness is a prophetic act; it restores the sound of Heaven through the vessel.

Testing Prophecy

Paul's instruction to the Thessalonian church remains vital today:

> *"Do not despise prophecies. Test all things; hold fast what is good."*
> **1 Thessalonians 5:20–21 (NKJV)**

Testing prophecy doesn't mean doubting God; it means valuing truth enough to verify it. Every prophetic word must be weighed according to Scripture, timing, fruit, and spirit.

How to test a prophetic word:

- **Scriptural Alignment**
  Does it align with the Word of God? His Spirit never contradicts His written truth.
- **Witness of Peace**
  Does it bring clarity and peace, or confusion and fear?
- **Confirmation**
  Does it agree with what the Holy Spirit has already been speaking through prayer or counsel?
- **Character of the Messenger**
  Does the vessel demonstrate humility, integrity, and submission?
- **Fruit of the Word**
  Does it produce faith, repentance, and love, or pride and division?

When prophecy is adequately tested, it strengthens faith rather than stirring confusion.

Prophetic Accountability

No prophetic voice, no matter how seasoned, is meant to operate in isolation. God designed prophetic ministry to function within community and counsel.

> *"Where there is no counsel, the people fall;*
> *But in the multitude of counselors there is safety."*
> **Proverbs 11:14 (NKJV)**

Accountability protects both the prophet and the hearer. Submitting prophetic insight to trusted spiritual leadership keeps motives pure and prevents misinterpretation. It also guards the Church from deception or spiritual pride.

True prophetic authority does not fear correction; it welcomes it. A teachable heart is a protected heart.

Prophetic Integrity and Character

Gifting can open doors, but only character can keep them open. Prophetic authority flows from integrity. If our lives don't reflect the nature of Christ, our words will lose their weight.

> *"Even so every good tree bears good fruit, but a bad tree bears bad fruit."*
> **Matthew 7:17 (NKJV)**

A prophetic person's greatest message is not what they say, it's how they live. Consistency, humility, and holiness testify louder than eloquence.

When the messenger embodies the message, people recognize God's voice in their words.

Summary for Study
- Prophetic purity is sustained through humility and intimacy.
- Mixture happens when emotion and revelation become entangled.
- Counterfeit prophetic flows arise through religious or political influence.
- Testing and accountability preserve authenticity.
- Character and integrity carry more weight than charisma.

Guarding the prophetic gift means protecting both the message and the messenger. Those who value purity above popularity will always carry Heaven's sound with authority and truth.

THE PROPHETIC INHERITANCE

The Covenant of Prophetic Continuity

From the beginning, God intended that His voice would never be silent among His people. The prophetic was not a temporary phenomenon; it is a perpetual covenant.

> *"As for Me," says the Lord, "this is My covenant with them:*
> *My Spirit who is upon you,*
> *And My words which I have put in your mouth,*
> *Shall not depart from your mouth,*
> *Nor from the mouth of your descendants,*
> *Nor from the mouth of your descendants' descendants," says the Lord,*
> *"from this time and forevermore."*
> **Isaiah 59:21 (NKJV)**

This divine promise reveals that the prophetic anointing is a generational inheritance. The Spirit and the Word were never meant to depart from God's people. Each generation is to carry the flame of divine communication further. The same Spirit that rested on the prophets of old now indwells every believer, ensuring that God's heart continues to be revealed on earth.

This is not merely a blessing—it is a mandate. The prophetic covenant means God has chosen to continually speak through His sons and daughters to reconcile, restore, and realign creation with His will.

The Inheritance of Sons and Daughters

When the Holy Spirit was poured out on the day of Pentecost, the Apostle Peter stood and declared that what was happening was the fulfillment of Joel's ancient prophecy:

> *"And it shall come to pass in the last days, says God,*
> *That I will pour out of My Spirit on all flesh;*
> *Your sons and your daughters shall prophesy,*

> *Your young men shall see visions,*
> *Your old men shall dream dreams.*
> *And on My menservants and on My maidservants*
> *I will pour out My Spirit in those days;*
> *And they shall prophesy."*
> **Acts 2:17–18 (NKJV)**

This announcement forever settled the question of who could prophesy. God said, "all flesh." Not a select group, not a spiritual elite, but every believer filled with His Spirit.

The prophetic inheritance belongs to every son and daughter of God. We were born again into a prophetic family. The moment the Spirit of God came to dwell within us, we became carriers of His voice.

This inheritance means that you can hear Him for yourself. You can discern His heart, receive His vision, and release His words. You are not a bystander in the Kingdom; you are a participant in the divine conversation between Heaven and earth.

But with this privilege comes responsibility. God will not put His words into the mouths of those who refuse to carry His character. Prophecy is not just an ability—it is an identity rooted in relationship. The Father reveals His secrets only to those who walk in reverence and love.

Prophets vs. Prophetic Believers

Although every believer can prophesy, not everyone is called to the office of a prophet.

The gift of prophecy is a grace made available to all Spirit-filled believers. The office of a prophet, however, is a governmental calling, one of the five ascension gifts given by Christ for the equipping of the saints and the establishment of the Church.

> *"And He Himself gave some to be apostles, some prophets, some evangelists, and some pastors and teachers, for the equipping of the saints for the work of ministry, for the edifying of the body of Christ."*
> **Ephesians 4:11–12 (NKJV)**

The distinction is not one of worth but of assignment.
- The gift of prophecy functions through inspiration.
- The office of a prophet functions through divine appointment.

Those who prophesy by gift release encouragement, edification, and comfort. Those who stand in the office of prophet are entrusted to bring correction, direction, and divine strategy to individuals, churches, and even nations.

A prophetic believer may sense God's heart for someone in a moment; a prophet may carry a word that shifts regions and generations.

Prophets are also responsible for training and activating others in hearing God's voice, helping the Body of Christ mature in prophetic discernment. Their words often establish new seasons, call the Church to repentance, or confirm what Heaven is about to do.

Both expressions are vital, but the office carries greater accountability. To hold the title of prophet without the character, testing, and commissioning of God is to carry a mantle without maturity.

The Sons and Daughters of the Prophets

In the Old Testament, we read about the sons of the prophets, groups of people who were trained under prophetic leadership to steward the word of the Lord with accuracy and humility. These were communities of learners who desired to carry the presence of God and understand His ways.

That same concept applies today. Every Spirit-filled believer is now a son or daughter of this prophetic lineage. The same Spirit that rested upon Elijah and Elisha now dwells within us, continuing the ministry of revelation through the Church.

"You are all sons of light and sons of the day. We are not of the night nor of darkness."
1 Thessalonians 5:5 (NKJV)

To be a son or daughter of light means to walk in truth and revelation, to carry divine insight into the darkness of the world. God's prophetic family lives not by assumption but by revelation, not by reaction but by discernment.

You have an inheritance of hearing. You are not abandoned to confusion; you are connected to the very Source of truth.

When believers understand this, their confidence in hearing God's voice grows, not from arrogance, but from awareness of identity. You are not striving to be prophetic; you already are prophetic because His Spirit dwells in you.

A Reminder About the Office

While all believers can prophesy, the office of prophet functions with a unique authority and weight. The prophet is not simply someone who gives words but one who shapes prophetic culture, guards doctrinal purity, and ensures that revelation aligns with God's nature.

Prophets are spiritual architects. They help the Church build according to Heaven's blueprint. They carry burdens for nations, regions, and movements, often standing in intercession until God's will is established on earth.

This responsibility carries both honor and humility. Prophets must model submission to God's timing and accountability to His people. Their words carry impact far beyond the moment; they influence spiritual direction for years to come.

Thus, every believer should honor prophetic voices without idolizing them, and prophets should serve humbly without controlling. Both must remember that the purpose of prophecy is always the same: to reveal Jesus Christ and bring glory to God.

Summary for Study
- The prophetic is a generational covenant (Isaiah 59:21).
- The outpouring of the Spirit enables all believers to prophesy (Acts 2:17–18).
- The gift of prophecy and the office of prophet differ in scope and responsibility.

- Every believer is a son or daughter of light, called to carry God's revelation.
- Prophets are architects and guardians of prophetic culture within the Church.

This inheritance is not reserved for a chosen few but extended to every child of God. The Spirit who once rested on prophets now abides within the Church, ensuring that the voice of the Lord will never be silenced.

GROWING IN THE PROPHETIC

Growth Through Intimacy

The prophetic life is a journey of continual growth. It matures not through striving, but through abiding. The more intimately you know the Lord, the more clearly you will recognize His voice. Prophetic depth flows from relational depth.

"Draw near to God and He will draw near to you."
James 4:8 (NKJV)

Growth in the prophetic begins in the secret place. The stillness of worship, the quiet of prayer, and the discipline of meditation train the believer's heart to discern His whisper. Every moment of intimacy refines spiritual perception.

The prophetic is not primarily about speaking; it's about *listening*. The deeper your fellowship with the Holy Spirit, the sharper your discernment becomes.

"He awakens Me morning by morning,
He awakens My ear
To hear as the learned."
Isaiah 50:4 (NKJV)

The Lord awakens the ears of those who walk in communion with Him. Revelation flows to those who prioritize relationship over recognition.

Practical Steps to Hearing and Growing

Growing in prophetic sensitivity is both spiritual and practical. God trains His people to hear Him through partnership and practice.

Here are seven ways to cultivate maturity in the prophetic:

- **Quiet Yourself Before the Lord**
  Create sacred space. Shut out distraction and center your focus on Jesus. Stillness is the soil where revelation grows.
- **Tune Into Spontaneity**
  Pay attention to thoughts, images, or scriptures that arise unexpectedly. The Holy Spirit often speaks through spontaneous impressions.
- **Record What You Hear**
  Keep a prophetic journal. Writing what God reveals helps you track accuracy and timing over time.
- **Celebrate Progress, Not Perfection**
  Every prophet in Scripture learned through a process. Don't fear mistakes—use them as lessons in discernment.
- **Embrace Community and Accountability**
  Submit prophetic words to trusted mentors and pastors. Feedback sharpens accuracy and builds humility.
- **Prophesy Over Yourself**
  Speak God's promises into your own life. This renews your faith and trains your mouth to agree with Heaven.
- **Activate Your Spiritual Senses** – Read Scripture aloud, pray in tongues, worship deeply. The more you engage your spirit, the more receptive you become.

Prophetic maturity develops like muscle, through consistent exercise and faithful obedience.

Staying Teachable and Humble

The greatest threat to prophetic growth is pride. The most excellent fuel for prophetic power is humility.

"Likewise you younger people, submit yourselves to your elders. Yes, all of you be submissive to one another, and be clothed with humility, for 'God resists the proud, but gives grace to the humble.'"
1 Peter 5:5 (NKJV)

Humility protects the prophetic from error. A teachable person never stops learning, and a humble prophet never stops listening. Even the most seasoned prophetic voices must remain open to correction and counsel.

Prophetic arrogance silences revelation. When we believe we no longer need accountability, we begin to hear ourselves more and Him less.

True prophetic maturity isn't measured by how often you are accurate; it's measured by how quickly you repent when you're wrong.

Cultivating the Fear of the Lord
The fear of the Lord is the foundation of all prophetic ministry. It guards purity, governs words, and anchors motives. Without holy reverence, revelation becomes reckless.

"The secret of the Lord is with those who fear Him,
And He will show them His covenant."
Psalm 25:14 (NKJV)

God entrusts His secrets to those He can trust with His heart. The fear of the Lord doesn't push us away; it pulls us closer with awe and responsibility.

When you carry holy fear, you treat His voice as sacred. You speak carefully, pray earnestly, and act with integrity. Every prophetic word becomes an act of worship.

Prophets and prophetic people must continually ask: *"Am I revealing His heart, or just my opinion?"* The answer determines whether the word brings transformation or confusion.

Embracing Process and Correction
God uses process to develop prophets. Before Joseph interpreted dreams for Pharaoh, he learned obedience in prison. Before Samuel spoke to kings, he learned to discern God's voice as a boy in the temple.

Every season of waiting, pruning, and testing refines your sensitivity to His Spirit. Prophetic accuracy grows in proportion to obedience in hidden places.

> *"Before I formed you in the womb I knew you;*
> *Before you were born I sanctified you;*
> *I ordained you a prophet to the nations."*
> ***Jeremiah 1:5 (NKJV)***

Calling is instant. Maturity takes time. The process turns gifting into authority.

Walking in Love While Growing in Power

Love must remain the foundation of all prophetic growth. As revelation increases, compassion must grow even more. Without love, revelation becomes mechanical, truth without tenderness.

> *"Though I have the gift of prophecy, and understand all mysteries and all knowledge, and though I have all faith, so that I could remove mountains, but have not love, I am nothing."*
> ***1 Corinthians 13:2 (NKJV)***

Prophecy reveals God's heart; love *is* God's heart. Growth in one without the other creates an imbalance. A mature prophetic believer will always choose kindness over control, grace over grandeur, and compassion over correctness.

Summary for Study

- Prophetic growth is rooted in intimacy, humility, and the fear of the Lord.
- Spiritual maturity develops through discipline and practice.
- Accountability and correction safeguard revelation.
- The fear of the Lord ensures that prophecy remains pure.
- Love must remain the motive and measure of all prophetic ministry.

The more we grow in intimacy and reverence, the more Heaven can trust us with its secrets. Prophetic maturity is not measured by power, but by purity, and the fruit of that purity is always love.

BECOMING HEAVEN'S ECHO

The Purpose Fulfilled

At the heart of prophetic ministry is a simple truth: God still speaks, and He desires to speak through His people.

From Genesis to Revelation, the voice of God has always been central to relationship with Him. The same voice that created the heavens and the earth continues to call His sons and daughters into divine partnership today.

> *"The Lord God has given Me*
> *The tongue of the learned,*
> *That I should know how to speak*
> *A word in season to him who is weary.*
> *He awakens Me morning by morning,*
> *He awakens My ear*
> *To hear as the learned."*
> ***Isaiah 50:4 (NKJV)***

This is the prophetic life: the posture of one who listens first and speaks only as the Spirit leads. Prophecy is not about possessing information; it is about releasing transformation. Every word inspired by the Holy Spirit carries the potential to heal hearts, restore hope, and reveal Jesus.

When believers learn to live as His messengers, the Church becomes a living conduit of Heaven's compassion. The prophetic is not the privilege of the elite; it is the expression of a people who walk closely with their God.

The Call to Represent Heaven

We live in a world filled with noise, so many opinions, distractions, and false voices. In this generation, the need for the unmistakable voice of the Lord has never been greater. Prophetic believers are Heaven's ambassadors, chosen to represent the heart of the King in the midst of confusion.

> *"Now then, we are ambassadors for Christ, as though God were pleading through us: we implore you on Christ's behalf, be reconciled to God."*
> ***2 Corinthians 5:20 (NKJV)***

When you speak prophetically, you are not just expressing thought; you are translating Heaven's heart. Your words become instruments of reconciliation, inviting others back into a relationship with their Creator. The prophetic ministry bridges the gap between humanity's brokenness and God's redemptive mercy.

To represent Heaven accurately, we must know the King intimately. Prophecy is not achieved by effort; it is birthed from encounter.

Prophecy: The Overflow of Relationship

The prophetic flow is the natural overflow of intimacy with the Holy Spirit. The closer you walk with Him, the easier it becomes to recognize His voice.

> *"The secret of the Lord is with those who fear Him,*
> *And He will show them His covenant."*
> **Psalm 25:14 (NKJV)**

Prophecy is the fruit of friendship with God. It is born in stillness, shaped in reverence, and spoken in love. Those who know His presence will carry His words.

The Lord reveals His secrets to those who dwell in the secret place, not to satisfy curiosity, but to release destiny. He does not confide in the arrogant or impulsive, but in the humble who handle His heart with care.

The Weight of Words

Heaven takes words seriously. Our speech carries power, whether natural or supernatural.

> *"For by your words you will be justified, and by your words you will be condemned."*
> **Matthew 12:37 (NKJV)**

When we release prophetic words, we are participating in divine creation. Just as God formed worlds through speech, we shape atmospheres through ours. Every word released in faith becomes a seed that bears eternal consequences.

> *"Let no corrupt word proceed out of your mouth, but what is good for necessary edification, that it may impart grace to the hearers."*
> **Ephesians 4:29 (NKJV)**

Prophetic people are called to steward words wisely. We speak to impart grace, life, and truth. Our words should heal, not harm; unify, not divide. The language of Heaven is kindness, even in correction.

Living as Heaven's Echo

To live prophetically is to become an echo of Heaven. This does not mean repeating phrases mindlessly, but reflecting the nature of the One who speaks. Prophetic believers mirror the heart, tone, and intent of their Father.

"If anyone speaks, let him speak as the oracles of God."
1 Peter 4:11 (NKJV)

When you live as Heaven's echo, your voice becomes secondary; His becomes primary. The goal of prophecy is never to impress; it is to express Him. Every prophetic act, word, or gesture should carry the fragrance of Christ.

Faithful prophetic ministry doesn't make people say, *"What a gifted person!"* It makes them say, *"What a glorious God!"*

Prophetic Maturity: Fruit That Remains

The true test of prophetic maturity is not accuracy, but fruit. Power may attract, but fruit transforms.

- Mature prophecy brings repentance, not rebellion.
- It births unity, not division.
- It produces faith, not fear.
- It magnifies Jesus, not the vessel.

When the prophetic matures, it moves from being event-based to lifestyle-based, from moments of inspiration to daily communion. The most prophetic people are those who reveal the character of Christ in how they live, love, and lead.

"Arise, shine; for your light has come!
And the glory of the Lord is risen upon you."
Isaiah 60:1 (NKJV)

Prophetic maturity means becoming light in dark places, revealing Jesus through every action, word, and response.

Becoming a Vessel of Truth and Love

The ultimate purpose of prophetic ministry is to reveal Jesus, His truth, His mercy, and His power. Every prophetic encounter should leave the hearer more in love with God and more aware of His nature.

Prophetic authority is not loudness, it's likeness. The more we resemble Christ, the more weight our words carry.

A prophetic voice should carry the fragrance of intimacy, not the noise of self-promotion. Heaven's authority flows through humility, not hype.

"He must increase, but I must decrease."
John 3:30 (NKJV)

The world doesn't need more noise; it requires clarity, purity, and love. True prophetic voices don't echo the chaos of culture; they release the calm of Christ.

Summary for Study and Reflection
- Prophecy flows from relationship, not performance.
- The voice of God brings reconciliation, direction, and transformation.
- Words carry spiritual weight; they must reflect Heaven's heart.
- Prophetic maturity is measured by fruit, not fame.
- The gift and the office of prophecy serve different purposes but reveal the same Spirit.
- The ultimate aim of prophecy is to reveal Jesus Christ.

The prophetic believer lives as a bridge between Heaven and earth, a reflection of the King's nature and a voice of His compassion in a broken world.

Closing Prayer

Father, thank You for entrusting me with Your voice. Teach me to listen with humility and to speak with love. Let my words reflect Your heart, and my life echo Your Kingdom.
Fill me with the fear of the Lord, the compassion of Christ, And the power of the Holy Spirit.
Make me a vessel of truth,

a messenger of mercy,
And a living testimony of Your glory.
In Jesus' name, Amen.

Appendix B: Understanding Prophetic Function

A Biblical Guide to the Difference Between Prophets and Those Who Prophesy

Introduction

In Scripture, prophecy is both a *gift* available to all believers and a *calling* given to some. Confusion arises when these two roles are blended together, yet the Bible makes a clear distinction between the gift of prophecy and the office of a prophet. This appendix provides a simple, biblical reference to help readers understand the unique purpose of each.

I. The Gift of Prophecy

Prophecy for Every Believer (1 Corinthians 12:10; 14:1)

The gift of prophecy is a grace the Holy Spirit distributes to the Body of Christ. It empowers believers to speak messages that edify, exhort, and comfort. Any Spirit-filled believer may prophesy as the Spirit leads.

Characteristics of Those Who Prophesy
- Operate in a spiritual gift, not a governmental calling.
- Speak words of encouragement, strengthening, and consolation.
- Minister prophetically occasionally or frequently, depending on spiritual maturity.
- Function primarily within their local church or community.
- Are responsible for the accuracy, humility, and motive of each prophetic word.
- Do not possess the authority to direct the broader Body of Christ.
- Bring revelation, but do not steward the prophetic direction of the Church.

This gift builds up individual believers and local congregations, releasing the heart of God in personal and practical ways.

II. The Office of the Prophet

A Leadership Calling Established by Christ (Ephesians 4:11)

The office of a prophet is far more than someone who frequently prophesies. It is a God-ordained mantle marked by authority, maturity, and responsibility. Prophets are foundational voices who equip, train, correct, and align the Body of Christ.

Characteristics of the Office of the Prophet

- Carry a distinct calling, not just a gift.
- Operate with consistent accuracy, spiritual authority, and discernment.
- Are entrusted to equip and mature prophetic believers within the Church.
- Provide direction, insight, and correction to the Body when needed.
- Help establish spiritual foundations in churches, ministries, and regions.
- Shift atmospheres, systems, and assignments through prophetic revelation.
- Bears greater accountability because of their wider influence.
- Carry understanding of times, seasons (1 Chronicles 12:32), and spiritual movements.

Prophets do not simply prophesy — they help guide the Church into alignment with God's purposes.

III. Summary: A Clear Distinction

A prophetic believer releases revelation, but a prophet stewards the flow of revelation across the Body of Christ. One brings encouragement; the other brings direction and alignment. One strengthens individuals, the other shapes the Church and/or Nations.

This difference is not superiority but stewardship. Each role carries a different measure of responsibility. Both are necessary for a healthy, balanced, Spirit-led Church.

IV. Walking in Your Measure

Every believer should eagerly desire to prophesy (1 Corinthians 14:1), but each must also discern their measure of faith, authority, and influence. Knowing your place fosters humility, protects your heart, and strengthens prophetic ministry as a whole.

Chapter 6: Imagination
The Eyes of Our Heart
Exploring the Sanctified Imagination and the Eyes of Faith

THE HIDDEN FACULTY OF FAITH

In the beginning, before there was light, sound, or form, there was the mind of God. Out of His invisible being came every visible thing. Creation itself began as an expression of divine thought, the Word made visible through the utterance of His will.

"By faith we understand that the worlds were framed by the word of God, so that the things which are seen were not made of things which are visible."
Hebrews 11:3 (NKJV)

Before the mountains rose, before the stars burned, before man ever opened his eyes, everything existed first in the imagination of the Creator.

Imagination, then, is not the invention of human fancy but a reflection of divine nature. It is the hidden faculty of faith, the spiritual sight through which invisible truth takes on form in the heart of man. The imagination is not an idle playground of thought, but the inner canvas upon which God paints His eternal purposes. When sanctified, it becomes a holy lens through which revelation is received and faith takes shape.

The Apostle Paul calls this sacred faculty *"the eyes of your understanding"* or, as other translations render it, *"the eyes of your heart."*

"The eyes of your understanding being enlightened; that you may know what is the hope of His calling, what are the riches of the glory of His inheritance in the saints."
Ephesians 1:18 (NKJV)

This phrase reveals that within the believer exists a set of inner eyes designed not for the physical realm, but for perceiving the unseen. Faith operates through these eyes. It sees beyond the horizon of circumstance and into the realm of promise. Faith believes what it sees inwardly before it ever sees it outwardly.

When we were born again, the Spirit of God awakened this inner life within us. We became new creations, equipped not only with a renewed spirit but also with spiritual faculties capable of perceiving the kingdom of God.

"Unless one is born again, he cannot see the kingdom of God."
John 3:3 (NKJV)

That "seeing" is not with the natural eye but with the eyes of faith, the sanctified imagination illuminated by the Spirit.

Through imagination, we can behold that which is eternal, though invisible. This is why faith and imagination are inseparable; one cannot believe for what one has not seen within. The prophet Habakkuk was instructed:

"Write the vision and make it plain on tablets, that he may run who reads it."
Habakkuk 2:2 (NKJV)

Before the vision could be written, it had to be seen, not with human sight, but with the inward eye.

Every significant act of faith begins in this hidden place. Abraham saw stars and understood they represented generations unborn. Joseph saw his brothers bowing before him in a dream long before he ever sat on a throne. Ezekiel saw dry bones come to life and form a living army. John, exiled on Patmos, saw the heavens open and the Lamb enthroned in glory. What God showed them on the inside became the faith that eventually shaped what they saw on the outside.

The imagination, therefore, is not optional to the believer; it is essential. It is the inner chamber where faith takes form, revelation unfolds, and divine promise becomes personal. Without the eyes of imagination, faith remains abstract, and hope remains distant. But when the heart begins to see, faith begins to live.

This is the hidden faculty of faith, the sanctified imagination, born of the Spirit, anchored in the Word, and fixed on the unseen realities of God. When the eyes of our heart are enlightened, we begin to perceive not only what God has said, but what He is still saying. The imagination, redeemed by the cross and filled with the Spirit, becomes the gateway of revelation and the language of divine communion.

FAITH AND THE UNSEEN REALM

Faith does not begin with what is seen; it begins with what is revealed. The natural world tells us what *is*; faith unveils what *shall be.* The unseen realm is not imaginary in the sense of illusion; it is the truest realm of all, the eternal dimension from which everything visible draws its origin.

"For the things which are seen are temporary, but the things which are not seen are eternal."
2 Corinthians 4:18 (NKJV)

When a believer steps into faith, they are not escaping reality; they are aligning with the highest reality: the eternal will and Word of God. But to behold that realm requires a faculty beyond the physical senses. This is where the imagination, sanctified by the Spirit, becomes essential. The imagination is the eye of faith. It gives substance to the unseen by forming an inner picture of what God has spoken.

"Now faith is the substance of things hoped for, the evidence of things not seen."
Hebrews 11:1 (NKJV)

Faith is not wishful thinking; it is divine assurance. Yet this assurance requires an image, something the heart can behold. Faith paints with the colors of revelation, and imagination is its canvas. When the Spirit speaks, He impresses images, concepts, and glimpses of divine reality upon our hearts. These impressions are not fantasy; they are previews of eternity.

Abraham: Seeing What Could Not Be Seen

When God declared to Abraham,

"I have made you a father of many nations"
Romans 4:17 (NKJV)

He was not describing Abraham's present reality but His eternal decree. Abraham's body was old, Sarah's womb was barren, and there was nothing in the natural realm to support the promise. Yet God invited Abraham to see, to lift his eyes above limitation and behold the stars. Each star became a visual prophecy; a symbol of what heaven had decreed.

When Abraham counted the stars, he was exercising sanctified imagination. God was teaching him to see with faith, to behold in the unseen what had not yet taken place. That vision became the image that sustained his belief. Before Isaac was ever born, Abraham had already held the promise in his heart. Faith gave life to what imagination had seen.

This principle is timeless. Faith requires the cooperation of imagination. We cannot believe for what we refuse to envision. If our inner eye remains blind, our faith remains confined. God calls us, as He called Abraham, to lift our eyes from the dust and fix them on the heavens, to see what He sees, even when the natural evidence declares otherwise.

Faith's Language: Calling Forth the Unseen

"God... gives life to the dead and calls those things which do not exist as though they did."
Romans 4:17 (NKJV)

This divine language of faith is not a denial of the present but a declaration of the eternal. It is the speech of one who has seen beyond time. Every prophetic utterance begins with vision, with something seen inwardly before it is spoken outwardly.

When we declare by faith, we are not inventing reality; we are aligning with Heaven's already established truth. This is why imagination must be grounded in the Word. Left to itself, imagination may wander, but when harnessed by Scripture, it becomes a tool of revelation. God's Word defines the limits of imagination, and imagination, in turn, helps the Word come alive inside us.

Faith expands imagination, and imagination feeds faith. Together, they form a living partnership that enables believers to walk in the unseen promises of God.

THE BRIDGE BETWEEN MIND AND SPIRIT

The human person is a masterpiece of divine architecture, a being woven together from spirit, soul, and body.
"Now may the God of peace Himself sanctify you completely; and may your whole spirit, soul, and body be preserved blameless at the coming of our Lord Jesus Christ."
1 Thessalonians 5:23 (NKJV)
Each part serves a sacred purpose in God's design. The spirit is the God-conscious part of man, capable of communion with the Holy Spirit. The soul holds the seat of intellect, emotion, and will. The body expresses outwardly what the inner life contains. When these three are rightly aligned under the lordship of Christ, the believer becomes a living temple through which God's glory flows unhindered.

But in this divine order, there exists a bridge between intellect and spirit, a faculty that allows revelation to move from concept to experience. That bridge is the imagination.

Imagination: The Inner Connector

When the Word of God enters the mind, it first takes form as knowledge. Knowledge informs, but imagination transforms. Knowledge gives us truth in principle; imagination lets us behold truth as reality. When the Holy Spirit anoints our imagination, understanding moves from the realm of intellect into the realm of encounter. We no longer merely *know* the truth; we *see* it.
"The eyes of your understanding being enlightened; that you may know what is the hope of His calling, what are the riches of the glory of His inheritance in the saints."
Ephesians 1:18 (NKJV)
The Apostle Paul calls this enlightened state "the eyes of your understanding." The Greek word translated "understanding" here is *dianoia*, meaning the deep faculty of perception or the mind's inner reasoning. In the Hebrew

mindset, this inner perception was rooted in the *leb*, the heart, the center of both thought and emotion. The biblical heart was not simply the seat of feeling but the inner chamber of meditation, reflection, and moral awareness.

When Paul prays for the "eyes of your heart" to be opened, he describes the awakening of this inner faculty —the imagination sanctified and illuminated by the Spirit. It is through this divine illumination that theology becomes revelation and revelation becomes transformation.

The imagination, then, is the place where divine truth and human comprehension meet. It stands between intellect and spirit as the living bridge that allows revelation to pass from thought into faith. Without imagination, doctrine remains distant and devotion remains dry. But when the heart's eye opens, understanding is no longer abstract; it becomes radiant.

Meditation: The Gateway of Illumination

Meditation in Scripture is not an emptying of the mind but a sanctified filling of it. The Hebrew word *hagah*, often translated "meditate," means to ponder, mutter, or envision. It carries the idea of rehearsing the Word in the heart until it becomes living within you.

"My meditation of Him shall be sweet; I will be glad in the Lord."
Psalm 104:34 (NKJV)

When David said this, he was describing more than mental reflection; he was engaging the imagination under the influence of the Spirit. As we meditate on Scripture, the imagination begins to visualize and experience the truth we are contemplating. When the psalmist spoke of God as a Shepherd, he did not merely define the word; he *saw* the Shepherd leading, protecting, and anointing.

When Isaiah beheld the Lord "high and lifted up," his imagination was not running wild; it was bowing in worship before unveiled reality. Meditation sanctifies the imagination by placing it under the authority of truth, allowing the Spirit to project divine images upon the screen of the heart.

> *"But we all, with unveiled face, beholding as in a mirror the glory of the Lord, are being transformed into the same image from glory to glory, just as by the Spirit of the Lord."*
> ***2 Corinthians 3:18 (NKJV)***

This is the difference between reading the Word and beholding the Word. Reading engages the intellect; beholding engages the whole person. Through this beholding, the believer is changed. Notice the pattern: we *behold*, and then we are *transformed*. The imagination, illuminated by the Spirit, becomes the mirror through which we behold His glory. The more clearly we see Him within, the more accurately we reflect Him without.

The Renewed Mind and the Enlightened Heart

> *"And do not be conformed to this world, but be transformed by the renewing of your mind."*
> ***Romans 12:2 (NKJV)***

This renewal is not only intellectual but spiritual and moral. The renewed mind is the mind whose imagination has been cleansed from defilement and brought under the reign of truth. It no longer visualizes sin, fear, or impossibility, but beholds purity, hope, and divine possibility.

When the mind and spirit unite through imagination, understanding becomes revelation, and revelation becomes transformation. This is why the enemy wages war so fiercely against our inner images. He knows that if he can corrupt the imagination, he can distort faith. A polluted imagination clouds spiritual sight. But a sanctified imagination clarifies it, enabling the believer to see as God sees.

To walk in mature faith, the believer must guard this inner bridge. The imagination cannot serve both light and darkness. It cannot carry the visions of God and the fantasies of the flesh simultaneously.

> *"The lamp of the body is the eye. If therefore your eye is good, your whole body will be full of light."*
> ***Matthew 6:22 (NKJV)***

The same is true of the inner eye. When the eyes of our heart are fixed upon Christ, the entire soul becomes radiant with His light.

Union of Knowledge and Spirit

The imagination allows the truths of theology to become the realities of spirituality. A person may study the omnipresence of God and yet live as if He were far away. But when that truth is seen inwardly, when the believer imagines His presence filling the room, surrounding, and indwelling them, the doctrine of omnipresence becomes the experience of communion.

In this way, imagination serves the Spirit as a vessel of revelation. It bridges the gap between the Word we read and the Presence we encounter. It joins intellect and intimacy, knowledge and wonder, teaching and transformation. The Spirit does not bypass the imagination, He sanctifies it so that divine knowledge may become divine encounter.

THE WAR FOR THE IMAGINATION

If imagination is the bridge between the mind and the spirit —the inner chamber where faith takes form —then it is no wonder it becomes the target of fierce spiritual warfare. The enemy understands that whoever controls the imagination controls the direction of faith. For faith operates by vision, and vision is born in the heart's imagery. If the adversary can corrupt what a person sees within, he can distort what they believe without.

"For the weapons of our warfare are not carnal but mighty in God for pulling down strongholds, casting down arguments and every high thing that exalts itself against the knowledge of God, bringing every thought into captivity to the obedience of Christ."
2 Corinthians 10:4–5 (NKJV)

The strongholds Paul describes are not made of stone; they are mental and spiritual fortresses built within the imagination. They are thought-structures, images, and inner narratives that resist divine truth. Satan rarely attacks first with action; he begins with suggestion. He paints false pictures in the mind, images of fear, impurity, doubt, failure, or pride, and seeks to seat them within the imagination. If these images take root, they become internal idols, shaping how we perceive reality.

A defiled imagination blinds spiritual sight, even while religious knowledge remains intact.

The Fall of the Mind's Eye

This corruption began in Eden.

"So when the woman saw that the tree was good for food, that it was pleasant to the eyes, and a tree desirable to make one wise, she took of its fruit and ate."
Genesis 3:6 (NKJV)

Before she touched the fruit, she imagined it, saw it inwardly as something desirable. The enemy implanted a false image of wisdom, and through that deception, humanity's inner vision was darkened.

Ever since that moment, the human imagination has been both powerful and perilous. Scripture testifies:

"The imagination of man's heart is evil from his youth."
Genesis 8:21 (NKJV)

But what sin has corrupted, grace has redeemed. In Christ, the fallen imagination can be cleansed, sanctified, and restored to its original purpose, to mirror the mind of God. The Spirit of Truth wages continual war to reclaim this inner territory. He does not merely inform the intellect; He transforms the imagination. When truth enters, darkness flees, and the heart begins to see clearly once again. The renewed believer learns to recognize false images, to discern when thoughts or impressions arise that contradict the nature or promises of God.

The Subtle Tactics of the Adversary

The enemy's strategy against the imagination can be traced through several subtle methods:

- **Fear:**
  The devil seeks to fill the imagination with images of disaster and doom. Fear projects false futures, persuading the believer to meditate on outcomes that contradict God's faithfulness.

  "Fear not, for I am with you; be not dismayed, for I am your God."
  Isaiah 41:10 (NKJV)

  Faith imagines presence; fear imagines absence. The Spirit of God replaces fear with vision rooted in divine assurance.

- **Lust and Corruption:**
  The enemy defiles the imagination through unholy images and desires.

  "Whoever looks at a woman to lust for her has already committed adultery with her in his heart."
  Matthew 5:28 (NKJV)

  The sin began not with the physical act, but with an image entertained within. Holiness begins in the imagination long before it manifests in behavior.

- **Pride and Self-Exaltation:**
  Satan's own fall began with imagination.

  "For you have said in your heart: 'I will ascend into heaven, I will exalt my throne above the stars of God.'"
  Isaiah 14:13 (NKJV)

  In the same way, pride paints a false picture of self-importance, enticing believers to trust in their own greatness rather than in God's grace.

- **Hopelessness and Despair:**
  The enemy darkens the inner vision with shadows of failure, convincing believers that what God has promised cannot come to pass. These images paralyze faith, keeping the heart fixated on what is lost rather than what is possible in Christ.

In every case, the adversary manipulates imagery to distort truth. But the Spirit restores imagery to illuminate truth. The battleground is the imagination; victory belongs to those who fill it with light.

The Cleansing of the Inner Vision
"Create in me a clean heart, O God, and renew a steadfast spirit within me."
Psalm 51:10 (NKJV)

The Hebrew word for "create" (*bara*) is the same word used in Genesis 1 to create from nothing. David was asking for a creative miracle within his inner life, a recreation of the imagination. When we pray for a clean heart, we are asking God to purge the inner images that defile us and restore divine vision.

Paul exhorted believers to:
"Be renewed in the spirit of your mind."
Ephesians 4:23 (NKJV)

Notice, it is not merely the *mind* that is renewed, but the *spirit* of the mind, the atmosphere of thought, the inward imagination. The Spirit of God cleanses not only what we think but also how we see. As He renews the inner landscape, images of fear are replaced by visions of faith, and lies give way to truth's brilliance.

Worship plays a powerful role in this renewal.
"One thing I have desired of the Lord, that will I seek: that I may dwell in the house of the Lord all the days of my life, to behold the beauty of the Lord."
Psalm 27:4 (NKJV)

The imagination, once used to envision sin, becomes a sanctified space for envisioning His glory. When the soul turns its gaze to Christ, the Spirit projects the image of the Son upon the heart. Over time, that image transforms the believer into His likeness.

The Sanctified Mind as a Fortress of Light
When the imagination is purified, it becomes a fortress of light rather than a stronghold of darkness. The believer learns to discern quickly when thoughts or images arise that do not

reflect God's nature. Such intrusions are brought "into captivity to the obedience of Christ."

This is not an act of repression but of redirection. We do not merely reject false images; we replace them with divine truth. We fill our inner world with Scripture, worship, and thanksgiving, allowing the Word to govern what the imagination beholds.

"Whatever things are true, whatever things are noble, whatever things are just… meditate on these things."
Philippians 4:8 (NKJV)

The imagination that once served sin now serves sanctity. It becomes a holy chamber of revelation where God's thoughts are welcomed and the enemy's projections are cast down. The believer whose imagination is submitted to Christ walks with unshakable clarity, no longer enslaved by fear, lust, or deception, but seeing with purity and confidence.

IMAGINATION AS A SPIRITUAL SENSE

In the natural world, we navigate life through five senses: sight, hearing, taste, touch, and smell. Each one translates the external world into internal experience. Yet Scripture teaches that man is more than flesh and blood; he is a living spirit. If we have natural senses to interact with the physical world, then surely the spirit possesses spiritual senses to perceive the invisible. The imagination is one of these sacred senses, the spiritual equivalent of sight.

"But solid food belongs to those who are of full age, that is, those who by reason of use have their senses exercised to discern both good and evil."
Hebrews 5:14 (NKJV)

Though this passage refers to discernment, it implies that the believer's inner faculties, spiritual senses, can be trained and sharpened. Just as physical sight can be strengthened through focus, so spiritual sight can be refined through holiness and intimacy with God.

The Imagination and Spiritual Perception
The imagination is not the birthplace of revelation, but it is often the screen upon which revelation is projected. When the Spirit communicates, He imprints divine impressions upon the heart, which the sanctified imagination interprets as vision, understanding, or inner knowing. This is why prophets often described what they "saw" even though their eyes were closed.

"The heavens were opened and I saw visions of God."
Ezekiel 1:1 (NKJV)
"Then I saw in my vision by night, and behold, the four winds of heaven were stirring up the Great Sea."
Daniel 7:2 (NKJV)
"I was in the Spirit... and I saw."
Revelation 1:10,12 (NKJV)

Each of these servants of God received revelation not merely as words but as divine imagery, truth clothed in symbol and picture. The imagination, illuminated by the Holy Spirit, becomes the eye through which the spirit beholds God's mysteries.

"We fix our gaze not on the things which are seen but on the things which are not seen. For the things which are seen are temporary, but the things which are not seen are eternal."
2 Corinthians 4:18 (NKJV)

This gaze is an act of spiritual imagination, seeing what cannot yet be seen. To perceive the invisible is not to fabricate illusion but to recognize eternal reality. Faith sees with the heart before it walks with the feet.

The Place of Revelation and Communion
In quiet prayer and worship, when the soul is still before God, the imagination becomes the meeting ground between divine revelation and human understanding. It is here that visions, impressions, or spiritual pictures often appear. These are not fantasies created by human will, but communications shaped by divine presence.

God designed this inner faculty as a language of communion. When we meditate on His Word, the Spirit breathes life into it, forming images and impressions that teach the heart more deeply than words alone. A believer might picture Christ on the cross, not because their mind invents it, but because the Spirit brings remembrance of what Jesus has done.

> *"The Helper, the Holy Spirit, whom the Father will send in My name, He will teach you all things, and bring to your remembrance all things that I said to you."*
> ***John 14:26 (NKJV)***

The imagination then becomes a temple where the Word dwells richly, alive with spiritual light and color. This is what David meant when he wrote:

> *"I have set the Lord always before me; because He is at my right hand I shall not be moved."*
> ***Psalm 16:8 (NKJV)***

To "set the Lord before you" requires the imagination — the continual inward awareness of His presence, the sight of faith that keeps the soul anchored in Him.

The Discipline of the Inner Eye

Just as natural sight can be strengthened or damaged, so the spiritual sense of imagination must be exercised and protected. The believer must learn to distinguish between true revelation and mere mental activity. This discernment develops through Scripture, obedience, and the fear of the Lord.

When the imagination is submitted to the Word, it becomes a servant of truth. When detached from the Word, it easily drifts into deception or emotional fantasy. The mature believer trains the inner eye to recognize the voice, nature, and pattern of God.

> *"The wisdom that is from above is first pure, then peaceable, gentle, willing to yield, full of mercy and good fruits, without partiality and without hypocrisy."*
> ***James 3:17 (NKJV)***

Revelation from the Spirit always aligns with Scripture, exalts Christ, and produces peace and purity in the soul. The training of this inner sense requires intentional practice. In contemplative prayer, one learns to quiet the mind so that God's impressions can surface without distortion. In worship, one fixes the gaze of the heart upon the beauty of the Lord, allowing His presence to paint the soul with peace.

Imagination and the Prophetic Dimension

Prophetic ministry depends heavily upon this sanctified sense. The prophet does not invent vision; he receives it. The Spirit of God communicates through pictures, parables, and patterns because these engage the imagination in divine revelation.

"Moreover the word of the Lord came to me, saying, 'Jeremiah, what do you see?' And I said, 'I see a branch of an almond tree.' Then the Lord said to me, 'You have seen well, for I am ready to perform My word.'"
Jeremiah 1:11–12 (NKJV)

Jeremiah saw what the Spirit revealed, and from that image, God imparted meaning. In the same way, the Holy Spirit may still communicate through inspired imagination, a mental picture, a symbolic scene, or an impression that carries divine truth. When interpreted through Scripture and tested by peace, these impressions can bring encouragement, correction, or insight.

But the goal is never spectacle; it is intimacy. God reveals Himself not to entertain but to transform.

The Quiet Revelation of God

Not all divine activity in the imagination comes in the form of visions. Sometimes it is a gentle awareness, a mental picture of someone who needs prayer, a sudden sense of light, a symbolic image in worship. The Spirit's movements are subtle yet unmistakable to the one whose inner eyes are open.

"For God may speak in one way, or in another, yet man does not perceive it."
Job 33:14 (NKJV)

The sanctified imagination restores this perception, teaching the believer to recognize God's voice in the imagery of the heart. The more this spiritual sense is exercised, the more attuned it becomes. Over time, the believer learns the rhythm of divine communication, how God speaks through Scripture, vision, impression, or inner knowing.

The imagination ceases to be a restless wanderer and becomes a consecrated instrument, devoted to perceiving the movements of Heaven.

Walking by the Eyes of the Heart

"For we walk by faith, not by sight."
2 Corinthians 5:7 (NKJV)

Ultimately, to live by faith is to walk by this inner sight. This does not mean walking in blindness; it means walking by a higher vision, the vision of the heart. The imagination, illuminated by the Spirit, allows us to perceive divine realities as more substantial than earthly appearances.

When the believer learns to rely upon this inner vision, the temporary gives way to the eternal, and the unseen becomes the anchor of hope. Such a life is no longer ruled by circumstance but governed by revelation. The eyes of the heart, trained to see God in all things, transform every moment into worship.

THE CREATIVE NATURE OF GOD REFLECTED IN MAN

At the dawn of time, when nothing yet existed but God Himself, the Almighty conceived within His own mind the design of creation. Every ocean, every star, every living creature began first as a thought in the heart of the Creator. Then, from the abundance of that divine imagination, God spoke, and the universe leapt into being.

"Then God said, 'Let there be light'; and there was light."
Genesis 1:3 (NKJV)

The act of creation reveals not only God's power but His nature. He is not merely a mechanical designer; He is the eternal Artist, the origin of all creativity, beauty, and expression. All that He made carries His signature, for creation is the visible expression of His invisible thought.

"For since the creation of the world His invisible attributes are clearly seen, being understood by the things that are made, even His eternal power and Godhead."
Romans 1:20 (NKJV)

The visible world mirrors the unseen mind of God.

Made in the Image of the Creator

When God formed humanity, He imparted this same creative capacity into us.

"Then God said, 'Let Us make man in Our image, according to Our likeness.'"
Genesis 1:26 (NKJV)

The Hebrew word for "image" (*tselem*) carries the sense of a shadow or reflection — not merely in form but in function. To be made in God's image means we were designed to mirror His attributes: His reasoning, His dominion, His moral nature, and yes, His imagination.

Our capacity to conceive, design, envision, and create is not a result of evolution or intellect; it is the imprint of divine likeness. Every invention, song, poem, or work of beauty that exalts what is good is an echo of the Creator's own voice within the human soul. But just as creation itself was marred by the fall, so too this faculty can be distorted when divorced from divine purpose.

The imagination, in its fallen state, becomes self-serving, using its creative power to glorify man rather than God. But when redeemed, it becomes the vessel through which God's Spirit continues His work of creation through us. We are co-laborers with Him, bringing forth beauty, innovation, and righteousness that reflect His glory upon the earth.

The Incarnation: God's Ultimate Expression

Nowhere do we see this divine creativity more clearly than in the mystery of the Incarnation. When the angel spoke to

Mary, declaring that she would bear the Son of God, the impossible was announced.

> *"Then Mary said to the angel, 'How can this be, since I do not know a man?'*
> *And the angel answered and said to her, 'The Holy Spirit will come upon you, and the power of the Highest will overshadow you.'"*
> **Luke 1:34–35 (NKJV)**

At that moment, the eternal Word was conceived in the womb of a virgin. The creative power of God intersected with human faith. Mary did not resist the unimaginable; she embraced it. Her reply reveals sanctified imagination joined with faith:

> *"Behold the maidservant of the Lord! Let it be to me according to your word."*
> **Luke 1:38 (NKJV)**

She pictured in her heart what had never existed before — God made flesh —and, by faith, what she saw became reality.

This is divine creativity in its purest form: the Spirit overshadowing human surrender to bring forth what eyes have not seen. Every act of faith that births God's purpose in our lives follows the same pattern. The Spirit conceives, the imagination beholds, and faith brings forth.

God's Beauty and the Human Soul

Because we are made in God's image, we are drawn naturally to beauty, wonder, and order. Beauty is not vanity; it is evidence of divine harmony. When the soul is attuned to the Creator, it perceives the glory of God in every aspect of creation, in music, art, poetry, craftsmanship, and nature.

> *"Worship the Lord in the beauty of holiness."*
> **Psalm 29:2 (NKJV)**

Scripture often connects beauty with holiness. True beauty flows from holiness because holiness restores the imagination to its original purpose, to reflect God's perfection and majesty. The redeemed imagination delights in that which honors the Creator.

When the imagination is ruled by truth, it perceives God's order even in what the world calls chaos. It begins to see divine potential where others see ruin. The artist, musician, or teacher filled with the Spirit can look at the brokenness of the world and envision restoration, for they share in the Creator's heart.

This is the essence of divine creativity: to bring forth life where there is death, light where there is darkness, and purpose where there is despair.

Creativity as Worship

Every expression of creativity, when offered in purity, becomes an act of worship. Whether one paints, writes, builds, or leads, the act of creating in alignment with God's nature is sacred. The believer's imagination, yielded to the Holy Spirit, becomes a brush in His hand, painting glimpses of heaven upon the canvas of earth.

"And whatever you do in word or deed, do all in the name of the Lord Jesus, giving thanks to God the Father through Him."
Colossians 3:17 (NKJV)

This means that all true creativity is ministry when it flows from a sanctified heart. When the imagination operates under the lordship of Christ, it becomes prophetic, revealing God's invisible realities through visible means.

The redeemed imagination turns every act of creation into a proclamation of God's goodness. It joins with the psalmist who declared:

"The heavens declare the glory of God; and the firmament shows His handiwork."
Psalm 19:1 (NKJV)

When believers create with purity, their work echoes the same song of the stars, the eternal testimony of divine glory made manifest through human vessels.

Participating in God's Ongoing Creation

God's act of creation did not cease on the seventh day; it continues in every life surrendered to Him. Each believer becomes a living extension of His creative work. The Spirit who hovered over the waters in Genesis now hovers over the hearts of His people, ready to bring forth new things in those who will yield their imagination to Him.

"The Spirit of God was hovering over the face of the waters."
Genesis 1:2 (NKJV)

Through the sanctified imagination, the Spirit forms visions of revival, strategies of ministry, inventions for good, and ideas that glorify Christ in every sphere of life. Creativity becomes not only expression but obedience, the continuation of God's command,

"Be fruitful and multiply."
Genesis 1:28 (NKJV)

We multiply not only physically but spiritually, producing works, words, and wonders that carry His imprint into the world.

When imagination is surrendered to divine purpose, it becomes one of the most significant forces for transformation on earth. It transforms dreams into reality, prayers into action, and revelation into manifestation. It joins heaven and earth in partnership, humanity creating not apart from God, but with Him.

RENEWAL AND REVELATION

Every divine gift must be renewed if it is to remain holy, and imagination is no exception. What the fall corrupted, redemption restores, but restoration requires participation. The imagination, like every part of the soul, must be continually brought under the cleansing influence of the Word and the sanctifying power of the Spirit. When renewed, it becomes not a playground for self, but a sanctuary for revelation.

"And do not be conformed to this world, but be transformed by the renewing of your mind, that you may prove

what is that good and acceptable and perfect will of God."
Romans 12:2 (NKJV)

This renewing of the mind includes the renewal of imagination. To be "transformed" (*metamorphoō*) is to be changed in form, to undergo an inward transfiguration. The Spirit does not merely correct our thinking; He re-creates the landscape of our inner world so that we may perceive and partner with the will of God.

The Word as the Cleansing Stream

The first work of renewal comes through the washing of the Word.

"That He might sanctify and cleanse her with the washing of water by the word."
Ephesians 5:26 (NKJV)

As we meditate on Scripture, it cleanses the inner eye, washing away images of fear, sin, and unbelief. The imagination that once mirrored the world begins to mirror the mind of Christ.

The Word of God is alive; it carries divine energy that purifies and illuminates. When read under the anointing of the Spirit, it does more than inform the intellect; it renews perception. The stories, parables, and promises of Scripture begin to unfold within the heart as living pictures. As we read of the Red Sea parting or the empty tomb, the sanctified imagination sees the hand of God at work, and faith rises. This process is not make-believe; it is participation. Through meditation, the Word moves from page to perception, from doctrine to encounter.

"Your word I have hidden in my heart, that I might not sin against You."
Psalm 119:11 (NKJV)

The hidden Word is not silent; it speaks within. It fills the imagination with truth until the enemy's false images are displaced.

Prayer and the Renewal of Vision

The second stream of renewal flows through prayer. Prayer is not merely speech; it is sight. When the believer prays in the Spirit, the imagination becomes a window through which the soul perceives the heart of God.

In the place of prayer, the Holy Spirit often brings visions, impressions, or inner pictures that carry divine instruction. The book of Acts is full of such moments.

"Peter went up on the housetop to pray, about the sixth hour... and saw heaven opened and an object like a great sheet bound at the four corners, descending to him."
Acts 10:9–11 (NKJV)

"And a vision appeared to Paul in the night. A man of Macedonia stood and pleaded with him, saying, 'Come over to Macedonia and help us.'"
Acts 16:9 (NKJV)

"I was in the Spirit on the Lord's Day, and I heard behind me a loud voice, as of a trumpet."
Revelation 1:10 (NKJV)

These were not the results of wishful thinking; they were the fruits of spiritual sensitivity, the imagination renewed and ready for revelation.

When the believer waits before God, the Spirit restores inner vision. Thoughts once chaotic become ordered, and images once dark become radiant with His presence. The renewed imagination learns to rest, to behold, and to receive. Prayer ceases to be one-sided communication and becomes communion, the exchange of sight for sight, thought for thought, heart for heart.

Quietness: The Soil of Revelation

Revelation does not bloom in noise but in stillness.
"Be still, and know that I am God."
Psalm 46:10 (NKJV)

In quietness, the imagination ceases striving and opens to divine impression. The Spirit often speaks in subtle ways, through gentle imagery, holy remembrance, or the illumination of a long-forgotten verse. These moments come not through force, but through rest.

In the ancient tabernacle, the golden lampstand burned continually before the veil, illuminating the holy place. The oil that fed it symbolizes the Spirit, and the flame represents revelation. When the believer cultivates inner stillness, the lamp of imagination begins to burn brightly again. It lights the soul, guiding the believer into a deeper understanding of God's Word and will.

"The work of righteousness will be peace, and the effect of righteousness, quietness and assurance forever."
Isaiah 32:17 (NKJV)

This "quietness" is not the absence of thought; it is order within thought, imagination brought into harmony with divine rhythm. Out of this holy stillness flows the whisper of revelation.

Revelation as Relationship

True revelation is not the pursuit of hidden information but the unveiling of divine relationship. The Greek word for revelation, *apokalypsis*, means "to unveil." God unveils Himself to those whose hearts are pure and whose eyes are single.

"Blessed are the pure in heart, for they shall see God."
Matthew 5:8 (NKJV)

The imagination, purified and renewed, becomes the chamber where this unveiling occurs. It is in this inner place that the Spirit interprets Scripture, unveils mysteries, and confirms divine guidance. Revelation is born not from intellectual mastery but from friendship with God.

"No longer do I call you servants... but I have called you friends, for all things that I heard from My Father I have made known to you."
John 15:15 (NKJV)

The sanctified imagination is the listening chamber of that friendship, the place where divine secrets are shared.

The Ongoing Work of Renewal

Renewal is not a single event but a continual process. Each day, the believer must submit the imagination to the Lord, allowing the Spirit to refresh and redirect it. As the natural eye tires and needs rest, so the spiritual eye must return often to the presence of God for restoration.

"Even though our outward man is perishing, yet the inward man is being renewed day by day."
2 Corinthians 4:16 (NKJV)

This daily renewal keeps the imagination aligned with heaven's perspective. The Spirit continually reorients our vision, teaching us to see circumstances not as obstacles but as opportunities for glory.

Over time, the renewed imagination becomes sensitive to divine rhythm. It discerns what grieves the Spirit and what delights Him. It no longer feeds on worldly images but delights in truth. It begins to dream with God, to perceive possibilities that reflect His heart rather than human ambition.

The believer who lives in this rhythm carries an atmosphere of revelation, walking through the world with the inner lamp always burning.

SEEING WITH THE EYES OF ETERNITY

There is a vision higher than sight, a perception purer than reason, a seeing that transcends time and touches eternity. This is the vision of the renewed heart, the eye of faith opened by grace. To walk with God is to walk by this vision. It is to live not by appearances, but by divine revelation; not by what the world declares, but by what the Word unveils.

"For we walk by faith, not by sight."
2 Corinthians 5:7 (NKJV)

Faith does not blind us to the natural; it opens our eyes to the *SUPER*natural. It shifts our focus from the fleeting to the everlasting. The believer who learns to see with the eyes of eternity perceives life not through the dim mirror of circumstance but through the unshakable reality of God's truth.

Living from the Unseen Realm

When a believer's imagination has been sanctified, it no longer drifts aimlessly between fantasy and fear. It becomes a vessel of divine perception, a lens through which eternity filters every earthly thing. To see as God sees is the goal of all spiritual growth. The more clearly we behold Him, the more clearly we understand everything else.

Faith does not deny what is seen; it interprets it. It recognizes that the visible world is temporary and that behind every moment, there stands the hand of the Eternal. The imagination redeemed by the Spirit learns to look through rather than merely at, to see beyond pain into purpose, beyond chaos into order, beyond the present into the promise.

When John was exiled on Patmos, he saw heaven open. The natural world called him forsaken, but his sanctified imagination saw glory. That vision sustained him in isolation and produced the Book of Revelation, a masterpiece of divine sight. So, it is with us: when our inner eyes are opened, exile becomes encounter, and suffering becomes sanctuary.

The Eye Fixed on Christ

"Looking unto Jesus, the author and finisher of our faith."
Hebrews 12:2 (NKJV)

The Greek word for "looking" (*aphorōntes*) means to gaze intently, to fix one's focus without distraction. The sanctified imagination has one supreme object: Christ in His glory.

When the eyes of the heart remain fixed upon Him, the believer walks in stability even in the storm. Peter walked on water until he looked away. Likewise, our faith falters only when our imagination turns to the waves rather than to the Savior. To "look unto Jesus" is to continually hold Him before the inner eye — to meditate upon His beauty, His cross, His triumph, and His soon return.

This continual inward gaze transforms the believer from within.

> *"But we all, with unveiled face, beholding as in a mirror the glory of the Lord, are being transformed into the same image."*
> **2 Corinthians 3:18 (NKJV)**

The more we behold Him inwardly, the more we reflect Him outwardly. The imagination, illuminated by glory, becomes the mirror of transformation.

The Eternal Horizon

All the saints of Scripture lived with their hearts fixed upon an unseen horizon.

> *"For he waited for the city which has foundations, whose builder and maker is God."*
> **Hebrews 11:10 (NKJV)**

> *"By faith he forsook Egypt, not fearing the wrath of the king; for he endured as seeing Him who is invisible."*
> **Hebrews 11:27 (NKJV)**

> *"But he, being full of the Holy Spirit, gazed into heaven and saw the glory of God, and Jesus standing at the right hand of God."*
> **Acts 7:55–56 (NKJV)**

They were not dreamers of unreality; they were visionaries of eternity. Their sanctified imagination became the compass that guided their obedience, courage, and worship.

To see with the eyes of eternity is to live as they lived, aware that every earthly moment is a shadow of a greater glory. It is to interpret every trial through the lens of divine promise, to respond to every difficulty with heaven's perspective. The believer who walks by such sight becomes immovable, for their gaze is fixed upon that which cannot be shaken.

The Sanctified Imagination as Eternal Fellowship

In the end, the sanctified imagination is not merely an instrument — it is a meeting place. It is where the Creator and His creation commune, where divine ideas become incarnate through human obedience. It is where eternity whispers to time and where the believer learns to live in two worlds at once — rooted in the earth but ruled by heaven.

"Open my eyes, that I may see wondrous things from Your law."
Psalm 119:18 (NKJV)

God does not reveal Himself only to the intellect; He reveals Himself to the heart that dares to see. This prayer must become our daily posture. For revelation is not a one-time gift; it is a continual unveiling. Every new dawn offers another opportunity to see as God sees.

The imagination that once served sin now serves worship. It beholds the majesty of God and translates that vision into prayer, obedience, and creativity. It dreams not for self-glory but for divine fulfillment. It becomes a lifelong companion of faith, a lamp that shines until the day dawns and the Morning Star rises in our hearts.

"And so we have the prophetic word confirmed, which you do well to heed as a light that shines in a dark place, until the day dawns and the morning star rises in your hearts."
2 Peter 1:19 (NKJV)

The Eyes of Our Heart Enlightened

To live with sanctified imagination is to live in unbroken fellowship with eternity. It is to walk through the temporal world carrying eternal sight. It is to see the invisible, hear the inaudible, and believe the impossible, not as a mystic fantasy, but as the normal inheritance of the Spirit-filled life.

"That the God of our Lord Jesus Christ, the Father of glory, may give to you the spirit of wisdom and revelation in the knowledge of Him, the eyes of your understanding being enlightened; that you may know what is the hope of His calling, what are the riches of the glory of His inheritance in the saints."
Ephesians 1:17–18 (NKJV)

May that prayer be fulfilled in us.
May our inner eyes be opened to behold the splendor of Christ,

the vastness of His purposes, and the beauty of His Kingdom. May we imagine with purity, believe with boldness, and walk with unwavering faith.

For the imagination sanctified is not fantasy, it is vision. And when the eyes of our heart are enlightened, we will see as God sees, and seeing, we will become what we behold.

CLOSING PRAYER

Father of Glory,
Illuminate the eyes of my heart.
Cleanse my imagination from every shadow and fill it with Your light.
Teach me to see as You see, beyond fear, beyond circumstance, into eternal truth.
Let my inner vision be fixed upon Jesus, the Author and Finisher of my faith.
May Your Spirit breathe upon the canvas of my soul until every thought reflects Your beauty,
and every dream echoes Your purpose.
Awaken within me the sight of eternity,
that I may walk by faith, live in wonder, and behold Your glory all my days.
In Jesus' name,
Amen.

Chapter 7: Angels

The Lord of Hosts and His Ministering Spirits

*"For He shall give His angels charge over you,
To keep you in all your ways."*
Psalm 91:11

There is an entire dimension of God's creation that most people rarely consider: the world of angels. Scripture calls them "ministering spirits" and speaks of the "host of heaven," a vast, organized, militant, worshiping realm that surrounds the throne of God and moves at His command. Angels are not decorative, delicate, storybook creatures. They are warriors, messengers, guardians, and worshipers, created to carry out the will of God and to partner with His people on the earth.

It is essential to see that angels are not just residents of heaven; they are part of how heaven speaks. God doesn't communicate only through sentences and syllables. He communicates through movements, messengers, dreams, visions, signs, and encounters. Angels are one way His voice is made visible. When an angel shows up with a message, a warning, a dream interpretation, a rescue, or a shift in atmosphere, it is God "speaking" through a living messenger. They are like living words, sent ones that carry His heart, His will, and His instruction.

Throughout Scripture, angels often show up at turning points in God's storyline, announcing births, warning of danger, interpreting visions, strengthening weary servants, and enforcing God's decrees. In that sense, they are part of heaven's vocabulary. Just as dreams, visions, signs, and prophetic words are expressions in God's language, so angelic activity is another dialect of that same language. When angels move, heaven is saying something.

When we begin to understand the ministry of angels, we realize two things at once: first, how small and limited we are in our own strength, and second, how secure and supported we are in God's. Heaven is not silent, and it is not empty. It is populated with a countless army of loyal, intelligent, powerful beings whose greatest joy is to glorify God and to assist in His plans, often by bringing His message, His protection, and His presence closer to us in very real ways.

This chapter will explore the Lord of hosts, the nature and ranks of angels, their responsibilities, their interaction with believers, and how they fit within the broader theme of God's language to His people. As we do, we will learn to recognize their role without worshiping them and to honor the God who speaks through them.

THE LORD OF HOSTS

Joshua 5 gives us a profound glimpse into the reality of the angelic hosts. As Joshua stood near Jericho, preparing for battle, he looked up and saw a man standing opposite him, a drawn sword in his hand. Joshua approached and asked, "Are you for us or for our adversaries?" The answer was startling: "No; rather I indeed come now as Captain of the host of the Lord." Joshua fell on his face and bowed down, recognizing he was not speaking with a mere angel, but with the Captain.

In Hebrew, the word translated as " hosts" is tseba'ah, meaning warriors or soldiers organized for military service and equipped for war. The "host of the Lord" is not a poetic metaphor; it refers to a real, organized angelic army. This passage reveals a highly structured, disciplined, and battle-ready company of angels under Christ's direct command.

We often unconsciously think of angels as sentimental or ornamental, but the Bible paints a very different picture. Angels are created to carry out God's plans under His command. Psalm 103:20 says,

> *"Bless the Lord, you His angels, who excel in strength, who do His word, heeding the voice of His word."*
> ***Psalm 103:20***

They listen for His commands and respond when His word is spoken, even when it is spoken through the mouths of His people in faith, through Spirit-inspired prayers, prophecies, and decrees. They are heavenly warriors, mobilized by the word of the King.

This is one of the purest pictures of heaven's language in motion. When God speaks, angels move. When His word is declared, heaven's armies respond. The angelic host does not act on emotion or impulse; they act on the language of the throne, which is the Word of God. Their obedience is instant and exact. They are living responders to His voice, demonstrating that the language of heaven is not only heard, but enacted. Every decree, every prophetic utterance, every Spirit-breathed word carries sound waves that mobilize the hosts of heaven to bring God's will into manifestation on earth.

Like any army, the angelic hosts have specific assignments. Armies guard and protect a king and his kingdom. They defend the inhabitants of that kingdom, implementing the king's strategies, plans, and laws. They patrol the boundaries and enforce jurisdiction, ensuring that what belongs to the king is not invaded or stolen. They steward the king's resources and see that what he decrees is carried out. They maintain weapons and war against threats to the kingdom. They protect and assist the king's family, his heirs.

In the same way, the hosts of heaven guard the kingdom of God, protect the saints, enforce God's decrees, and war against demonic powers that threaten His purposes on the earth. They move in rhythm with a divine voice. The Lord of hosts, of the angel armies, speaks, and His word becomes action. When He commands, heaven's army becomes the sound of His authority in motion. Through them, heaven's language becomes visible on earth.

ANGELS: CREATED MESSENGERS OF GOD

The Greek word for angel, angelos, means "messenger." Angels are first and foremost messengers and servants of God who do His will. They are part of the universe God created; they are not *above all things* in the way God is. But He did create them before the foundation of the world.

Genesis 2:1 declares,
"Thus the heavens and the earth, and all the host of them, were finished."
Genesis 2:1

Nehemiah 9:6 says,
"You alone are the Lord; You have made heaven, the heaven of heavens, with all their host... and the host of heaven worships You."
Nehemiah 9:6

Paul tells us that God created all things,
"visible and invisible, whether thrones or dominions or principalities or powers"
Colossians 1:16

This includes the angelic realm.

The word host is also used for angels, meaning a mass of people or things prepared for war. When Genesis speaks of God creating the sun, moon, and "all the host of them," we see that even before Adam and Eve ever fell, God had already created His warrior angels. Heaven's army was established long before sin entered the world; God was never caught off guard.

They are living extensions of God's voice. Every angelic assignment is a sentence in the ongoing language of heaven. When an angel appears, heaven is speaking. When an angel moves, heaven is declaring something on the earth. They embody divine messages —sometimes of comfort, sometimes of warning, sometimes of warfare —but always as a direct expression of what God is saying and doing.

Just as the Holy Spirit breathes the prophetic word through human vessels, angels carry the vibrational tone of God's speech into creation. They deliver His instructions, execute His decrees, and confirm His promises. Every appearance of an angel in Scripture carries with it a revelation of God's heart.

THE NATURE OF ANGELS: SPIRITUAL AND FIERY

Angels are not like us. The author of Hebrews suggests that all angels are spirits: spiritual beings, not physical like humans. They operate in a realm unseen yet deeply real, interacting with ours whenever heaven desires to speak or move.

Scripture shows that angels are usually invisible to humans unless God opens our eyes. Balaam did not see the angel blocking his path until the Lord opened his eyes (Numbers 22). Elisha prayed for his servant's eyes to be opened, and suddenly the young man saw the mountain full of horses and chariots of fire all around (2 Kings 6:17). At the birth of Jesus, *"a multitude of the heavenly host"* suddenly appeared with an angel, praising God (Luke 2).

"And suddenly there was with the angel a multitude of the heavenly host praising God and saying:
'Glory to God in the highest,
And on earth peace, goodwill toward men!'"
Luke 2:13–14 (NKJV)

Yet from time to time, angels took on bodily form and appeared to people. The angel at the tomb of Jesus appeared like a man, with clothing white as snow (Matthew 28:5). Hebrews 13:2 warns us that some have

"entertained angels unawares,"
Hebrews 13:2

implying that angels can appear in ways that look ordinary and human.

Scripture often associates angels with light, fire, and wind, revealing their nature as powerful spiritual beings. The Bible speaks of horses of fire and chariots of fire, glimpses of the unseen realm intersecting with the natural one. The Hebrew word *ruach* means breath, wind, and spirit, and Scripture uses this language symbolically to describe the movement and nature of spiritual beings. Likewise, the Greek word *pneuma*, used in the New Testament, carries the same meanings—spirit, breath, and wind.

Angels are referred to as "winds" and "flames of fire," emphasizing their swiftness, purity, and radiant glory:

"Who makes His angels spirits [ruach], His ministers a flame of fire"
Psalm 104:4 (NKJV)

"And of the angels He says:
'Who makes His angels spirits [pneuma]
And His ministers a flame of fire.'"
Hebrews 1:7 (NKJV)

Many angelic encounters are accompanied by brilliant light, underscoring that they belong to the realm where God's glory dwells.

God did not breathe life into angels as He did with humanity; rather, He created them directly as spiritual beings—pure spirit, without physical bodies unless they take on form as He wills. They are crafted by His power.

"Praise Him, all His angels…
For He commanded and they were created."
Psalm 148:2, 5 (NKJV)

To understand angels is to glimpse one of the purest dialects of heaven's language. They are not only carriers of messages; they are messages embodied—living flames of communication, radiant expressions of God's glory whose very presence communicates what words cannot contain.

CHERUBIM: GUARDIANS OF THE HOLY

One of the most awe-inspiring descriptions of angels in Scripture is the vision of the cherubim in Ezekiel 1:5-14. Ezekiel saw living creatures with human-like forms, yet each had four faces and four wings. Their legs were straight, and the soles of their feet were like the soles of a calf's foot, sparkling like burnished bronze. Under their wings, they had human hands. Each face represented a different aspect: a human face, a lion's face, an ox's face, and an eagle's face. Their wings touched one another as they moved straight forward, without turning. Their appearance was like burning coals of fire, like torches moving to and fro, and lightning went out from the fire. The creatures darted back and forth like flashes of lightning.

The word cherub (plural cherubim) likely derives from a term meaning "to guard," which fits their role perfectly. After Adam and Eve were driven from the garden, God placed cherubim with a flaming sword to guard the way to the tree of life (Genesis 3:24). God is described as enthroned above the cherubim (Ezekiel 10). Two golden cherubim were fashioned above the ark of the covenant, overshadowing the mercy seat, where God promised to dwell among His people (Exodus 25:22).

In Psalm 18, David poetically describes God riding upon a cherub, soaring on the wings of the wind, bending the heavens to come down in rescue. The imagery is dramatic: the earth shaking, smoke and fire surrounding Him, thunderclouds and darkness under His feet, a cherub as His steed, and the winds carrying Him swiftly. All of this emphasizes the strength, speed, and fearful majesty that surround God's presence. Where He moves, the angelic realm moves with Him.

SERAPHIM: BURNING ONES AROUND THE THRONE

Isaiah 6 records another stunning encounter with the angelic realm. In the year King Uzziah died, Isaiah saw the Lord seated on a high and exalted throne, and the train of His robe filled the temple. Above Him stood seraphim, each with six wings. With two, they covered their faces, with two, they covered their feet, and with two, they flew. They called to one another,
> "Holy, holy, holy is the Lord of hosts; the whole earth is full of His glory."
> ***Isaiah 6:3***

At the sound of their voices, doorposts shook, and the temple was filled with smoke. When Isaiah cried out in awareness of his own sinfulness, one of the seraphim flew to him with a burning coal from the altar, touched his lips, and declared that his guilt was taken away and his sin atoned for.

The word seraphim (singular seraph) means "burning ones" or "nobles." These angels burn with holy love and zeal in the immediate presence of God. They are all about the presence and holiness of God, crying out day and night, filling the atmosphere of heaven with worship and purification.

THE LIVING CREATURES AROUND THE THRONE

In Revelation 4, John sees four living creatures around the throne of God. They are covered with eyes, front and back. One is like a lion, one is like an ox, one has a face like a man, and one is like a flying eagle. Each has six wings and is full of eyes around and within. Day and night, they never cease to say,
"Holy, holy, holy, Lord God Almighty, who was and is and is to come!"
Revelation 4:8

Whenever they give glory, honor, and thanks to Him who sits on the throne, the twenty-four elders fall before Him and cast their crowns.

These living creatures, sometimes called "living beasts" or simply "the four beasts," minister by worshiping and glorifying God without ceasing. Their many eyes speak of deep perception and awareness; their forms reflect strength, service, humanity, and soaring vision.

MINISTERING ANGELS AND GUARDIAN HELP

Hebrews 1:13-14 asks,
"Are they not all ministering spirits sent forth to minister for those who will inherit salvation?"
Hebrews 1:13–14

Angels are servants sent out by God to accompany, protect, and help His people. Hebrews 13:2 tells us not to forget to show hospitality to strangers, because some have entertained angels without realizing it. Angels can come in forms that look ordinary, yet they carry heavenly assignments to comfort, warn, direct, or protect.

We see this awareness in Acts 12, when Peter is miraculously released from prison by an angel. He comes to the house where believers are praying, and when the servant girl insists that Peter is at the door, those inside say, "You are beside yourself!" Then they conclude, "It is his angel." Their first assumption was not that Peter had escaped, but that his angel had appeared. This suggests they were so accustomed to the reality of angels that they considered a visit from Peter's angel more likely than his physical arrival.

God always intended His kingdom to be intertwined with our realm. It is normal in the kingdom of God for the supernatural, including angelic activity, to be woven into the everyday lives of His people, even when we are not aware of it.

ANGELIC HIERARCHY AND RANK

Scripture suggests that angels have rank and order. Jude 9 calls Michael "the archangel," a title that indicates rule or authority over other angels. Daniel 10:13 describes him as "one of the chief princes," and in Revelation 12, he leads God's angelic army in war against the dragon and his angels. Paul tells us that the Lord will return "with the voice of an archangel" (1 Thessalonians 4:16).

Over time, theologians and teachers have summarized the idea of ranks into what is often called the "nine choirs of angels." While not all of this structure is laid out explicitly in Scripture, it expresses a traditional understanding of heavenly order:

• Seraphim – attendants before God's throne, burning with worship.
• Cherubim – those who praise God's glory and guard His presence and holy places.
• Thrones – living symbols of God's justice and authority.
• Dominions – those who regulate the duties of lower angelic orders.

- Virtues – angels associated with governing nature and heavenly bodies.
- Powers – warrior angels who defend the cosmos from spiritual forces of evil.
- Principalities – guardians of realms and regions on earth.
- Archangels – chief angels who often interact directly with humans.
- Angels – the general order of messengers and ministering spirits.

Ancient Jewish writings, such as 1 Enoch, even list names and functions of various angels—Uriel over the world and Tartarus, Raphael over the spirits of men, Raguel over luminaries, Michael over the best part of mankind and chaos, Saraqael over rebellious spirits, Gabriel over Paradise, serpents, and cherubim, and Remiel over those who will rise.

While these texts provide historical insight into how earlier generations understood the angelic realm is important to remember that the book of Enoch is *not* part of the biblical canon. It should be viewed only as an ancient Jewish work—not as Scripture, not authoritative for doctrine, and not equal to the Word of God.

My inclusion of this material is not to elevate it to the level of Scripture, but to highlight the historical perspective of past generations—how they thought about angels, how they structured the unseen realm, and how seriously they took the idea of an ordered heavenly hierarchy.

These writings demonstrate how early Jewish tradition regarded the idea of an ordered, structured angelic hierarchy—something Scripture itself affirms in passages referring to "principalities," "powers," "thrones," and "dominions."

In the Bible itself, only two angels are named directly:
- Michael, the archangel and warrior leader (Jude 9; Daniel 10:13, 21; Revelation 12:7–8).
- Gabriel, the messenger who interprets visions and announces key moments in salvation history (Daniel 8:16; 9:21; Luke 1).

ANGELS ARE NOT OMNIPRESENT—BUT THEY ARE POWERFUL

Unlike God, angels are not omnipresent. They travel from one place to another. In Daniel 10, an angel appears to Daniel and explains that from the first day Daniel began to pray, his words were heard in heaven, and the angel was sent in answer. However, for twenty-one days, the "prince of the kingdom of Persia" resisted him until Michael, one of the chief princes, came to help. If angels were everywhere at once, there would be no need for help to arrive or for one angel to "leave" another engaged in battle.

God alone is omnipresent. Angels, though incredibly fast and powerful, are still finite created beings.

Scripture gives us glimpses into the swiftness of angelic movement. In Daniel 9:21, Gabriel is described as coming to Daniel "swiftly," and in Ezekiel 1:14, the living creatures—angelic beings—are said to move *"like a flash of lightning."* Lightning is one of the fastest natural phenomena we know, and light travels roughly 186,000 miles per second. For comparison, the Earth's circumference is about 25,000 miles.

As for the likeness of the living creatures, their appearance was like burning coals of fire and like the appearance of torches. Fire was going back and forth among the living creatures; the fire was bright, and out of the fire went lightning. And the living creatures ran back and forth, in appearance like a flash of lightning.
Ezekiel 1:13–14 (NKJV)

If a being moved even *comparable* to the speed of light, it could circle the globe several times in a single second. So, while Scripture does not give us exact measurements of angelic speed, these illustrations help us grasp one simple truth: angels are not slow, weak, or confined by the limitations of human movement.

In the time it takes you to whisper the name of Jesus, an angel sent on assignment could—within the bounds of God's command—move with a speed and precision far beyond anything we can comprehend.

As for how many angels exist, the Bible does not give a total count, but every description suggests an immeasurable number. Deuteronomy 33 speaks of the Lord coming with "myriads" of holy ones. Hebrews 12:22 refers to "countless thousands of angels in joyful gathering." Revelation 5:11 speaks of "thousands of thousands" and "ten thousand times ten thousand." In other words, beyond human counting.

Their power is also staggering. Angels are called "mighty ones who do His word" (Psalm 103:20), "powers," "dominions," and "authorities." They are "greater in might and power" than humans (2 Peter 2:11). Angels battle against Satan's forces (Daniel 10:13; Revelation 12:7–8; 20:1–3).

Consider the story in 2 Kings 18–19: an army threatens Jerusalem, and in a single night, the angel of the Lord strikes down 185,000 Assyrian soldiers. One angel, 185,000 men. Jesus said that He could call on more than twelve legions of angels to rescue Him from the cross if He desired. A Roman legion consisted of about 6,000 soldiers, so 12 legions of angels would be approximately 72,000 angels. If one angel can deal with 185,000 men, then 72,000 angels could theoretically handle billions. In fact, far more than the current population of the Earth.

When God says He will protect you, He means it. He has the numbers, the power, and the heavenly army to back every promise.

HOW ANGELS CARRY OUT GOD'S PLANS

Angels serve God in many ways as He directs the course of history and salvation:

They frequently bring God's messages to people. An angel appears to Zechariah to announce John the Baptist's birth, to Mary to announce Jesus' conception, and to Joseph in dreams to give direction. Angels instruct Philip to go to a specific road (Acts 8:26), speak to Cornelius (Acts 10:3–8), and stand by

Paul in a storm, assuring him that all aboard the ship will be spared (Acts 27:23–24).

They carry out divine judgments. An angel brings a plague upon Israel when David sins (2 Samuel 24:16–17). An angel strikes the leaders of the Assyrian army (2 Chronicles 32:21). Another strikes Herod because he failed to give glory to God (Acts 12:23). In Revelation 16, angels pour out the bowls of God's wrath upon the earth.

When Christ returns, angels will come with Him as a great army accompanying their King and Lord (Matthew 16:27; Luke 9:26; 2 Thessalonians 1:7). They patrol the earth as God's representatives (Zechariah 1:10–11), war against demonic forces (Daniel 10:13; Revelation 12:7–8), seize the dragon and bind him (Revelation 20:1–3), and proclaim significant moments in God's plan (1 Thessalonians 4:16; Revelation 18:1–2; 19:17–18).

Angels are deeply involved in both the unseen spiritual battles and the visible events of history.

ANGELS AND WORSHIP: GLORY TO GOD ALONE

Angels themselves are worshipers. Psalm 103:20 calls them to bless the Lord. The four living creatures in Revelation 4:8 never rest day or night, crying,
"Holy, holy, holy, Lord God Almighty, who was and is and is to come!"
Revelation 4:8
Isaiah saw seraphim declaring,
"Holy, holy, holy is the Lord of hosts; the whole earth is full of His glory!"
Isaiah 6:3
At Jesus' birth, angels proclaim,
"Glory to God in the highest, And on earth peace, goodwill toward men!"
Luke 2:14
Hebrews 1:6 says,

"Let all the angels of God worship Him."
Hebrews 1:6

Paul even reminds us that our lives and obedience are carried out in the presence of angelic witnesses. He charges Timothy "before God and the Lord Jesus Christ and the elect angels" (1 Timothy 5:21), and he says the apostles have been made a spectacle to the world, to angels and to men (1 Corinthians 4:9). Heaven is watching.

Yet angels are not to be worshiped. At Colossae, "worship of angels" was one of the false teachings Paul confronted (Colossians 2:18). In Revelation 19:10, when John falls at an angel's feet to worship him, the angel immediately responds,

"You must not do that! I am a fellow servant with you and your brethren who hold the testimony of Jesus. Worship God."
Revelation 19:10

We do not pray to angels; we pray to God, who commands His angels. If an angel of the Lord appears, we may speak with them, just as people in Scripture did, but we do not honor them as we honor God. They are our fellow servants, not our God.

WHAT ANGELS ARE LIKE

Scripture and experience reveal many "facts" about angels. They were created to live forever; they do not age or die the way humans do. They observe God's people with interest and are deeply involved in His redemptive work. Angels ministered to Jesus in the wilderness and in Gethsemane. They help humans, report back to God, and will join believers in the heavenly kingdom.

Angels are described as messengers, watchers, military hosts, sons of the mighty, and chariots. They do not marry. They are wise and intelligent, with far greater understanding than we possess, yet they are still learning as God unfolds His plan. They are faster than humans and can move between realms. They have a will; some, like Satan and his followers, chose to rebel (Isaiah 14:12–14), while the holy angels chose to remain loyal.

Angels are sometimes called "sons of God" in the Old Testament. When Satan fell with some of the angels, that identity was marred. God then created Adam and called him a son of God. When Adam fell, God called Israel His son and raised up a covenant people. Israel also fell into idolatry. Finally, God brought forth One who would never fall: Jesus, the only begotten Son. He is the true and perfect Son of God, and through Him, redeemed humans are brought into sonship in a way angels never were.

Angels are rational, intelligent beings with unique personalities. They display a full range of emotions: joy, sorrow, anger, and compassionate love. Jesus said there is

"joy in the presence of the angels of God over one sinner who repents"
Luke 15:10

Unlike us, their emotions are not impaired by sin. Our emotions and bodies carry the wounds of the fall; we wrestle with fear, anxiety, anger, and sorrow. Angels' emotions function perfectly, as God intended, in alignment with His will.

Angels are humble, obedient, patient, pure, fiercely loyal to God, and eager to serve Him. Whether or not you have been conscious of their presence or assistance, these mighty warriors have helped you many times. Being in the presence of angels increases awareness of the kingdom of God. Abiding in God draws the realm of heaven and the ministry of angels closer.

Angels point us to God, lifting our souls toward Him, encouraging us to fix our eyes on the One who is our strength. Their holiness touches our minds, bodies, and emotions as they pass on the encouraging messages God gives them for us.

RESPONSIBILITIES OF ANGELS

Scripture outlines many responsibilities given to angels:
They will return with Jesus when He comes in glory (2 Thessalonians 1:7). They guard the church, represented by the "angels" of the churches in Revelation 1:20. They execute judgments, as seen when an angel strikes Herod for his pride

(Acts 12:23), and when they carry out God's justice in other passages.

Angels were involved in the giving of the law (Acts 7:53; Deuteronomy 33:2; Galatians 3:19; Hebrews 2:2). They also exalt, worship, and glorify God (Hebrews 1:6) and act as His messengers to His people.

They function as guardians and protectors (Psalm 91:11). They are involved in deliverance from evil as they enforce Christ's victory over the works of the devil. They participate in bringing God's purposes to pass in areas of healing, guidance, protection, and breakthrough. Again and again, we see them show up at critical moments, announcing births, steering servants, strengthening weary hearts.

DISCERNING ANGELIC ACTIVITY

Believers can become more aware of angelic activity through the Holy Spirit's help. We may see, feel, or hear evidence of their presence. While we never chase experiences for their own sake, we can ask God to make us more sensitive to what He is doing.

Many people have prayed, "Lord, send Your angels ahead of me. Send Your warring angels, Your guarding angels, Your ministering angels." This is a faith-filled way of agreeing with what Scripture already says about their ministry.

Many teachers encourage believers to ask the Lord to open their eyes to see the angels already assigned to them, reminding us that our eyes are blessed to see (Matthew 13:16). We do not demand or command angels; we seek God, and He is the One who sends them.

Seeing Angelic Activity

Angels appear hundreds of times in Scripture. Elijah saw an angel who cooked for him. Zechariah saw an angel who announced the birth of his son. That same angel appeared to Mary to announce her miraculous pregnancy.

Today, many people report seeing brief flashes of light in their peripheral vision, in colors such as blue, white, or gold. Others see small white feathers appearing out of nowhere during worship or prayer. These can be manifestations of angelic presence. Sometimes angels appear in human form, ordinary-looking people who show up at just the right time and then disappear.

Angels are created spirit beings who can become visible when necessary. Scripture presents them as actively involved in our world, though usually unseen. Cornelius, a Roman centurion, experienced this when he had a vision in which he clearly saw an angel of God come to him and call him by name (Acts 10:1–4). The angel told him that his prayers and gifts to the poor had risen as a memorial before God.

Feeling Their Presence

Sometimes we feel angels. Have you ever experienced a sudden breeze indoors where no natural wind was possible? Felt a brush like a hand on your shoulder when no one was there? Angels are described as winds and flames of fire (Hebrews 1:7). People often report feeling a gentle wind, a warmth like fire, or a tangible strength when angelic presence is near.

Before Jesus' crucifixion in Gethsemane, an angel appeared to strengthen Him. Similarly, angels can strengthen us noticeably in times of intense pressure, prayer, or warfare.

Hearing Angelic Activity

The Hebrew word for angel, mal'ak, carries the idea of a messenger—one who is sent. Angels sometimes speak audibly, bringing instruction, warning, or encouragement. Philip heard an angel give him specific directions (Acts 8:26). Hagar, when she had lost all hope, heard an angel speak to her, asking what was wrong and assuring her that God had heard the boy's cry.

Ezekiel heard the sound of the angels' wings, like the noise of many waters, and the voice of the Almighty, like the roar of an army. Throughout history, believers have testified to hearing angelic choirs, mysterious harmonies, or even sounds like wind chimes with no natural source.

ANGELS IN DREAMS AND SYMBOLISM

Angels also appear in dreams, visions, and symbolic language. In a dream context, angels can represent messengers of God, guardians, ministers, God's presence, warriors, or worshipers. It is vital to discern carefully, because the enemy can masquerade as an angel of light, or a familiar spirit may mimic the appearance of an angel. Discernment and the witness of the Holy Spirit are necessary.

Images of angels ascending and descending may speak of an open heaven —a portal to God's presence —or of the establishment of His kingdom in a place, as in Jacob's dream of a ladder between heaven and earth.

Feathers in dreams or symbolic experiences may point to covering, protection, trust, the Holy Spirit, or the evidence of angelic activity.

Wings can symbolize being carried by the Spirit, protection, intimacy under God's covering, warmth, refuge, worship, service, heavenly beings, escape, joy, or being lifted to a higher place. They can also picture riches that vanish quickly or come under the dominion of someone whose wings are stretched out. Wings on fire might speak of the fire of God being imparted or of spiritual judgment.

All of these symbols must be submitted to Scripture and the Holy Spirit. Angels always point back to Jesus and to the Word of God, never away from Him.

ANGEL OF THE LORD: A PRE-INCARNATE CHRIST

One of the most intriguing figures in Scripture is "the Angel of the Lord." When the definite article "the" is used with this title, it often refers to a unique person distinct from other angels. The Angel of the Lord speaks as God, identifies Himself with God, and exercises the responsibilities of God (see Genesis 16:7–12; 21:17–18; 22:11–18; Exodus 3:2; Judges 2:1–4; 5:23; 6:11–24; 13:3–22; 2 Samuel 24:16; Zechariah 1:12; 3:1; 12:8).

In several of these appearances, the people who encounter the Angel of the Lord fear for their lives because they believe they have "seen the Lord." In Exodus 23:20–23, God speaks of "My Angel" who will go before Israel, warning them not to provoke Him because He will not pardon their transgressions and saying, "My name is in Him." Forgiveness and the name of God belong to God alone.

Many believers understand "the Angel of the Lord" as Old Testament appearances of Christ before His incarnation, the eternal Word manifesting Himself in a temporary, visible form. Jesus declared that He existed before Abraham (John 8:58), so it is logical that He would be active in the world before being born in Bethlehem.

Interestingly, the specific title "the Angel of the Lord" disappears after the birth of Christ. Angels are still mentioned in the New Testament, but that particular figure no longer appears. This fits the idea that once the Word became flesh, the pre-incarnate manifestations under that title were no longer needed.

In Matthew 28:2, some translations (like the KJV) say "the angel of the Lord" rolled away the stone, but in the original Greek, there is no definite article; it simply says, "an angel." Other translations reflect this, which strengthens the view that the unique Angel of the Lord in the Old Testament was a special manifestation, not just any angel.

LIVING NATURALLY SUPERNATURAL WITH ANGELS

God never intended His kingdom to be disconnected from our everyday lives. Angels are not meant to be an odd side topic we debate, but a real part of how His kingdom works. They are not to replace the Holy Spirit, overshadow Jesus, or become the focus of our devotion. But they are part of our spiritual family, fellow servants, warriors, and worshipers who love the same King we love.

Whether you have clearly seen angels, felt their presence, heard their voices, or believed by faith that they are near, you have been helped by them more times than you know. They have guarded you, protected you, strengthened you, and delivered messages, all at the command of the Lord.

Our response is not to obsess over angels but to:
• Worship God alone.
• Walk in obedience, knowing heaven backs His word.
• Ask the Lord to send His angels to accomplish His purposes in and through our lives.
• Remain sensitive to the gentle ways He may allow us to see, feel, or hear their activity.

As we abide in Christ, the realm of heaven comes closer. The Lord of hosts stands as Captain over the armies of heaven, and His ministering spirits are dispatched on behalf of those who will inherit salvation. You are not alone. Heaven's host is real, active, and aligned with God's assignment on your life.

Appendix C: Angelic Encounters
A Biblical Reference Guide (NKJV)

Introduction

From Genesis to Revelation, angels appear as divine messengers, protectors, and warriors—heavenly beings sent to carry out the purposes of God. They announce His plans, strengthen His people, and execute His judgments. These encounters reveal the reality of a Kingdom unseen and remind us that Heaven is actively involved in the affairs of earth.

"Bless the Lord, you His angels, who excel in strength, who do His word, heeding the voice of His word."
Psalm 103:20 (NKJV)

This appendix serves as a resource for study and devotion, listing the key angelic visitations and encounters throughout Scripture. Each appearance reveals an aspect of God's heart—His holiness, mercy, power, and covenant faithfulness.

I. Old Testament Angelic Encounters
A. Early Appearances and Patriarchal Encounters

- The Angel of the Lord speaks to Hagar: *Genesis 16:7–12*
- Two angels visit Lot in Sodom: *Genesis 19:1–22*
- The Angel of the Lord stops Abraham from sacrificing Isaac: *Genesis 22:11–12*
- An angel appears to Jacob in a dream: *Genesis 31:11–13*
- Jacob wrestles with the Angel of the Lord: *Genesis 32:24–30*

  "For I have seen God face to face, and my life is preserved."
  Genesis 32:30 (NKJV)

- An angel leads Israel out of Egypt: *Exodus 14:19*
- An angel promises to guide and protect Israel: *Exodus 23:20–23*

- The Angel of the Lord appears in the burning bush: *Exodus 3:2–4*
- The Angel of the Lord confronts Balaam: *Numbers 22:22–35*

B. Angelic Appearances in the Time of the Judges and Kings
- An angel rebukes Israel for disobedience: *Judges 2:1–4*
- The Angel of the Lord calls Gideon and commissions him – *Judges 6:11–23*
- An angel foretells the birth of Samson: *Judges 13:3–21*
- The Angel of the Lord strikes 70,000 after David's census: *2 Samuel 24:15–17*
- The Angel of the Lord protects Elisha and reveals fiery chariots: *2 Kings 6:15–17*

"And behold, the mountain was full of horses and chariots of fire all around Elisha."
2 Kings 6:17 (NKJV)

- The Angel of the Lord destroys the Assyrian army: *2 Kings 19:35*

C. Angelic Encounters in the Prophets and the Exile
- Isaiah's vision of the seraphim crying "Holy, holy, holy:" *Isaiah 6:1–7*
- An angel touches Elijah to strengthen him in the wilderness: *1 Kings 19:5–7*
- An angel shuts the lions' mouths for Daniel: *Daniel 6:22*
- Gabriel interprets Daniel's visions: *Daniel 8:16–26; 9:21–27*
- Michael contends for Israel: *Daniel 10:13, 21; 12:1*
- Ezekiel sees the cherubim and the glory of God's throne: *Ezekiel 1:4–28; 10:1–22*
- Zechariah's visions guided by an interpreting angel: *Zechariah 1–6*

"The angel who talked with me said to me, 'I will show you what these are.'"
Zechariah 1:9 (NKJV)

II. New Testament Angelic Encounters
A. The Birth and Life of Christ
- Gabriel announces the birth of John the Baptist to Zechariah: *Luke 1:11–20*
- Gabriel announces the birth of Jesus to Mary: *Luke 1:26–38*
- An angel appears to Joseph in a dream: *Matthew 1:20–24*
- A multitude of angels proclaim Jesus' birth to shepherds: *Luke 2:8–14*
- An angel warns Joseph to flee to Egypt: *Matthew 2:13*
- An angel later instructs Joseph to return: *Matthew 2:19–21*

B. Angels in the Ministry of Jesus
- Angels minister to Jesus after His temptation: *Matthew 4:11*
- An angel strengthens Him in Gethsemane: *Luke 22:43*
- Angels appear at the tomb following His resurrection: *Matthew 28:2–6; Luke 24:4–7; John 20:12–13*

"He is not here; for He is risen, as He said. Come, see the place where the Lord lay."
Matthew 28:6 (NKJV)

- Two angels speak at His ascension: *Acts 1:10–11*

C. Angelic Activity in the Early Church
- An angel releases the apostles from prison: *Acts 5:19–20*
- An angel instructs Philip to meet the Ethiopian eunuch: *Acts 8:26*
- An angel appears to Cornelius with a message from God: *Acts 10:3–6*
- An angel frees Peter from prison: *Acts 12:6–11*

- An angel strikes down Herod for pride: *Acts 12:23*
- An angel encourages Paul during the storm at sea: *Acts 27:23–24*

"For there stood by me this night an angel of the God to whom I belong and whom I serve."
Acts 27:23 (NKJV)

D. Angels in Revelation and the Last Days
- Angels worship before the throne of God: *Revelation 5:11–12*
- Four angels hold back the winds of judgment: *Revelation 7:1–3*
- Angels sound the seven trumpets of judgment: *Revelation 8–9*
- Michael and his angels cast down the dragon: *Revelation 12:7–9*
- An angel proclaims the everlasting gospel: *Revelation 14:6*
- An angel shows John the New Jerusalem: *Revelation 21:9–10*

"Then one of the seven angels… came to me and talked with me, saying, 'Come, I will show you the bride, the Lamb's wife.'"
Revelation 21:9 (NKJV)

III. Roles and Characteristics of Angels
- Messengers of God's will: *Luke 1:19; Hebrews 1:14*
- Worshipers before His throne: *Isaiah 6:3; Revelation 5:11–12*
- Protectors and ministers to believers: *Psalm 91:11–12; Acts 12:7–10*
- Warriors who battle for righteousness: *Daniel 10:13; Revelation 12:7*
- Guides in revelation and prophecy: *Zechariah 1:9; Revelation 22:8–9*
- Executors of divine judgmentL *2 Samuel 24:16–17; Revelation 15–16*

"Are they not all ministering spirits sent forth to minister for those who will inherit salvation?"
Hebrews 1:14 (NKJV)

Closing Reflection

From Eden to Revelation, angels remind us that Heaven is nearer than we imagine. They stand as witnesses of God's majesty, servants of His will, and companions of His presence. Through every age, they have declared one message: God is holy, faithful, and sovereign.

"Then I looked, and I heard the voice of many angels around the throne, the living creatures, and the elders; and the number of them was ten thousand times ten thousand, and thousands of thousands, saying with a loud voice: 'Worthy is the Lamb who was slain.'"
Revelation 5:11–12 (NKJV)

Angels still minister today—not to draw attention to themselves, but to point all glory to the One they serve. Their presence is a reminder that the unseen realm is alive with God's activity, and that His Kingdom is ever advancing on earth as it is in Heaven.

Chapter 8: The Bride of Christ

"Let us be glad and rejoice and give Him glory, for the marriage of the Lamb has come, and His wife has made herself ready."
Revelation 19:7 (NKJV)

THE MYSTERY OF DIVINE UNION

Before there was ever a Church, there was a Bride in the heart of God. Before the foundations of the world were laid, before light pierced the darkness, Christ already desired a people who would know Him, love Him, and share in His glory. From the very beginning, God's ultimate purpose has been union, heaven and earth joined, Creator and creation reconciled, the Bride and the Bridegroom made one.

When Scripture speaks of the Church as the Bride of Christ, it unveils one of the greatest mysteries of the Kingdom, the eternal covenant of love between Jesus and His people. This is not a mere poetic metaphor; it is divine reality. The relationship between Christ and His Church is the model and meaning behind every covenant in Scripture. Just as Adam received Eve from his own side, Christ purchased His Bride from the wound in His side.

At Calvary, when blood and water flowed from His side, it was not only an act of redemption but of divine romance, the moment the Bride was birthed. In His suffering, He was preparing a people who would be joined to Him forever. Salvation, then, is not just rescue from sin; it is entrance into union. We were not merely forgiven, we were betrothed.

"Husbands, love your wives, just as Christ also loved the church and gave Himself for her, that He might sanctify and cleanse her with the washing of water by the word, that He might present her to Himself a glorious church, not having spot or wrinkle or any such thing, but that she should be holy and

without blemish."
Ephesians 5:25–27 (NKJV)

This passage is not only instruction for marriage; it is a window into the divine romance that defines all of history. Christ gave Himself to purify His Bride, to wash her with His Word until she radiates His likeness. The same love that held Him to the cross now calls us to the altar.

The Church, then, is not an organization but an organism — a living body united by love, animated by His Spirit, and adorned by His righteousness. We are not merely followers of Christ; we are joined to Him. The mystery of the Bride reveals our most authentic identity. We are His beloved, the ones chosen, pursued, and prepared for eternal fellowship.

To be the Bride of Christ is to live from this place of divine belonging. It reshapes our purpose, our priorities, and our perception of the world. We are not wandering souls seeking acceptance; we are a chosen people called into covenant. This is why Scripture declares:

"You are a chosen generation, a royal priesthood, a holy nation, His own special people, that you may proclaim the praises of Him who called you out of darkness into His marvelous light."
1 Peter 2:9 (NKJV)

The Bride of Christ is the embodiment of this truth. She exists to display His glory and to carry His heart into the world. Her beauty is not in outward splendor but in her reflection of His character, humility, mercy, truth, and purity. The more she beholds Him, the more she becomes like Him.

"But we all, with unveiled face, beholding as in a mirror the glory of the Lord, are being transformed into the same image from glory to glory, just as by the Spirit of the Lord."
2 Corinthians 3:18 (NKJV)

This is the mystery of divine union: Christ in us, the hope of glory. The Bride is not waiting for union; she is being united day by day, as His Spirit conforms her to His likeness. We are becoming what we behold.

When the world looks upon the Church, it should see a reflection of the Bridegroom — a people in love, a people of purity, a people whose lives sing of covenant and faithfulness. This is not religion; it is a relationship in its purest form, the eternal love story between God and humanity.

The Betrothal of the Church

In the days of Jesus, a marriage covenant was not a casual agreement; it was a sacred vow sealed with purpose, preparation, and promise. Understanding the ancient Jewish betrothal reveals the beauty of what it means to be the Bride of Christ.

When a young man desired to take a bride, he and his father would approach the young woman's family to propose a covenant. A bride price was negotiated, a sum demonstrating the groom's deep commitment and value for his bride. Once the price was paid, the covenant was sealed with a cup of wine. The bride would drink, symbolizing her complete acceptance of the covenant, and from that moment, she was set apart, legally bound to her future husband, though they would not yet live together.

This was the betrothal period, often lasting about a year. During that time, the groom would return to his father's house to prepare a place for his bride, a new dwelling, often an addition built onto his father's home. He could not return for her until his father declared the room finished and suitable. Meanwhile, the bride waited, devoted and expectant, never knowing the exact day or hour when her groom would come.

This custom is rich with prophetic imagery. When Jesus spoke to His disciples before His crucifixion, He used this exact language:

"In My Father's house are many mansions; if it were not so, I would have told you. I go to prepare a place for you. And if I go and prepare a place for you, I will come again and receive you to Myself; that where I am, there you may be also."
John 14:2–3 (NKJV)

In essence, Jesus was saying, "You are My betrothed. I have paid the bride price with My blood. Now I return to My Father's house to prepare a place for you — and when it is ready, I will come again for My Bride."

The parallels are breathtaking:

- The bride price represents the sacrifice of the cross, Christ's own life poured out for our redemption.
- The cup of wine recalls the Last Supper, when Jesus said, "This cup is the new covenant in My blood, which is shed for you." *(Luke 22:20, NKJV)*
- The waiting period mirrors the Church Age, our season of faithfulness and preparation as we await His return.
- And the Father's approval echoes the divine timing of the Second Coming, for as Jesus said, "But of that day and hour no one knows, not even the angels of heaven, but My Father only." *(Matthew 24:36, NKJV)*

When the groom's father finally gave permission, the bridegroom would gather his wedding party and go out at night, carrying torches. The streets would fill with shouts of joy, "Behold, the bridegroom is coming!" and the bride, who had been waiting with her bridesmaids, would rise quickly to meet him. Together, they would process through the streets to the wedding feast, where celebration, song, and covenant rejoicing would last for days.

This is the prophetic picture of the rapture of the Church, the moment the heavenly Bridegroom comes to receive His Bride. Paul describes it this way:

"For the Lord Himself will descend from heaven with a shout, with the voice of an archangel, and with the trumpet of God. And the dead in Christ will rise first. Then we who are alive and remain shall be caught up together with them in the clouds to meet the Lord in the air. And thus we shall always be with the Lord."
1 Thessalonians 4:16-17 (NKJV)

The Bride's posture during this time is one of watchful devotion. She does not occupy herself with worldly distractions or lose sight of her covenant. She keeps her lamp full, her garments pure, and her eyes fixed on the horizon.

"Then those who were ready went in with him to the wedding; and the door was shut."
Matthew 25:10 (NKJV)

In this divine betrothal, the Church learns what true love looks like, a love that waits, that prepares, that endures. The Bridegroom's delay is not abandonment; it is mercy and preparation. He is perfecting His Bride through every season of testing, cleansing, and refining.

The ancient Jewish bride would often spend her days sewing her wedding garments, trimming her lamps, and listening for the sound of the shofar, the trumpet that would announce the bridegroom's arrival. Likewise, we are called to live in readiness, cultivating hearts that burn for His presence.

To be the betrothed of Christ means living in the tension of promise and fulfillment, faithful in the waiting, joyful in the testing, steadfast in love. The Bride of Christ does not grow weary; she grows radiant. Every act of obedience, every moment of surrender, and every tear of longing becomes part of her preparation for the eternal wedding feast.

When that trumpet sounds and the heavens split open, there will be no more separation. The Bridegroom will return, the waiting will be over, and the cry will fill the heavens:

"Alleluia! For the Lord God Omnipotent reigns! Let us be glad and rejoice and give Him glory, for the marriage of the Lamb has come, and His wife has made herself ready."
Revelation 19:6–7 (NKJV)

THE CALL TO HOLINESS AND THE FEAR OF THE LORD

To be the Bride of Christ is to be marked by love, but also by holy fear. The end-time Bride will not only sing about His goodness; she will tremble at His holiness. Intimacy with Jesus and the fear of the Lord are not opposites; they are two parts of the same covenant. The closer we draw to His heart, the more we burn with a longing to be clean before Him.

Isaiah prophesied of Jesus, our Bridegroom King:

"There shall come forth a Rod from the stem of Jesse,
And a Branch shall grow out of his roots.
The Spirit of the Lord shall rest upon Him,
The Spirit of wisdom and understanding,
The Spirit of counsel and might,
The Spirit of knowledge and of the fear of the Lord.
His delight is in the fear of the Lord,
And He shall not judge by the sight of His eyes,
Nor decide by the hearing of His ears."
Isaiah 11:1–3 (NKJV)

The very Spirit that rested on Jesus culminates in this: His delight is in the fear of the Lord. The fear of the Lord is not beneath Him; it is His pleasure. If the Son of God delights in the fear of God, how much more should His Bride? We are not called to live off momentary touches of His presence or occasional convicting moments at an altar. We are called to live under the continual resting of the Holy Spirit, and part of that resting is a constant awareness of His holiness.

In our human experience, fear is usually negative —an unpleasant emotion that arises when we feel threatened or in danger. There is a destructive fear that torments, paralyzes, and lies to us about threats that may not even be real. There is also a natural, constructive fear that warns us of danger and keeps us from foolishness. But above all these, there is a different kind of fear altogether: the fear of the Lord. This is not terror of a distant Judge, but awestruck reverence for a holy God. It is the profound, trembling realization that He is God and we are not, that His word is final, His judgments are true, and His presence is not to be treated casually.

Scripture is very clear:

"The fear of the Lord is the beginning of knowledge,
But fools despise wisdom and instruction."
Proverbs 1:7 (NKJV)

*"The fear of the Lord is the beginning of wisdom;
A good understanding have all those who do His commandments.
His praise endures forever."*
Psalm 111:10 (NKJV)

If the fear of the Lord is the beginning of wisdom and knowledge, then a church that loses this fear will drift into deception, pride, and confusion. Many chase after revelation, knowledge, and spiritual experiences, but bypass the very gate through which true understanding flows: the fear of the Lord. To reach for knowledge without surrendering to holy fear is to eat from the tree of the knowledge of good and evil without the covering of God.

The fear of the Lord touches every part of life. The book of Proverbs ties it to protection, longevity, and freedom from destruction:

*"The fear of the Lord prolongs days,
But the years of the wicked will be shortened."*
Proverbs 10:27 (NKJV)

*"The fear of the Lord is a fountain of life,
To turn one away from the snares of death."*
Proverbs 14:27 (NKJV)

*"The fear of the Lord leads to life,
And he who has it will abide in satisfaction;
He will not be visited with evil."*
Proverbs 19:23 (NKJV)

*"The fear of the Lord is to hate evil;
Pride and arrogance and the evil way
And the perverse mouth I hate."*
Proverbs 8:13 (NKJV)

The fear of the Lord does not make us miserable; it makes us wise, clean, and safe. It leads us away from sin's snares and into true life. It teaches us to hate what He hates, not from legalism, but from love. The Bride who fears the Lord doesn't stand on the edge of compromise, asking, "How close can I get to the line and still be saved?" She asks, "How close can I get to His heart? How far can I get from anything that grieves Him?"

Holiness, then, is not a legalistic cage; it is the freedom of belonging fully to Him. Holiness means being set apart, separated unto God. It is the fruit of the Spirit of the fear of the Lord at work in us.

"The fear of the Lord is clean, enduring forever;
The judgments of the Lord are true and righteous altogether."
Psalm 19:9 (NKJV)

The fear of the Lord cleanses. It washes our motives. It purifies our desires. It keeps our outward behavior aligned with our inward devotion. When we walk in holy fear, we cannot treat sin lightly, because we value His presence too much to risk losing the sense of His nearness.

This fear is not only an Old Testament theme; it is the atmosphere of the early church. In the book of Acts, after Ananias and Sapphira fell dead for lying to the Holy Spirit, we read:

"So great fear came upon all the church and upon all who heard these things. And through the hands of the apostles, many signs and wonders were done among the people. And they were all with one accord in Solomon's Porch. Yet none of the rest dared join them, but the people esteemed them highly. And believers were increasingly added to the Lord, multitudes of both men and women, so that they brought the sick out into the streets and laid them on beds and couches, that at least the shadow of Peter passing by might fall on some of them. Also, a multitude gathered from the surrounding cities to Jerusalem, bringing sick people and those who were tormented by unclean spirits, and they were all healed."
Acts 5:11–16 (NKJV)

Notice this carefully: great fear came on the church, and what followed was power, unity, respect from the world, multitudes being saved, and mass deliverance and healing. The fear of the Lord did not shut down revival; it intensified it. When the church returned to holy fear, the world had to take the church seriously again.

This is a word for our generation. Many churches rightly celebrate God's goodness, love, and joy, but in many places the message has been cut in half. The holiness, severity, and fear of the Lord are often ignored or dismissed as "Old Covenant." Yet the New Testament commands are clear:

"Therefore, my beloved, as you have always obeyed, not as in my presence only, but now much more in my absence, work out your own salvation with fear and trembling."
Philippians 2:12 (NKJV)

"Therefore, having these promises, beloved, let us cleanse ourselves from all filthiness of the flesh and spirit, perfecting holiness in the fear of God."
2 Corinthians 7:1 (NKJV)

"Therefore, since we are receiving a kingdom which cannot be shaken, let us have grace, by which we may serve God acceptably with reverence and godly fear."
Hebrews 12:28 (NKJV)

"And if you call on the Father, who without partiality judges according to each one's work, conduct yourselves throughout the time of your stay here in fear."
1 Peter 1:17 (NKJV)

Jesus Himself said:

"And do not fear those who kill the body but cannot kill the soul. But rather fear Him who is able to destroy both soul and body in hell."
Matthew 10:28 (NKJV)

The Bride of Christ cannot afford to treat these words lightly. Yet in our generation, many have reshaped Jesus into a more comfortable version of themselves. We hear phrases like, "My Jesus just wants me to be happy," or "My Jesus wouldn't judge anyone," or "God understands my heart," even while choosing to live in ways the Word clearly calls sin. This is not the Jesus of Scripture; it is an idol made in our own image. When we take His name but not His nature, we misuse that holy name.

To "take the Lord's name in vain" is not only to speak it carelessly; it is to **carry His name** without reflecting His character. It is to call ourselves "The Bride of Christ" yet live in opposition to His ways. Every time we claim to belong to Him but refuse to obey His Word, we take His name in vain. The true Bride, however, bears His name with reverence and truth. She knows that to belong to Him is to represent Him, to carry His presence, His purity, and His truth wherever she goes.

When the Church forgets this, she loses her distinction and her power. But when she remembers whose name she carries, she walks in holy fear, not as one bound by rules but as one bound by love. This fear of the Lord is what frees us from every other fear. When we live in awe of Him, we no longer tremble before the opinions of people.

The fear of the Lord delivers us from the fear of man. When we know that God's eyes are on us, and His opinion is what matters eternally, we stop bending our convictions to keep people comfortable. A church that fears the Lord more than public opinion becomes bold, pure, and uncompromising. This is the kind of Bride who can carry His glory in these last days.

The fear of the Lord and the bridal identity belong together. As His Bride, we are not flirting with the world; we are consecrated to One Man. We refuse to live lukewarm, halfway lives because we understand that all we do will be tested by fire. Paul wrote:

> *"If anyone's work is burned, he will suffer loss; but he himself will be saved, yet so as through fire."*
> ***1 Corinthians 3:15 (NKJV)***

We do not want to step into eternity as those who are "barely escaping through flames," saved but with a lifetime of wasted opportunities scorched away. The Bride lives differently because she knows she will see Him face to face.

To fear the Lord is to love what He loves and hate what He hates. It is to turn from sin, not because we are afraid of being caught, but because the thought of grieving Him is unthinkable. It is to say, "I would rather lose everything than lose the tenderness of Your presence."

In these days, the Spirit of the Lord is restoring this holy fear to the Church. It is not to crush us, but to cleanse us. It is not to push us away, but to draw us into deeper union. The Bride who walks in the fear of the Lord will be a pure, powerful, radiant Bride, ready for the coming of her King.

PREPARATION OF THE BRIDE

From Genesis to Revelation, preparation has always been the pattern of God's people. Noah built an ark before the rain ever came. Moses sanctified the people before the glory descended on Sinai. John the Baptist prepared the way for Jesus's revelation. In the same way, the Spirit is now preparing a Bride, one who reflects the purity, devotion, and power of her Bridegroom.

To prepare is not simply to wait; it is to align our lives with heaven's rhythm. Just as a bride adorns herself in anticipation of her wedding day, so we must clothe ourselves with righteousness, humility, and faithfulness.

"Let us be glad and rejoice and give Him glory, for the marriage of the Lamb has come, and His wife has made herself ready. And to her it was granted to be arrayed in fine linen, clean and bright, for the fine linen is the righteous acts of the saints."
Revelation 19:7–8 (NKJV)

The garments of the Bride are not made of earthly fabric. They are woven through every act of obedience, every unseen prayer, and every moment of surrender. Heaven measures beauty not by outward adornment, but by inward purity. Christ is coming for a Bride whose heart burns for Him above all else — one who walks in holiness and love, unspotted by the world.

Oil for the Lamps

In Matthew 25, Jesus tells the parable of the ten virgins: five wise and five foolish. Each carried a lamp, but only the wise carried extra oil. When the midnight cry rang out, "Behold, the Bridegroom is coming," the wise entered the wedding, while the foolish were left outside, scrambling in the dark.

This oil represents intimacy with the Holy Spirit, the hidden life of communion that cannot be borrowed or bought at the last minute. The Bride keeps her lamp burning because she values His presence above all else. She guards her time with Him, cherishes His voice, and lets His fire refine her.

"But the wise took oil in their vessels with their lamps... And while they went to buy, the bridegroom came, and those who were ready went in with him to the wedding; and the door was shut."
Matthew 25:4,10 (NKJV)

The preparation of the Bride is deeply personal. Each believer must tend their own flame. Church attendance, ministry activity, or good works cannot replace the oil of intimacy. The true Bride knows her Beloved's voice because she spends time in His presence.

The Refining of Esther

Before Esther could stand before the king, she endured a year of preparation: six months with oil of myrrh and six months with perfumes and cosmetics (Esther 2:12). This was not mere vanity; it was a process of purification and transformation. She entered the palace as a captive but, through obedience and favor, emerged as a queen.

Likewise, the Church is being purified and perfumed by the Holy Spirit. The oil of myrrh represents dying to self — the surrender of our own desires so that His will might prevail. The fragrance of perfume represents the beauty of His nature being formed within us.

God is raising up a Bride like Esther, pure, bold, and positioned for such a time as this. Her preparation is not wasted time; it is the hidden work that precedes divine promotion. When the King calls for her, she will already be ready.

The Bride's Awakening

The Spirit is awakening the Bride in this generation. For too long, the Church has been content with religion instead of relationship, performance instead of presence. But the cry of the Bridegroom is stirring the hearts of believers around the world, calling them out of compromise, out of apathy, and into the fullness of love.

This awakening is not about fear of His coming, but joy in His appearing. It is the sound of hearts returning to their first love. The Bride is awakening to her identity, not as a servant striving for approval, but as a beloved one already chosen.

"You did not choose Me, but I chose you and appointed you that you should go and bear fruit."
John 15:16 (NKJV)

When the Bride knows who she is, she walks differently. She loves deeply, forgives quickly, worships passionately, and lives with eternity in view. She reflects the nature of her Bridegroom, radiant in holiness, fearless in love, steadfast in truth.

This preparation is leading to the ultimate moment, the union of heaven and earth, when the Bride and the Spirit will cry together:

"And the Spirit and the bride say, 'Come!' And let him who hears say, 'Come!'"
Revelation 22:17 (NKJV)

APPLICATION AND PRAYER

The revelation of the Bride of Christ is not distant theology; it is a living call to intimacy. To be His Bride is to live in daily communion, walking in holiness and reverent love. The Church is not waiting for the return of a stranger, but for the One her soul adores. Every moment of surrender, every step of obedience, draws us closer to that eternal union.

This truth shapes how we live right now. The Bride keeps her lamp full. She guards her heart against compromise and distraction. She lives with eternity in view, not merely surviving, but shining as a testimony of love. Her devotion transforms her lifestyle: purity becomes her adornment, humility her fragrance, and worship her language.

The fear of the Lord and the love of Christ are not opposites; they are the heartbeat of the same covenant. The more we know His love, the more we revere His holiness. The closer we draw to His presence, the more we long to please Him. Holiness becomes a joy, not a burden, the overflow of being deeply loved.

Let the Church awaken to her identity once more. We are not a defeated, divided people; we are a chosen Bride, being made ready for the wedding of the Lamb. Our Bridegroom is not delayed; He is preparing a place and a people. And soon, the cry will echo across heaven and earth:

"Behold, the Bridegroom is coming; go out to meet Him!"
Matthew 25:6 (NKJV)

Until that day, may we live as those betrothed, faithful, pure, and passionately in love with Jesus.

Prayer

Heavenly Bridegroom,
Prepare our hearts for Your return. Teach us to live with holy anticipation and pure devotion. Let the oil of intimacy never run dry within us. Remove every distraction, every compromise, and every affection that competes with You.

Clothe us with garments of righteousness and fill our hearts with reverent love. Let Your Bride, the Church, awaken in glory and unity. Teach us to fear You rightly, to walk humbly, and to reflect Your beauty on the earth.

Come, Lord Jesus. May our lives echo the cry of heaven: **"The Spirit and the Bride say, 'Come.'"**
Amen.

Part III

The Counterfeit Unveiled
Exposure · Discernment · Truth Revealed

Every truth has an imitation.

This section confronts the counterfeit languages of darkness that seek to distort God's voice: witchcraft, New Age philosophy, and false spirituality. Through biblical discernment, the believer learns to recognize and reject deception, understanding that not every supernatural manifestation is divine. Here, truth stands as light in contrast to imitation, and Jesus is revealed as the only trustworthy source of wisdom, power, and freedom.

- Chapter 9:   Witchcraft
- Chapter 10: New Age
- Chapter 11: Deliverance

Chapter 9: Witchcraft
The Ancient Rebellion Revived
*"For rebellion is as the sin of witchcraft,
And stubbornness is as iniquity and idolatry."*
1 Samuel 15:23 (NKJV)

WHAT WITCHCRAFT REALLY IS

Witchcraft is a vast and complex subject, one that could easily fill an entire book on its own. The history, deception, and spiritual dynamics surrounding it reach into every part of culture and faith. In this chapter, we will uncover as much as possible within one section, exposing what witchcraft truly is, how it operates, and why God calls His people to be separate from it.

Most people think of witchcraft as cauldrons, curses, and dark rituals, something far removed from everyday life. While it is those things, witchcraft is not limited to those who openly practice the occult in this way. It is far more subtle, disguised, and widespread than most realize.

At its core, witchcraft is rebellion against God. It is an attempt to gain spiritual power, wisdom, or control apart from submission to His Spirit. Humanity desires to access the supernatural without surrender. From the very beginning, this was Lucifer's downfall: he wanted God's power without God's presence.

The word *occult* means *hidden*. It refers to what is secret, unseen, and outside the natural realm, practices that seek supernatural power through forbidden means. This includes witchcraft, divination, spiritism, and every attempt to manipulate the unseen world apart from the authority of Christ.

Witchcraft thrives in secrecy, yet the enemy no longer hides it in the shadows; he conceals it in plain sight. It is behind entertainment, culture, and even self-help, but to the discerning, its disguise is transparent. It appears harmless, spiritual, and sophisticated, but its goal has never changed: to draw hearts away from dependence on God. The same voice that whispered to Eve still whispers today, "Did God really say?" (Genesis 3:1).

What makes witchcraft dangerous is not only what it does, but what it replaces. It turns worship into self-will, prayer into manipulation, and faith into formula. It is the counterfeit of a divine relationship.

"Now the Spirit expressly says that in latter times some will depart from the faith, giving heed to deceiving spirits and doctrines of demons."
1 Timothy 4:1 (NKJV)

Many believe they are safe because they do not cast spells or join covens, yet witchcraft is everywhere, in horoscopes, crystals, mantras, and "manifestation." Even the passive acceptance of these things gives the enemy room to influence the heart. When we participate in what God calls forbidden, we invite spiritual compromise.

The occult has been woven into modern life so seamlessly that it often goes unnoticed. Movies, television, and music casually glorify sorcery, rebellion, and supernatural power apart from God. What was once hidden in darkness is now presented as harmless entertainment. This constant exposure dulls discernment and normalizes what God calls detestable.

"But I fear, lest somehow, as the serpent deceived Eve by his craftiness, so your minds may be corrupted from the simplicity that is in Christ."
2 Corinthians 11:3 (NKJV)

The goal of witchcraft has never changed: to distort the truth and destroy intimacy with God. The devil's greatest deception is not convincing people to worship him; it is convincing them that they can walk in power without Him.

THE ROOTS OF WITCHCRAFT

Witchcraft did not begin with humans; it started with rebellion in heaven. Before the world was formed, Lucifer sought to exalt himself above God. His desire was not to serve, but to rule. When he was cast out, he brought with him one-third of the angels who shared in his pride. That same spirit of rebellion became the root of witchcraft, the pursuit of power without submission, authority without relationship.

When Satan entered the garden, he passed this rebellion to humanity. He tempted Eve with the promise of secret wisdom and self-exaltation: *"You will be like God."* (Genesis 3:5). From that moment, humanity has been drawn toward forbidden knowledge, seeking spiritual power apart from dependence on the Creator.

"So when the woman saw that the tree was good for food, that it was pleasant to the eyes, and a tree desirable to make one wise, she took of its fruit and ate. She also gave to her husband with her, and he ate."
Genesis 3:6 (NKJV)

The desire for independence from God grew through generations. At Babel, mankind again united in pride, determined to reach the heavens by their own strength. It was not merely a tower; it was an altar of self-exaltation. From that spirit of pride came the birth of paganism, idolatry, and occult religion.

As the world's empires rose, witchcraft became organized, manifesting in the magicians of Egypt, the sorcerers of Babylon, and the prophets of false gods. These practices all shared one root: spiritual rebellion. Pharaoh's magicians imitated Moses' miracles through demonic power, but their counterfeit was consumed by the true.

"Then Pharaoh also called the wise men and the sorcerers; so the magicians of Egypt, they also did in like manner with their enchantments. For every man threw down his rod, and they became serpents. But Aaron's rod swallowed up their rods."
Exodus 7:11–12 (NKJV)

Even Israel struggled with the pull of occult influence. When King Saul disobeyed the Lord and could no longer hear His voice, he turned to a medium for answers. That single act of desperation marked his downfall. Every time we reach for guidance apart from God, we repeat Saul's mistake, exchanging divine direction for demonic deception.

"Then Saul said to his servants, 'Find me a woman who is a medium, that I may go to her and inquire of her.' And his servants said to him, 'In fact, there is a woman who is a medium at En Dor.'"
1 Samuel 28:7 (NKJV)

Throughout Scripture, God consistently warns His people not to imitate the occult practices of surrounding nations. These rituals —divination, conjuring the dead, and interpreting omens — were more than cultural traditions; they were acts of allegiance to demonic powers. God's command to separate from them was not to restrict His people, but to protect them from the spiritual consequences that follow rebellion.

"When you come into the land which the Lord your God is giving you, you shall not learn to follow the abominations of those nations. There shall not be found among you anyone who makes his son or his daughter pass through the fire, or one who practices witchcraft, or a soothsayer, or one who interprets omens, or a sorcerer, or one who conjures spells, or a medium, or a spiritist, or one who calls up the dead."
Deuteronomy 18:9–11 (NKJV)

The New Testament continues the same warning. In Acts 8, Simon the sorcerer tried to purchase the power of the Holy Spirit. His actions revealed the same sin that began with Lucifer, a lust for divine power without divine surrender.

"But Peter said to him, 'Your money perish with you, because you thought that the gift of God could be purchased with money! You have neither part nor portion in this matter, for your heart is not right in the sight of God.'"
Acts 8:20–21 (NKJV)

From Lucifer to Babel, from Pharaoh to Simon, the story repeats: witchcraft is humanity's rebellion disguised as spirituality. It offers power, knowledge, and control, but every promise is rooted in deception. True power is never found apart from submission to the King.

FORMS AND FACES OF WITCHCRAFT

Witchcraft wears many disguises, but its source is always the same. Whether it appears dark and violent or bright and benevolent, all of it flows from one spirit, the desire to access supernatural power apart from God. The Bible does not distinguish between "good" and "bad" magic. The moment power is sought outside the authority of the Holy Spirit, it becomes rebellion.

"There shall not be found among you anyone who makes his son or his daughter pass through the fire, or one who practices witchcraft, or a soothsayer, or one who interprets omens, or a sorcerer, or one who conjures spells, or a medium, or a spiritist, or one who calls up the dead."
Deuteronomy 18:10–11 (NKJV)

Dark Magic and Satanic Rituals

This is the most blatant expression of witchcraft, open allegiance to darkness. It involves spells, curses, blood rituals, and demonic invocation. These practices may appear extreme, but they represent the same rebellion that lives quietly in less obvious forms. Few begin at this level; most are drawn here gradually, deceived by practices that seem harmless at first.

Dark magic takes many forms across cultures and religions, but its core purpose is always the same: to access power through submission to demonic forces. It includes ritualistic sacrifice, hexes, incantations, spirit channeling, astral travel, and summoning entities to harm, manipulate, or dominate others. In modern times, it manifests in Satanic worship, Luciferianism, voodoo curses, blood pacts, and black ritual magic. Some use symbols such as pentagrams, sigils, or occult circles to open portals and invite spirits to empower their will.

These practices often promise revenge, control, or supernatural strength, but every promise is a trap. Those who step into this realm quickly discover that they do not control the spirits they summon; the spirits control them. The "power" of dark magic is parasitic; it consumes the very soul of the one who wields it. Behind every spell and ritual is a demonic covenant designed to enslave, not empower.

White Magic – The Beautiful Lie
"White magic" disguises rebellion beneath the illusion of good intentions. Its practitioners claim to heal, protect, or bring blessings through rituals and spells. But good motives do not purify a corrupted source. Any spiritual power not rooted in Christ is demonic by nature. Satan does not care whether people practice "dark" or "light" magic; he only cares that they seek power apart from God.

"And no wonder! For Satan himself transforms himself into an angel of light."
2 Corinthians 11:14 (NKJV)

White magic often takes the form of "harmless spirituality." It preys on compassion and curiosity. It appeals to those who long for peace, connection, or justice. It whispers that your intentions determine righteousness and that as long as you "use your gift for good," you are safe.

Wicca and Pagan Spirituality
Wicca and modern paganism revive the ancient worship of nature and the divine feminine. They honor the elements, the moon, and earth as sacred powers, blending witchcraft with environmental reverence and self-deification. These movements often use the language of peace, healing, and harmony, but behind them lies the same deception that led humanity to bow before creation rather than the Creator.

"They exchanged the truth of God for the lie, and worshiped and served the creature rather than the Creator, who is blessed forever. Amen."
Romans 1:25 (NKJV)

Wicca teaches that divinity exists in all things, trees, water, the sun, and even humanity itself. Many Wiccans follow rituals tied to lunar cycles or the "Wheel of the Year," celebrating seasonal festivals such as Samhain, Yule, Ostara, and Beltane. These ceremonies often involve the casting of circles, lighting candles or incense to invoke elemental spirits (earth, air, fire, and water), and chanting spells to draw down the "goddess" or "horned god." Crystals, herbs, wands, and pentagrams are frequently used as tools to focus energy and summon power.

Modern paganism extends far beyond Wicca. It includes Druidism, Norse or Celtic polytheism, and various forms of earth-based spirituality that call upon ancestral gods or spirits. Some pagans honor deities such as Isis, Gaia, Artemis, or Pan, claiming to reconnect with ancient wisdom or restore balance to the planet. While these movements often appear peaceful and poetic, their foundation is the same as every form of witchcraft, seeking spiritual power and connection apart from submission to the true and living God.

Divination and Fortune-Telling

Divination is one of the oldest and most widespread forms of witchcraft. It seeks knowledge of the future or hidden information through supernatural means, bypassing God as the source of wisdom. Tarot cards, horoscopes, pendulums, psychic readings, and astrology all promise secret knowledge and insight, but their source is not divine; it is demonic.

Divination feeds humanity's desire for control. It whispers, *"You can know what comes next. You can guide your destiny."* When people look to fortune-tellers, spirit guides, or zodiac signs for direction, they open a spiritual door that only God should hold the key to. Even those who read horoscopes "just for fun" or consult online astrology apps participate in a system rooted in ancient idolatry.

Modern forms of divination are often disguised as entertainment or self-discovery. Tarot cards are sold as spiritual therapy, psychic readings are streamed live on social media, and astrology is promoted as harmless personality insight. Crystal pendulums, runes, and "oracle cards" are marketed as tools to "tune in" to the universe or one's "higher self." Yet every one of these practices calls upon spirits that do not belong to God.

Divination may look different across cultures, but its essence never changes. Whether through psychic intuition, palm reading, astrology charts, tea leaves, or so-called "angel cards," the goal is the same—to receive revelation without repentance, wisdom without worship. But every attempt to gain supernatural knowledge apart from God invites deception.

"And when they say to you, 'Seek those who are mediums and wizards, who whisper and mutter,' should not a people seek their God? Should they seek the dead on behalf of the living?"
Isaiah 8:19 (NKJV)

Necromancy and Spirit Communication

Necromancy, the attempt to communicate with the dead, is one of the most dangerous and deceptive forms of witchcraft. It seeks comfort, guidance, or knowledge from spirits that claim to be departed loved ones, but Scripture makes it clear: the dead do not return to speak with the living. The voices that answer are not human souls; they are demonic impersonations meant to deceive and entangle.

For centuries, people have sought to bridge the gap between life and death through mediums, seances, and rituals. The Bible records this in 1 Samuel 28, when King Saul, desperate for answers, sought out the witch of En Dor to summon the prophet Samuel. Though something appeared to respond, Saul's act of rebellion marked the end of God's favor on his life. His choice to consult the dead rather than the living God opened a door to destruction.

Today, necromancy has been rebranded. It appears through psychic mediums, ghost-hunting, and paranormal investigation shows that treat the spirit world as entertainment. People visit "angel whisperers" or "afterlife readers" to receive comfort messages from deceased relatives. Many of these experiences feel emotional, even loving, but the source is demonic imitation. Evil spirits are masters of mimicry; they know how our loved ones spoke, acted, and even the private details of their lives. Their goal is not to comfort, but to connect, and once that connection is made, the deception deepens.

Some cultures practice ancestral worship, believing that family members who have passed can bring blessings or protection. Others use charms, altars, or offerings to "honor" or "appease" the dead. Though these practices are often rooted in tradition and family devotion, they directly contradict God's Word. Scripture teaches that there is one Mediator between God and man, Jesus Christ (1 Timothy 2:5). All other forms of communication with the spirit world outside of Him are forbidden.

Necromancy may promise closure, but it delivers confusion. It offers contact (with demons) but produces bondage. Those who entertain communication with spirits often begin to experience torment, strange dreams, fear, anxiety, and a growing distance from peace. The enemy's ultimate goal is always the same: to shift our focus from God's presence to the world of the dead, replacing divine comfort with counterfeit connection.

Sorcery and Spellcraft

Sorcery seeks to alter outcomes through rituals, words, or objects. It appears in "manifestation," "positive affirmations," and "energy alignment" — modern names for ancient practices. The problem is not imagination or hope; it is invoking power through will rather than surrender. Even minor acts of superstition, such as throwing salt for luck, wearing charms, or burning sage, are forms of agreement with fear, and are witchcraft.

In the Bible, sorcery was closely tied to the use of potions, enchantments, and spells designed to influence people or events. The Greek word for sorcery, *pharmakeia*, is where we get the word *pharmacy*. It referred not only to the use of mind-altering substances but also to the blending of chemicals and rituals to open gateways to the spirit world. These practices were central to pagan religions that used drugs, chants, and sacrifices to induce trances and receive messages from demons.

In today's culture, sorcery is no longer confined to temples or rituals; it's been repackaged as "self-empowerment" and "spiritual wellness." Social media and bookstores overflow with content teaching people how to "speak things into existence," "manifest their reality," or "shift energy through words." While these ideas sound inspiring, they subtly replace dependence on God with self-reliance. Declaring your own will into being is not faith; it is sorcery in disguise.

Modern sorcery can be found in manifestation journals, crystal grids, "money spells," vision boards used for spiritual attraction, or the popular "law of attraction" movement, which teaches that the universe responds to your words and energy. Even when framed in positive language, these practices draw from the same demonic roots as ancient magic; they center the will of man instead of the sovereignty of God.

Superstition is another subtle form of sorcery. Many people wear bracelets to ward off the "evil eye," hang dreamcatchers to trap negative spirits, or burn sage to cleanse energy—all while believing they are being cautious or spiritual. But Scripture teaches that protection comes only from the presence of God, not from objects or rituals. Every attempt to use material items for spiritual safety is a rejection of the Holy Spirit's authority as our Defender.

Sorcery is not about wands and potions; it's about influence. It teaches that words, symbols, or actions can control the unseen world apart from obedience to God. But the believer's power is not in formulas; it is in faith. Our words carry Heavenly authority *only* when they align with His Word, and our strength flows not from the energy around us, but from the Spirit within us.

"The works of the flesh are evident, which are: adultery, fornication, uncleanness, lewdness, idolatry, sorcery…"
Galatians 5:19–20 (NKJV)
"And they did not repent of their murders or their sorceries or their sexual immorality or their thefts."
Revelation 9:21 (NKJV)

Occultism and Secret Societies

Remember, the word *occult* means "hidden" or "secret." It refers to the pursuit of knowledge and power that is concealed from the uninformed, knowledge that promises enlightenment but leads to bondage. Occultism teaches that truth is discovered through secret rituals, symbols, and initiations rather than revealed by God.

Throughout history, this pursuit of hidden wisdom has taken many forms, such as alchemy, Kabbalah, Hermeticism, Theosophy, Freemasonry, and other esoteric orders that claim to hold "the ancient mysteries." These movements often blend fragments of truth with lies, mixing philosophy, astrology, and mysticism to create systems that glorify intellect and self-deification. They promise spiritual awakening through secret knowledge (*gnosis*), but Scripture calls this the "knowledge that puffs up" and warns that it leads to pride and rebellion.

Modern occultism thrives in universities, media, and even entertainment, cloaked in symbolism most people do not recognize. All-seeing eyes, pyramids, pentagrams, and sacred geometry fill music videos, brand logos, and films, not as harmless art, but as spiritual language. Secret societies throughout history have used these same symbols to communicate allegiance to hidden powers and to spread ideologies that subtly oppose the authority of Christ.

Freemasonry, for example, presents itself as a moral fraternity dedicated to brotherhood and service. Yet its deeper degrees reference deities, rituals, and oaths that conflict with the exclusivity of the gospel. Theosophy and the occult revival of the 19th and 20th centuries introduced doctrines that laid the groundwork for much of today's New Age movement, ideas of "ascended masters," spirit evolution, and self-divinity. Even modern "manifestation" teachings and energy-based spiritualities borrow heavily from these same occult roots.

The danger of occultism is not only in its rituals but in its worldview. It denies absolute truth and replaces divine revelation with human discovery. It teaches that salvation comes through enlightenment rather than repentance. But Jesus declared,

"I am the way, the truth, and the life. No one comes to the Father except through Me."
John 14:6 (NKJV)

No amount of hidden knowledge can substitute for the transforming power of His Spirit.

Occultism always promises freedom, but its secrecy is a snare. What begins as curiosity quickly becomes covenant. What appears to be wisdom becomes a form of self-worship. The moment truth is hidden behind levels, symbols, or secret codes, it ceases to be truth; it becomes manipulation. The gospel of Jesus Christ requires no initiation, no secret words, and no hidden knowledge. It is light made plain for all who will see.

SUBTLE WITCHCRAFT IN THE CHURCH

Witchcraft is not limited to covens or pagan rituals; it can also operate within the walls of the Church. The enemy knows that if he cannot destroy the Church from the outside, he will attempt to influence it from within. His most effective strategy is subtle, spiritual manipulation disguised as zeal, pride disguised as discernment, and control disguised as leadership.

"O foolish Galatians! Who has bewitched you that you should not obey the truth, before whose eyes Jesus Christ was clearly portrayed among you as crucified?"
Galatians 3:1 (NKJV)

Paul's question to the Galatians reveals how witchcraft can influence believers without resorting to rituals or spells. They had begun in the Spirit but tried to finish in the flesh, trading dependence on God for human effort. Witchcraft always seeks to produce spiritual results through natural strength. It is the sin of independence wrapped in religious language.

Whenever we try to manipulate outcomes, control people, or manufacture spiritual experiences, we step into the same spirit that first rebelled. This is why Scripture equates rebellion with witchcraft—it flows from the same root of self-will.

"For rebellion is as the sin of witchcraft,
And stubbornness is as iniquity and idolatry."
1 Samuel 15:23 (NKJV)

The Spirit of Control and Manipulation

Control is one of the most evident signs of witchcraft operating in the Church. It appears in many forms: leaders who rule through fear, intercessors who dominate prayer with manipulation, or individuals who twist Scripture to get their way. Sometimes it looks spiritual, but its fruit is bondage, not freedom.

It can also appear in more subtle ways, through emotional manipulation disguised as "spiritual concern," through guilt-driven obedience that demands loyalty to a person rather than to God, or through flattery that entangles others in obligation.

God's authority never manipulates; it liberates. The Holy Spirit leads; He never forces. True authority protects people; false authority possesses them. When control replaces freedom, witchcraft has found a seat in the house of God.

"Now the Lord is the Spirit; and where the Spirit of the
Lord is, there is liberty."
2 Corinthians 3:17 (NKJV)

Christianized Witchcraft

A new and dangerous form of witchcraft has crept into modern Christianity: a blending of biblical terms with occult methods. Practices like "manifestation," "energy healing," or "prophetic declarations" that aim to force outcomes are often rooted in human will rather than in the Spirit's leading.

The difference between faith and witchcraft is surrender. Faith trusts God's timing; witchcraft tries to control it. Faith rests in relationship; witchcraft relies on ritual. The Holy Spirit cannot be commanded; He can only be obeyed.

When believers use Scripture like incantations or prayer like a formula to bend God's will to theirs, they cross from faith into manipulation. True prayer is not about control but communion—aligning our hearts with His.

"Not everyone who says to Me, 'Lord, Lord,' shall enter the kingdom of heaven, but he who does the will of My Father in heaven."
Matthew 7:21 (NKJV)

This "Christianized witchcraft" often begins with good intentions. People want breakthrough, healing, or provision, but instead of waiting on God, they reach for spiritual shortcuts. In doing so, they exchange intimacy for influence and purity for performance. God's true power never requires mixture.

There is also a growing fascination with mystical experiences, angel numbers, vibrations, or "Christian energy." These things may sound spiritual, but they echo the language of the New Age, not the Holy Spirit. The Spirit of God brings revelation through Scripture and holiness, not through secret signs or frequencies.

When believers replace purity with power, discernment with sensation, and submission with spectacle, they invite the same deception that fuels the world's witchcraft.

"Therefore submit to God. Resist the devil and he will flee from you."
James 4:7 (NKJV)

Submission is the antidote to witchcraft. Pride fuels rebellion, but humility restores authority. Every time we yield to the Spirit instead of striving, the counterfeit loses its grip. The Church does not need control to display power—it needs surrender to reveal glory.

The pure Bride Christ is returning for will not manipulate or perform; she will love, obey, and reflect Him. The most significant spiritual authority flows through the deepest humility.

The Cult of Celebrity in the Church

Another subtle form of witchcraft in the Church today is the worship of personalities. When preachers become *"celebrities,"* pride begins to replace purity. The altar becomes a platform, and the ministry becomes a brand. Influence, once meant to point people to Jesus, starts pointing them to a person.

This is not the leadership of Christ; it is the deception of Lucifer. The same spirit still seeks a stage today.

"I will ascend...I will exalt my throne above the stars of God,"
Isaiah 14:13 (NKJV)

When ministers begin to crave applause more than presence, when their worth is measured in followers rather than fruit, the enemy has already gained ground.

When leaders use charisma, emotional manipulation, or spiritual authority to draw people's devotion to themselves, it is a form of witchcraft operating in pride. They may still preach the name of Jesus, but they have begun to build their own kingdoms instead of His.

This spirit breeds comparison, competition, and jealousy among believers. Churches begin to measure anointing by popularity, sermons by soundbites, and truth by trends. The goal quietly shifts from transforming hearts to entertaining crowds. Yet the Holy Spirit cannot share the stage with pride.

True authority in God's Kingdom looks like servanthood. Jesus, who had all power, took the towel and washed the feet of His disciples. He did not build a following to be worshiped; He raised disciples to carry His presence. When leaders lose that humility, they risk becoming idols themselves, and where there is idolatry, witchcraft is already at work.

WITCHCRAFT IN EVERYDAY CULTURE

What once was whispered in secret circles is now celebrated in mainstream culture. Movies, music, and social media have transformed the occult from something feared into something fashionable. The enemy no longer needs to disguise witchcraft as evil; he repackages it as art, empowerment, and entertainment.

Television and film are saturated with imagery of magic and sorcery. Shows about witches, vampires, and "chosen ones" blur the line between fantasy and spiritual reality. Children grow up cheering for characters who cast spells, summon spirits, and use enchantments to overcome evil, unaware that they are being desensitized to the very things God calls abominations. Franchises like *Harry Potter*, *Chilling Adventures of Sabrina*, *Hocus Pocus*, and even, yes, *Doctor Strange* may seem harmless or creative. Still, their consistent theme is the same: that supernatural power apart from God can be used for good.

What begins as entertainment subtly becomes indoctrination. Even animated films and children's programming now include spells, magical creatures, and pagan symbolism, introducing the next generation to witchcraft as early as possible. The goal is not just to entertain, but to normalize the supernatural outside of God's design.

Social media has made witchcraft more accessible than ever before. Millions of users follow "#WitchTok," "#Manifestation," or "#EnergyHealing" accounts, where spell tutorials and rituals are shared as casually as cooking recipes. Crystals, tarot cards, and moon rituals are sold as lifestyle accessories, spiritual rebellion merchandised for the masses. Many who would never join a coven now practice modern witchcraft from their phones.

Music carries the same influence. What was once created to glorify God has been hijacked to exalt man. Witchcraft has found a new platform, not just in rituals or temples, but in microphones, stages, and screens. Through music, media, and even ministry, the enemy is shaping culture through sound and influence.

Sound has always carried spiritual power. Heaven was formed with it; creation responds to it. Worship hosts the presence of God, and rebellion distorts it. Many theologians believe, based on interpretations of Ezekiel 28, that Lucifer once held a role in heavenly worship. If so, it is no surprise that he continues to use music and influence as two of his greatest weapons.

Music was meant to move the human heart toward worship. But in the hands of the enemy, it becomes a tool to pervert affection and direct glory away from the Creator. Today's music industry is one of the most potent spiritual forces on earth. Its lyrics, rhythms, and performances often glorify rebellion, pride, lust, and greed, the very nature of Satan himself. The melodies may sound good, but the message is corrupt. What enters through the ears begins to dwell in the heart.

We see artists openly using occult symbols—pentagrams, serpents, all-seeing eyes—and even performing ritualistic acts on stage. Some speak openly about channeling "muses" or "spirit guides," acknowledging that their inspiration comes from another realm. Their concerts become modern altars of worship to self and sensuality, and the world calls it art. Yet what the world celebrates as creativity, heaven calls corruption.

Even more deceptive is when witchcraft operates under the guise of light. Not all music, sermons, or platforms that mention God are aligned with His Spirit. Pride has crept into pulpits, and performance has replaced presence. What began as worship becomes self-promotion; what started as service becomes spectacle.

The spirit of witchcraft always seeks to dominate and draw devotion. It thrives in environments where fame replaces faith and charisma replaces character. It manipulates emotions, controls crowds, and seduces hearts into admiration of man rather than adoration of Christ. Whether through a concert or a sermon, its aim is the same: to redirect worship from God to humanity.

True authority in God's Kingdom does not demand attention; it carries presence. Jesus, though all-powerful, humbled Himself to wash feet. He never sought fans; He made disciples. The Holy Spirit does not entertain; He transforms. The sound of heaven is not fame or noise; it is holiness.

Music and media are not neutral. Every song, message, and broadcast carries a spirit, either one that honors God or one that opposes Him. The believer must learn to discern the atmosphere behind what they hear and see. The question is never just "Does it sound good?" or "Is it popular?" but "What spirit does it carry?"

When we fill our lives with the sounds of heaven — worship, truth, and purity —darkness loses its grip. But when we allow the noise of pride and rebellion to become our soundtrack, we agree with the very witchcraft God calls us to resist.

This normalization is not harmless; it is intentional. The enemy has weaponized entertainment to dull spiritual sensitivity. What we repeatedly watch, listen to, or agree with begins to shape our beliefs. That is why Scripture warns,

"I will set nothing wicked before my eyes."
Psalm 101:3 (NKJV)

Witchcraft's greatest trick is not convincing people to serve Satan outright; it is convincing them that darkness is harmless, or even fun.

Pop culture witchcraft may look like fiction, but its influence is real. It trains a generation to laugh at sin, to call rebellion creativity, and to accept sorcery as normal. But the true children of God must see through the disguise. What the world calls entertainment, heaven calls war.

The enemy doesn't care which disguise a person chooses; he only cares that they choose something other than Christ.

"Abstain from every form of evil."
1 Thessalonians 5:22 (NKJV)

"Woe to those who call evil good, and good evil;
Who put darkness for light, and light for darkness;
Who put bitter for sweet, and sweet for bitter!"
Isaiah 5:20 (NKJV)

"He must increase, but I must decrease."
John 3:30 (NKJV)

"I will set nothing wicked before my eyes;
I hate the work of those who fall away;

> *It shall not cling to me."*
> **Psalm 101:3 (NKJV)**

The Battle for the Next Generation

The enemy knows that if he can shape a child's imagination, he can shape their destiny. From the very beginning, Satan has targeted identity and wonder—because whoever forms a child's imagination will form their worldview. Many cartoons, movies, and video games introduce concepts of spells, spirit guides, and magical powers long before children can discern truth from deception.

Shows like *Harry Potter*, *The Owl House*, *Sailor Moon*, *Encanto*, and *Frozen* normalize magic as harmless fun. Characters cast spells, speak to spirits, or channel unseen power to solve problems and find belonging. Children's television and streaming platforms include "cute" witches, sorcerers, and fortune-telling animals, training the next generation to see witchcraft as exciting, funny, or even heroic.

Toys and décor follow the same trend. Ouija boards are marketed as party games. Dreamcatchers, crystals, and evil-eye charms are sold in children's stores and school fairs. Astrology-themed coloring books and "beginner spell kits" are packaged to look innocent and empowering. Yet all of these items have roots in paganism and the occult. What the world sells as harmless décor or pretend play, the kingdom of darkness uses as initiation.

This is not harmless play; it is spiritual conditioning. The enemy is patient. He doesn't need a child to start casting spells; he only needs them to stop resisting them. Fascination becomes acceptance, and acceptance becomes agreement. Once the imagination has been softened to darkness, discernment weakens, and deception takes root without resistance. What is accepted in innocence becomes celebrated in adulthood.

Even education and entertainment promote "magical thinking" and self-deification, teaching children that power, purpose, and truth come from within rather than from God. When a generation grows up believing that they can speak things into being without His Spirit or create their own moral truth, they have unknowingly embraced the first doctrine of witchcraft: self as god.

The Word of God calls parents, teachers, and spiritual leaders to guard the gates of a child's imagination. What children see, hear, and play with forms their view of the unseen realm. The same creativity that can be used to worship can also be corrupted to wander. That is why Scripture commands us:

> *"Train up a child in the way he should go,*
> *And when he is old he will not depart from it."*
> **Proverbs 22:6 (NKJV)**

Yoga and Eastern Mysticism

What many consider harmless exercise is, in its origin, a form of worship. The word *yoga* means "to yoke," to unite with divine consciousness. Every pose and chant in traditional yoga was designed as an offering to Hindu gods and to awaken *kundalini*, a serpent energy believed to reside at the base of the spine.

Yoga originated in ancient India as part of Hindu spiritual practice more than 3,000 years ago. It was never meant to be merely physical. Each posture, breath pattern, and mantra was a sacred act of devotion to deities such as Shiva, Vishnu, Krishna, or Kali. The ultimate goal of yoga was to merge the practitioner's consciousness with Brahman, the Hindu concept of universal divinity, thereby erasing the distinction between creator and creation. In Hinduism, this "union" is considered enlightenment; in Scripture, it is rebellion against the Creator.

Over time, yoga spread to Buddhist and Jain traditions, absorbing their beliefs about meditation, reincarnation, and detachment from the material world. In the 19th and 20th centuries, teachers such as Swami Vivekananda and Paramahansa Yogananda introduced yoga to the West as a philosophy of spiritual awakening. They intentionally presented it as a system of personal peace and physical health to make it more acceptable to Western audiences, but its spiritual roots remained intact.

Even the physical postures—known as *asanas*—are not neutral. Each one was originally dedicated to a specific deity or spiritual concept. For example, *Surya Namaskar*, or "Sun Salutation," is a sequence designed to honor the Hindu sun god *Surya*. Chanting the sacred syllable *Om* is believed to vibrate with the frequency of the universe and connect the practitioner with divine consciousness. Breathwork (*pranayama*) was intended to regulate life force energy, not just oxygen flow.

Although God used a bronze serpent in the wilderness as a prophetic picture of Christ taking the curse upon Himself, Scripture never presents the serpent as a source of healing, energy, or divine awakening. The people were healed by faith in God's promise, expressed in obedience. Outside that moment, the serpent remains the emblem of deception, Satan, and rebellion. This is EXACTLY why kundalini's serpent power is a deception.

The biblical serpent represents the curse, represents Satan, and represents deception. The bronze serpent was simply a shadow of Christ taking the curse. It was NEVER a spiritual "serpent power" and NEVER meant to be repeated, replicated, symbolized in healing, or sought after.

Because people began to worship it, Scripture tells us:

"He broke in pieces the bronze serpent... for they burned incense to it."
2 Kings 18:4 (NKJV)

God refused to let it become a symbol of healing, energy, or power. Greek paganism turned it into an idol. Eastern mysticism turned it into a false "energy." New Age turned it into "awakening." Yoga turned it into kundalini. The world now treats it as a wellness symbol—yet medicine's serpent emblem does not come from Moses at all, but from pagan Greek mythology (the Rod of Asclepius), not the bronze serpent.

The Bible has always been clear: *healing comes from God alone.*

The "kundalini awakening," (*serpent spirit*) sought in advanced yoga is said to rise through the chakras—energy centers of the body—and bring enlightenment. But biblically, the serpent spirit represents pride, rebellion, and counterfeit revelation. The supposed "awakening" that yoga promises is not communion with God; it is a spiritual counterfeit leading to self-deification.

Many Christians attempt to separate yoga from its spiritual origins, using it as a form of stretching or relaxation. But you cannot sanctify what was designed for worship to other gods. Adding Christian music or Scripture verses to yoga does not make it holy; it simply mixes light with darkness. God does not share His glory with idols.

The modern wellness industry has repackaged Eastern mysticism as mindfulness, energy alignment, and self-healing, yet these practices still carry the same essence of yoga: awakening the "divine within." Whether called *kundalini*, *chi*, or *universal energy*, it all points to one message: that salvation and power come from within, not from Christ. But Scripture tells us that only the Holy Spirit gives true peace, power, and rest.

"You shall have no other gods before Me."
Exodus 20:3 (NKJV)
"What agreement has the temple of God with idols? For you are the temple of the living God."
2 Corinthians 6:16 (NKJV)

Symbols and Superstitions

Witchcraft hides behind symbols that most people wear or use without thought. Pentagrams, the all-seeing eye, the "evil eye" jewelry, astrological signs, and moon cycles all trace back to ancient occult worship. Even simple traditions like throwing salt, burning sage, or carrying crystals for protection are rooted in superstition, not Scripture.

Symbols are not merely art—they are spiritual language. Throughout history, symbols have been used to invoke, honor, or align with specific spiritual forces. In ancient pagan religions, every image, shape, and mark held meaning. The pentagram, now popular in jewelry and fashion, represented the five elements—earth, air, fire, water, and spirit—and was used in rituals to summon power and protect against spirits. Inverted, it symbolized man's dominance over God and became a sign of Satanic worship.

Every believer should ask three simple questions:
1. Where does this power come from?
2. Would I do this or wear this if Jesus were standing beside me?
3. Does this invite any spirit other than the Holy Spirit?

If the answer to any of these is uncertain, it must be rejected. The presence of God leaves no room for mixture.

"What accord has Christ with Belial? Or what part has a believer with an unbeliever? And what agreement has the temple of God with idols? For you are the temple of the living God."
2 Corinthians 6:15–16 (NKJV)

WHY GOD HATES WITCHCRAFT

God's hatred of witchcraft is not rooted in anger; it is rooted in love. He despises it because it separates His children from Him. Witchcraft is spiritual adultery; it replaces a relationship with imitation and worship with manipulation. It teaches people to depend on counterfeit power rather than on the presence of the Holy Spirit.

Every act of witchcraft, no matter how subtle, is an invitation to darkness. When people seek healing, guidance, or protection apart from God, they surrender themselves to demonic influence. Witchcraft doesn't just open a door; it builds a bridge for the enemy to access the mind, emotions, and spirit. That is why God speaks so firmly against it.

"When you come into the land which the Lord your God is giving you, you shall not learn to follow the abominations of those nations. There shall not be found among you anyone who makes his son or his daughter pass through the fire, or one who practices witchcraft, or a soothsayer, or one who interprets omens, or a sorcerer, or one who conjures spells, or a medium,

or a spiritist, or one who calls up the dead. For all who do these things are an abomination to the Lord."
Deuteronomy 18:9–12 (NKJV)

Witchcraft is rebellion at its root—a declaration of independence from the Creator. It whispers the same lie the serpent told Eve: *"You can be like God."* It feeds pride, giving the illusion of control while stripping away true peace. God hates witchcraft because it promises light but delivers darkness, because it blinds His children to truth and leads them away from His love.

"The coming of the lawless one is according to the working of Satan, with all power, signs, and lying wonders, and with all unrighteous deception among those who perish, because they did not receive the love of the truth, that they might be saved."
2 Thessalonians 2:9-10 (NKJV)

The Counterfeit Power

Witchcraft imitates what belongs to God. Pharaoh's magicians could mimic some of Moses' miracles, but their imitation ended where the true power of the Lord began. The devil cannot create, but can only corrupt. The supernatural power of witchcraft may look impressive, but it is always a distortion of what was meant to flow from God's Spirit.

True power brings freedom. Counterfeit power brings bondage. Witchcraft's "signs" are empty performances that glorify man, not God. The power of the Holy Spirit restores, redeems, and points to Jesus; witchcraft manipulates, deceives, and draws attention to self.

"Then Pharaoh also called the wise men and the sorcerers; so the magicians of Egypt, they also did in like manner with their enchantments. For every man threw down his rod, and they became serpents. But Aaron's rod swallowed up their rods."
Exodus 7:11–12 (NKJV)

Spiritual Adultery

To practice witchcraft is to break covenant with God. It is to trust another spirit instead of the Holy Spirit, to look for answers in the dark rather than the Light. God calls this idolatry, and idolatry always brings destruction.

He is not jealous because He is insecure; He is jealous because He is protective. The Lord knows that every false god, every false power, and every false light leads to death. His jealousy is love refusing to share us with what will destroy us.

"You shall not go after other gods, to serve them and worship them, and I will not provoke you to anger."
Jeremiah 25:6 (NKJV)

People no longer seek the voice of God—they seek experiences that make them feel divine. The more they chase enlightenment apart from truth, the deeper the darkness grows.

God hates witchcraft because it destroys intimacy, defiles purity, and deceives His creation. It is rebellion disguised as revelation, a counterfeit kingdom that seeks to rival His own. But no matter how strong deception becomes, it cannot outshine the truth.

God's judgment against witchcraft is not vengeance; it is mercy. It is His refusal to let darkness claim what He died to redeem.

THE POWER OF REPENTANCE AND THE WAY OUT

No matter how far someone has wandered into darkness, the power of Jesus Christ is greater. There is no curse, spell, or deception that the cross cannot break. The enemy's authority only lasts as long as our agreement with him does. The moment we repent, that agreement is dissolved.

Repentance is not a word of shame; it is the invitation to come home. It is not merely saying, *"I'm sorry,"* but turning completely toward God. It is the decision to reject every counterfeit source of power and to receive His mercy instead.

"If we confess our sins, He is faithful and just to forgive us our sins and to cleanse us from all unrighteousness."
1 John 1:9 (NKJV)

God never exposes sin to humiliate us; He reveals it to heal us. Conviction is not condemnation; it is the voice of a loving Father drawing His children back into His embrace. The same God who warned against witchcraft is the same God who forgives it when repentance is genuine.

When we turn to Him, He restores everything that deception tried to destroy.

"Draw near to God and He will draw near to you. Cleanse your hands, you sinners; and purify your hearts, you double-minded."
James 4:8 (NKJV)

Renouncing Darkness

True repentance requires renunciation, breaking agreement with the powers we once submitted to. Witchcraft cannot simply be "ignored" or "outgrown"; it must be confronted with truth. The believers in Acts understood this clearly. When they came to Christ, they publicly burned their books of magic. They did not try to redeem what was demonic; they destroyed it.

"And many who had believed came confessing and telling their deeds. Also, many of those who had practiced magic brought their books together and burned them in the sight of all."
Acts 19:18–19 (NKJV)

This act was more than symbolism; it was deliverance through obedience. When we remove every object or practice tied to darkness, we close the doors that once gave the enemy permission to operate. What we destroy in obedience, God replaces with peace.

Repentance empties the heart so that the Holy Spirit can fill it. Every space once occupied by deception becomes a dwelling place for truth.

The Freedom of Forgiveness

God's forgiveness is not partial; it is complete. Once you repent, the blood of Jesus covers your past entirely. He does not label you by what you once practiced; He calls you by who you are becoming.

Witchcraft thrives on shame and guilt, but both are silenced at the cross. No matter what agreements were made, no matter how deep the deception, the blood of Jesus is enough. Freedom is not earned through striving; it is received through surrender.

"Therefore if the Son makes you free, you shall be free indeed."
John 8:36 (NKJV)

Living in the Light

Repentance does not end at confession; it begins a lifestyle of alignment with truth. The more we pursue His Word and presence, the less room there is for darkness to return. Every time we choose obedience, we reinforce the victory of the cross in our lives.

God calls His people not just to reject witchcraft, but to replace it with worship, prayer, and intimacy with Him. The cure for darkness is not avoidance but affection for the Light.

"Submit to God. Resist the devil and he will flee from you."
James 4:7 (NKJV)

Repentance is the key that unlocks freedom. When the heart turns entirely toward God, every chain of deception breaks. He is not asking for perfection. He is asking for pursuit. The same Jesus who delivered Mary Magdalene from seven demons still delivers today. The same Spirit who filled the disciples in Acts still fills surrendered hearts.

The call is simple: leave the shadows and live in the light.

"Come out of her, My people, lest you share in her sins, and lest you receive of her plagues."
Revelation 18:4 (NKJV)

Repentance is not the end of your story; it is the beginning of restoration. Once you step out of deception and into His truth, you discover that freedom is not the absence of darkness; it is the presence of Jesus.

THE RISE OF MODERN WITCHCRAFT – PROPHECY FULFILLED

What we are witnessing in our generation is not a trend; it is prophecy unfolding. Scripture warns that in the last days, deception will increase, and many will turn away from the truth, embracing a false spirituality that denies God's power. The explosion of witchcraft, sorcery, and occult fascination in our culture is not random; it is evidence that the Word of God is being fulfilled before our eyes.

"But know this, that in the last days perilous times will come: For men will be lovers of themselves, lovers of money, boasters, proud, blasphemers, disobedient to parents, unthankful, unholy, unloving, unforgiving, slanderers, without self-control, brutal, despisers of good, traitors, headstrong, haughty, lovers of pleasure rather than lovers of God, having a form of godliness but denying its power."

2 Timothy 3:1–5 (NKJV)

Paul's warning describes the world we live in—a culture that claims to be "spiritual," yet denies the power and purity of the Holy Spirit. Modern witchcraft no longer hides behind secrecy; it parades itself as enlightenment, empowerment, and freedom. Its message is everywhere: *"You are your own god."*

Witchcraft today calls itself by many names: manifestation, astrology, energy work, the law of attraction, and even "shadow healing," and more. These movements promise transformation through self-focus rather than repentance. They teach that divinity comes from within, that salvation can be achieved through "higher consciousness." But the serpent's lie remains unchanged: *"You will be like God."*

"Then they said, 'Come, let us build ourselves a city, and a tower whose top is in the heavens; let us make a name for ourselves.'"

Genesis 11:4 (NKJV)

The Tower of Babel was humanity's first attempt at unity without God—an altar to pride disguised as progress. Today's spiritual movements carry that same spirit: people striving to reach heaven through their own means, convinced that enlightenment can replace obedience. But the Word of God reveals that self-exaltation always ends in confusion.

Witchcraft has become the religion of self, the worship of human potential without divine dependence. It rejects moral absolutes, redefines truth, and teaches people to trust energy rather than the Holy Spirit. It is the same spirit that fueled Babylon: seductive, intelligent, and deadly.

"For the time will come when they will not endure sound doctrine, but according to their own desires, because they have itching ears, they will heap up for themselves teachers; and they will turn their ears away from the truth, and be turned aside to fables."
2 Timothy 4:3–4 (NKJV)

The Rising Divide

As darkness increases, so will the light. The Word of God declares that deep darkness will cover the earth, but the glory of the Lord will rise upon His people. The rise of witchcraft is not just a sign of evil; it is a signal that revival is near. The counterfeit grows bold when the genuine is about to be revealed.

"Arise, shine;
For your light has come!
And the glory of the Lord is risen upon you.
For behold, the darkness shall cover the earth,
And deep darkness the people;
But the Lord will arise over you,
And His glory will be seen upon you."
Isaiah 60:1–2 (NKJV)

The increase of witchcraft and deception in the world is not the end of the story; it is the prelude to awakening. God is exposing the counterfeit to reveal His authentic power. The Church must not respond in fear, but in discernment. The true sons and daughters of God will shine brighter as the false light of witchcraft burns out.

The rise of modern witchcraft is proof that prophecy is being fulfilled and proof that the King is soon to return.

THE TRUE POWER OF GOD VS. THE FALSE FIRE

The enemy has always tried to counterfeit what is holy. Witchcraft offers power without purity, excitement without obedience, and experiences without transformation. It is the world's imitation of what can only be found in the presence of the Holy Spirit. The answer to witchcraft is not fear—it is fire. Not the strange fire of rebellion, but the holy fire of God that purifies, exposes, and consumes everything false.

"Then Nadab and Abihu, the sons of Aaron, each took his censer and put fire in it, put incense on it, and offered profane fire before the Lord, which He had not commanded them. So fire went out from the Lord and devoured them, and they died before the Lord."
Leviticus 10:1–2 (NKJV)

Strange fire still burns today, manifestations and experiences that claim to be divine but are rooted in pride or self-promotion. The difference between the false and the true is surrender. The false seeks control, the true bows in reverence. The counterfeit glorifies man; the authentic glorifies Christ.

Witchcraft and the occult cannot reproduce holiness. They can mimic miracles, stir emotions, and counterfeit revelation—but they cannot produce the fruit of the Spirit. The devil does not create; he corrupts. His false fire dazzles the eye but destroys the soul.

"For false christs and false prophets will rise and show great signs and wonders to deceive, if possible, even the elect."
Matthew 24:24 (NKJV)

The Source of True Power

The power of God is not summoned; it is entrusted. It flows through relationship, not ritual. It cannot be bought, borrowed, or manipulated—it is released through surrender. The Holy Spirit is not an energy to be channeled but a Person to be known. He empowers those who are humble, fills those who are empty, and uses those who are yielded.

True power always points back to Jesus. It restores the broken, heals the sick, raises the dead, and sets captives free—not to glorify man, but to glorify the King. It does not seduce; it sanctifies.

"But you shall receive power when the Holy Spirit has come upon you; and you shall be witnesses to Me in Jerusalem, and in all Judea and Samaria, and to the end of the earth."
Acts 1:8 (NKJV)

Witchcraft seeks power to serve self. The Spirit gives power to serve others. Witchcraft controls; the Spirit compels. Witchcraft manipulates; the Spirit liberates. The proof is in the fruit. The works of witchcraft produce pride, fear, and confusion, but the fruit of the Spirit produces love, joy, and peace that no demonic power can imitate.

"Now the Lord is the Spirit; and where the Spirit of the Lord is, there is liberty."
2 Corinthians 3:17 (NKJV)

The Call to Choose

Every believer must decide which fire they will live by, the false fire of self-will or the holy fire of surrender. One destroys; the other refines. God is calling His people to walk in authentic power, the kind that flows from purity, humility, and intimacy with Him.

The world is fascinated by the supernatural because it was designed to hunger for it. That hunger is holy, but it must be filled with truth. When the Holy Spirit moves in purity, no counterfeit can compete. The answer to witchcraft is not retreat, it is revival. The greater the darkness, the brighter the true light shines.

"For our God is a consuming fire."
Hebrews 12:29 (NKJV)

God's fire purifies; Satan's fire pollutes. One produces glory; the other, deception. The false fire offers power without presence, but the true fire reveals the presence that transforms everything it touches.

Now is the time for the Church to burn with holy fire again, not the fire of performance or pride, but the flame of consecration that consumes compromise. The world does not need more spiritual spectacle; it requires the real presence of God.

The rise of witchcraft is not a reason to fear; it is a call to awaken. For when light rises, darkness cannot remain. The Holy Spirit is still the only true power, and Jesus is still the only name that saves.

"And the light shines in the darkness, and the darkness did not comprehend it."
John 1:5 (NKJV)

CLOSING PRAYER

Heavenly Father,

I come before You in the name of Jesus, the One who conquered every power of darkness and triumphed over the enemy through the cross. Lord, I thank You for Your light that exposes deception and for Your truth that sets us free.

I renounce every form of witchcraft, occult influence, and counterfeit power that has touched my life—whether knowingly or unknowingly. I close every door that has been opened to darkness, and I break every agreement I have made with fear, manipulation, or rebellion. I choose to walk in the light of Your Spirit, where there is liberty and peace.

Father, purify my heart and my home. Let no unclean thing dwell in me or around me. Guard my mind from deception, my ears from lies, and my eyes from images that defile. Teach me to discern the spirits at work in this world and to cling to what is holy, pure, and true.

I invite Your Holy Spirit to fill every place that darkness once occupied. Restore my imagination, my worship, and my desires to reflect Your glory alone. I dedicate my gifts, my influence, and my voice to You, Lord—use them only for Your Kingdom.

I declare that Jesus Christ is Lord over my life. His blood covers me, His Word guides me, and His power keeps me. I will not fear the enemy, for greater is He who is in me than he who is in the world.

Let Your fire burn away all compromise, and let Your light expose every hidden work of darkness. Teach me to walk in holiness and truth, so that my life becomes a testimony of Your freedom.

In Jesus' mighty name,
Amen.

Chapter 10: Exposing the New Age Movement

The Old Lie in a Modern Disguise

THE RISING TIDE OF DECEPTION

In today's world, deception often masquerades as enlightenment. The very philosophies that claim to "awaken" humanity are, in truth, leading millions into spiritual darkness. The New Age movement, once considered a fringe ideology, has now seeped into nearly every corner of modern life: music, media, wellness culture, self-help books, and even churches. What once hid behind the curtain of *mysticism* now parades openly under the banner of "spiritual freedom."

What many do not realize is that the New Age movement is not separate from witchcraft; it is one of its branches. It is witchcraft dressed in softer colors and spiritual language, repackaged for a generation that craves "energy," "healing," and "awakening" but wants nothing to do with repentance and the cross. New Age offers spells without calling them spells, divination without calling it divination, and spirit contact without calling it demons.

In the last chapter, we exposed different expressions of the enemy's language and tactics. In this chapter, we are zooming in specifically on the New Age because it has become one of Satan's most effective weapons in our generation. It doesn't just lure those in blatant rebellion; it also seduces the spiritually curious, the wounded, and even those sitting in church pews who are searching for "more" but lack discernment.

Recent studies reveal that 62% of Americans embrace at least one New Age belief, whether astrology, crystals, energy healing, or faith in "universal oneness." This is striking, considering that roughly 70–80% of Americans still identify as Christian. This overlap reveals just how subtle and deceptive the movement truly is. It's not a distant danger; it's already in our neighborhoods, our social feeds, and our schools.

The Bible warns us,

"Now the Spirit expressly says that in latter times some will depart from the faith, giving heed to deceiving spirits and doctrines of demons"
1 Timothy 4:1 (NKJV)

These aren't just philosophical ideas; they're spiritual strategies of the enemy, designed to replace the truth of God with the oldest lie ever told: "You shall be like God." (Genesis 3:5)

Why Expose the New Age Movement?

We expose darkness because the Word of God commands it.

"And have no fellowship with the unfruitful works of darkness, but rather expose them."
Ephesians 5:11 (NKJV)

The New Age is not a harmless set of "positive" spiritual practices; it is a **counterfeit gospel** that leads souls away from Christ. It must be exposed:

- **Because people deserve the truth.**
  Many who dabble in New Age teachings do so out of genuine spiritual hunger. They long for peace, healing, and meaning, but are unknowingly opening doors to spiritual bondage.
- **Because it is a counterfeit form of spirituality.**
  It mimics biblical language, words like "light," "love," "peace," and "energy," yet redefines them into something entirely different from the gospel.
- **Because people are spiritually oppressed through it.**
  Behind "energy work," "spirit guides," and "manifestation" lie demonic forces masquerading as light.
- **Because it is rooted in satanic practice.**
  The heart of New Age teaching is the same lie whispered in Eden, that humanity can become divine apart from God.

- **Because Jesus Christ directly contradicts every core belief of the New Age.**
  He alone is "the way, the truth, and the life" (John 14:6), and no spiritual path outside of Him leads to salvation.

  The modern rise of New Age spirituality is not a new enlightenment; it is an ancient deception repackaged for the 21st century. The enemy changed his marketing.

  What makes it so dangerous is that it often appeals to emotion and intellect rather than rebellion. It does not always look evil. It looks good. It sounds peaceful. It feels loving. But Scripture reminds us,

  "Satan himself transforms himself into an angel of light."
  2 Corinthians 11:14 (NKJV)

WHAT IS THE NEW AGE MOVEMENT?

To understand the danger of the New Age, we must first understand its true nature and origin. Most people—Christians included—have little idea what the term even means. Yet its influence has quietly saturated our culture for generations.

The New Age Movement takes its name from the belief that the world is entering a new astrological era, the *Age of Aquarius*, a supposed utopian age of peace and enlightenment. Behind its colorful language and soothing aesthetics, however, lies a spiritual philosophy that denies the truth of God's Word.

At its core, New Age belief combines occult practices, Eastern mysticism, and modern self-deification, offering humanity the illusion of control and divine status. In essence, it is ancient paganism dressed in modern vocabulary: an alluring blend of yoga, crystals, astrology, "energy healing," "manifestation," and "higher consciousness."

It borrows heavily from Hinduism, Buddhism, and occult traditions, fused by 19th-century mystics and teachers who brought Eastern spirituality to the West. Its modern spread came through the influence of occultists, cult leaders, "enlightened" gurus, yoga instructors, and even pop culture icons.

If we were to summarize the movement in one sentence, it would be this:

The New Age is humanity's attempt to reach divinity without God.

But the Bible makes this distinction clear:

"There is a way that seems right to a man, but its end is the way of death."
Proverbs 14:12 (NKJV)

The Spiritual Counterfeit

The New Age appeals to those who crave spiritual meaning in a broken world. It promises inner peace, personal empowerment, and harmony with the universe, but replaces the Creator with creation itself. It teaches that we are all part of a universal consciousness, that "all is one," and that "divinity lies within." These statements may sound inspiring, but they are direct contradictions to the Word of God.

The New Age Movement claims that truth is relative, that all paths lead to the same spiritual destination, and that sin is "low energy" or "negative thinking." This seductive philosophy draws people into self-worship, the very deception that led to Lucifer's rebellion:

"For you have said in your heart: 'I will ascend into heaven, I will exalt my throne above the stars of God... I will be like the Most High.'"
Isaiah 14:13–14 (NKJV)

It is the same lie recycled for every generation.

Core Beliefs of the New Age

At its core, the New Age movement is built on a collection of ideas that blur every line between the Creator and His creation. Its foundational belief is that a single divine essence connects everything in existence, and that the universe, the earth, and humanity are one. This thinking removes the holiness and individuality of God and replaces it with a pantheistic view that everything and everyone *is* god in some form. Humanity is taught not to worship God, but to discover the "divine within," convincing people that salvation comes through awakening their own higher potential rather than through repentance and faith in Jesus Christ.

Another key theme of New Age philosophy is the pursuit of "enlightenment." Instead of surrendering to the Holy Spirit, people are told they can raise their level of consciousness and evolve into a higher spiritual state. In this system, sin is simply ignorance, and salvation is replaced with self-realization. The idea of one ultimate truth is rejected; instead, all religions and belief systems are said to lead to the same destination. This distortion promotes tolerance not of people, but of falsehood, merging light and darkness into one deceptive message of "universal unity."

Underneath these beliefs lies an entirely different view of God and the world. In the New Age, God is not a personal Father but an impersonal force, a kind of energy that flows through all things. The universe is believed to be eternal and self-sustaining, matter is seen as an illusion, and life is portrayed as a continuous cycle of reincarnation rather than a single appointed life followed by judgment. Humanity, according to this belief, is evolving toward godhood over countless lifetimes, growing closer to divine perfection with each cycle.

The practices that stem from this worldview are deeply spiritual but dangerously deceptive. Followers seek guidance through spirit communication, channeling, and altered states of consciousness achieved through meditation or substances. They explore astrology, tarot cards, and psychic readings in search of answers that only God can give. "Healing" is redefined through energy manipulation and vibration work rather than faith in Christ. The movement promotes a false peace, a calm that comes from detachment rather than surrender. Its end goal is a world unified under one religion, one consciousness, and one spiritual authority that denies the Lordship of Jesus Christ.

In truth, there is nothing "new" about these ideas. They are the same ancient lies recycled in modern language, the same rebellion that began in Eden, where creation sought to become equal with the Creator. The New Age is simply old idolatry wearing new clothing.

New Age = Satanic Occult

Even those within the occult world recognize the New Age as a mirror image of Satanism. Anton LaVey, founder of the Church of Satan and author of The Satanic Bible, once admitted:

"New Agers have really drawn all manner of satanic material, adapting it to their own hypocritical purposes. But, in truth, all New Age labeling is, again, trying to play the devil's game without using his infernal name."

Anton LaVey was not just a random voice on the fringe. He was a leading figure in modern Satanism. In 1966, he established the Church of Satan in San Francisco and became known as the "Black Pope" of Satanism. His philosophy blended ritual, occult symbolism, and radical self-worship. He promoted a worldview where the self is the highest authority, where "do what you want" becomes a moral code, and where traditional Christianity is openly mocked and opposed. Through *The Satanic Bible*, he laid out principles of indulgence, rebellion, and empowerment apart from God, principles that echo strongly in New Age thought, even when they are dressed up in softer, more "positive" language.

Among the central ideas found within satanic and occult philosophy are several themes that perfectly mirror the teachings of the New Age. One of these, which we've already discussed, is the Age of Aquarius, the belief that humanity is entering a new era of peace, enlightenment, and unity, in which mankind will evolve into its divine self. To the natural mind, it sounds like a vision of hope, but at its core, it preaches salvation apart from Christ. It replaces the Second Coming of Jesus with the rise of human consciousness, leading people to believe they can build heaven on earth without repentance or redemption. The so-called Age of Aquarius is not a prophetic awakening but a counterfeit gospel that denies the power of the Cross and the authority of Christ's return.

Another central tenet is the reliance on spirit guides, often described as benevolent beings of light who assist in spiritual growth or deliver hidden wisdom. These entities may appear peaceful, but they are not from God. They are deceiving spirits posing as messengers of truth, echoing Paul's warning that,

"Satan himself transforms himself into an angel of light."
2 Corinthians 11:14 (NKJV)

When people open themselves to these spirits, they are not gaining guidance; they are granting access to demonic influence.

The doctrine of pantheism also runs through both New Age and satanic beliefs. It teaches that everything, every planet, tree, and person, is divine, part of one universal essence. This erases the line between Creator and creation, leading humanity to worship the created rather than the Creator. In pantheism, man becomes his own god, able to define truth and morality as he pleases.

The idea of "Lucifer as light" is perhaps the most blatant distortion of truth within occult philosophy. It presents Lucifer not as the enemy of God but as the bringer of wisdom and freedom, the one who opens humanity's eyes to hidden knowledge. In this narrative, rebellion becomes enlightenment. Yet Scripture makes the truth clear:

"The god of this age has blinded the minds of unbelievers."
2 Corinthians 4:4 (NKJV)

What the world calls illumination is in reality deception.

Closely connected to this is the symbol of the All-Seeing Eye, an image found throughout occult writings. Often surrounded by light or enclosed in a pyramid, it represents divine knowledge and ultimate awareness, the idea that man can attain godlike perception. But only God possesses all-seeing vision:

"The eyes of the Lord run to and fro throughout the whole earth."
2 Chronicles 16:9 (NKJV)

The All-Seeing Eye symbolizes humanity's desire to possess divine sight without divine submission.

The belief in rebirth through mysteries follows the same pattern. It teaches that through hidden wisdom, rituals, or initiations, a person can ascend into higher consciousness and be spiritually reborn. This is a counterfeit of Jesus' words,

> *"Unless one is born again, he cannot see the kingdom of God"*
> **John 3:3 (NKJV)**

Instead of grace, it offers secret knowledge, instead of salvation, self-elevation. It promises transformation but delivers bondage.

Finally, the doctrine of being one's own redeemer stands as the cornerstone of both New Age and satanic teaching. It insists that humanity is not fallen but merely unaware of its divine potential, that sin is an illusion, and that every person holds within themselves the power to save and perfect their own soul. This belief strips away the necessity of the Cross and replaces worship with self-adoration. It is the ultimate deception, the worship of self in the place of God.

Each of these philosophies, though clothed in the language of light, wisdom, and freedom, is a thread woven from the same false spiritual fabric. They are not separate streams of belief but tributaries flowing into the same river of rebellion. What many today call "New Age spirituality" is simply the occult hiding behind a modern face of the same ancient doctrines that have always opposed the truth of Christ.

The "Mother" of New Age: Helena Blavatsky

The modern New Age movement can be traced back to Helena Petrovna Blavatsky, a 19th-century Russian occultist and mystic often regarded as the *Mother of the New Age.* She was a writer, philosopher, and medium who claimed to receive revelations from "ascended masters," spiritual beings she said existed on higher planes of consciousness. These supposed beings guided her to synthesize the world's religions into a single universal system.

Blavatsky arrived in New York City in 1872, bringing with her an eclectic mix of Hinduism, Buddhism, occultism, and Western esoteric thought. In 1875, she co-founded the Theosophical Society, an organization dedicated to exploring "divine wisdom" through the blending of science, religion, and mysticism. Its stated goals were to form a universal brotherhood of humanity, to study comparative religion and ancient writings, and to investigate the hidden laws of nature and the latent powers of man. Though these aims sounded noble, they were built on a foundation that rejected the authority of Scripture and replaced the worship of God with the pursuit of secret knowledge.

Her writings, particularly *The Secret Doctrine* (1888) and *Isis Unveiled* (1877), became the blueprint for nearly every New Age idea that followed. Through these works, she introduced the Western world to reincarnation, karma, ascended masters, energy planes, and cosmic evolution. She taught that all religions were merely fragments of one great truth and that man's destiny was to evolve into godhood through spiritual awakening. These teachings later influenced movements like Transcendental Meditation, yoga, holistic healing, astrology, and the belief in "higher consciousness."

Blavatsky was also the editor of a magazine called Lucifer, where she openly praised the devil as the "light-bringer" of wisdom and enlightenment. In her writings, she described Lucifer not as God's adversary, but as the misunderstood liberator of mankind, echoing the same lie the serpent told in Eden. Her own words left no room for confusion: she called Satan "the god of our planet" and "the highest divine spirit."

From the very beginning, the foundation of what we now call the New Age was built upon these occult philosophies. Blavatsky's teachings elevated Lucifer as the symbol of knowledge, rebellion, and light, while rejecting the authority of Jesus Christ. She saw Christianity as an obstacle to human evolution, claiming that biblical faith suppressed spiritual freedom.

Her disciples and successors—such as Annie Besant, Alice Bailey, and later, leaders within the human potential movement—continued to expand her doctrines. Alice Bailey, in particular, a Theosophist and self-proclaimed channeler, developed what she called "The Plan" for humanity: a coming New World Order that would unite all religions under a single spiritual system. She even coined the term "New Age" in the early 20th century, describing it as the dawning of the Age of Aquarius, a new era when humanity would collectively awaken to its divine nature.

Through these figures, Blavatsky's influence rippled across generations. Her ideas shaped modern spiritualism, the rise of occult fraternities, and the development of Eastern mysticism in Western culture. The language of energy, vibration, universal consciousness, and spiritual evolution—all of it—traces directly back to her. What began in her drawing rooms and séances has now become mainstream philosophy.

From its inception, the New Age movement has carried the same spiritual DNA: a rejection of the Creator, a glorification of self, and the elevation of Lucifer as the source of enlightenment. What the world now embraces as "spiritual awakening" is nothing more than the continuation of the oldest rebellion, man seeking godhood without God.

Aleister Crowley: The Prophet of Self-Worship

After Helena Blavatsky, Aleister Crowley (1875–1947), a British occultist, magician, and writer, carried Blavatsky's doctrines into the modern world. Crowley called himself *"The Great Beast 666,"* openly mocked Christianity, and sought to replace biblical morality with what he called *"The Law of Thelema."* Its core command was deadly yet straightforward: "Do what thou wilt shall be the whole of the law."

Crowley taught that the highest act of spirituality was the discovery and expression of one's "True Will," the inner divine self. This concept became the seed for the modern gospel of self-empowerment, self-discovery, and "living your truth." Through Thelema, he blended ceremonial magic, Eastern meditation, sexual ritual, astrology, and mysticism into one system, which he claimed would usher humanity into a *New Aeon* of enlightenment.

He drew heavily from Blavatsky's writings, especially her belief in ascended masters and Lucifer as the bringer of light. Where she wrapped the deception in philosophical mysticism, Crowley tore off the mask and embraced rebellion outright. His practices involved channeling spirits, invoking Egyptian deities, and performing rituals meant to transcend human limitation.

Crowley's influence stretched far beyond the secret lodges of England. His writings inspired the founders of modern Wicca, many later occult fraternities, and eventually the philosophy behind the New Age movement's self-divinization. His emphasis on personal will and spiritual evolution became the backbone of twentieth-century humanism and the "age of Aquarius" mindset: that man is his own god, his own law, and his own light.

By the 1960s, his legacy bridged the gap between the dark rituals of occultism and the polished spirituality of New Age mysticism.

In short, Blavatsky built the foundation, Crowley lit the torch, and the modern world carried the flame. His teachings continue to echo through every New Age slogan that elevates "the divine within" over the Lordship of Christ.

Symbols and Practices of the New Age Movement
The world of the New Age is filled with imagery, rituals, and objects that appear peaceful, creative, or deeply spiritual, but behind their beauty lies a dangerous spiritual power. These are not harmless symbols or artistic expressions; they are remnants of ancient paganism and occult worship, revived and disguised under the banner of "wellness," "energy," and "enlightenment." Each one subtly invites the soul to participate in practices that open spiritual doors never meant to be opened.

The symbols themselves carry deep meaning in the spirit realm. The pentagram, once used in witchcraft to invoke elements and spirits, is often seen as a charm for protection or balance. The all-seeing eye, also known as the Eye of Horus or the Eye of Providence, symbolizes illumination and hidden knowledge. This image directly echoes Satan's promise in Eden that man could "see" as God sees. The ankh of Egypt, shaped like a cross with a loop, symbolizes eternal life without the Creator who gives it. Likewise, the triquetra, or triple knot, represents the pagan goddess in her three forms: maiden, mother, and crone.

Other popular emblems include the yin-yang, which teaches that light and darkness are equal and necessary, denying God's separation of the two. The lotus flower symbolizes self-enlightenment rising above the "mud" of earthly limitation, while the mandala serves as a visual portal for meditation, drawing the mind into trance-like states. Even simple designs like the hamsa hand, the peace sign, or the infinity symbol are often repurposed for spiritual meaning in the New Age, promoting the idea of protection, energy balance, and eternal cycles of life and rebirth, each one reflecting the same false message that divinity exists within creation itself.

The same deception appears in objects and practices. Crystals and gemstones are used as tools for energy healing, emotional balance, or attracting love and prosperity, as though God's blessing could be summoned by holding a stone. Dreamcatchers and charms are hung as symbols of spiritual protection, though only the presence of the Holy Spirit guards the believer. Pyramids and obelisks, relics of ancient sun worship, are used to focus energy or represent ascension to higher consciousness.

Beyond symbols, the practices of the New Age movement are even more spiritually invasive. Astrology, horoscopes, and numerology promise divine guidance through the stars and numbers, but Scripture calls such divination an abomination before the Lord (Isaiah 47:13-14). Meditation, when stripped of its biblical grounding, encourages the emptying of the mind, creating a spiritual vacuum into which deception can enter. Yoga, far from being merely physical exercise, was designed in

Hinduism as worship of the gods, with each pose an act of surrender to a false deity. Reiki and energy healing claim to channel universal power through the hands, while chakra balancing and kundalini awakening attempt to stir the so-called serpent energy within, directly echoing the serpent's role in Genesis.

New Agers also seek wisdom through spirit guides, angels, and "ascended masters," spiritual beings they believe bring messages of light and truth. In reality, these are demonic impersonations cloaked in goodness (2 Corinthians 11:14). Others practice tarot, runes, pendulum readings, and automatic writing, seeking answers that belong only to God. Aura reading, frequency healing, and sound baths are promoted as tools for emotional or spiritual cleansing. Yet, they rely on vibrations and energy rather than the sanctifying work of the Holy Spirit.

Even common rituals like burning sage, lighting incense, or moon ceremonies are promoted as spiritual cleansings, imitations of biblical purification, but without the presence of God. The use of crystal grids, altar setups, or manifestation boards mimics the altar of worship, but instead of exalting Christ, they elevate the self. The teaching of manifestation and the law of attraction promises that by visualizing or speaking positively, a person can create their own reality. It replaces "Thy will be done" (Matthew 6:10) with "My will be manifested."

Even modern "self-care" trends are often infused with New Age philosophy. Practices like mindfulness, energy cleansing, and affirmation rituals encourage people to look inward for strength rather than upward for salvation. Feng Shui arranges homes to invite spiritual energy, while herbal magic and spell jars use God's creation as tools of manipulation instead of worship. Astral projection and lucid dreaming tempt people to explore realms outside their physical bodies, yet these experiences leave them vulnerable to spiritual attack.

In our generation, this spiritual language has been carefully rebranded. What once belonged to witchcraft is now presented as wellness. What was once an occult ritual is now sold as self-discovery. The same practices that Scripture condemns as sorcery and divination are now disguised as therapy and mental health tools. The deception has become so normalized that even believers share New Age phrases without realizing their roots, speaking of "energy," "vibrations," "the universe," and "manifesting destiny."

But behind every symbol and ritual lies the same spirit, the ancient rebellion that says humanity can achieve divine power without submitting to God. The Bible warns clearly,

"You shall not learn to follow the abominations of those nations... For all who do these things are an abomination to the Lord."
Deuteronomy 18:9, 12 (NKJV)

No charm, stone, ritual, or chant can protect or purify the soul. Only the blood of Jesus Christ has the power to cleanse, to heal, and to restore. What the world calls "light work" is nothing more than the oldest darkness wearing new names. The practices of the New Age promise connection and peace, but they deliver confusion and captivity. It is the same lie spoken in Eden, the promise of divine power apart from divine obedience.

"Woe to those who call evil good, and good evil; who put darkness for light, and light for darkness."
Isaiah 5:20 (NKJV)

THE COUNTERFEIT OF TRUTH: NEW AGE VS. CHRISTIANITY

The New Age movement is one of the most subtle and seductive forms of deception in modern history because it often borrows Christian words and truths but twists them just enough to destroy their meaning. It speaks of "love," "light," "spirit," and even "Christ consciousness," yet it denies the power, divinity, and exclusivity of Jesus Christ.

The apostle Paul warned that such distortions would come:

"For if he who comes preaches another Jesus whom we have not preached, or if you receive a different spirit which you have not received, or a different gospel which you have not accepted—you may well put up with it!"
2 Corinthians 11:4 (NKJV)

Many believers today unknowingly entertain "another gospel," one wrapped in spirituality, positivity, and peace, yet utterly devoid of repentance, holiness, and the cross. Let's examine how the New Age philosophy directly opposes the truth of God's Word.

God

To New Agers, "God" is not a personal Creator but an impersonal force or "universal energy." They teach that everything is God: trees, animals, stars, and humans, all part of one divine essence. This belief, called monism (from the Greek word monos, meaning "one"), is common in Hinduism and Buddhism.

But the Bible is clear: God is not the universe—He is its Creator. He is holy, separate, and sovereign.

"In the beginning God created the heavens and the earth."
Genesis 1:1 (NKJV)

"For I am God, and there is no other; I am God, and there is none like Me."
Isaiah 46:9 (NKJV)

To reduce the Almighty to a cosmic energy is to deny His nature as a personal, relational, and living God, a Father who loves, disciplines, and redeems His children.

Jesus Christ

In the New Age world, Jesus is not the Son of God but merely a "spiritual teacher," "ascended master," or an enlightened guru. They claim He was a man who reached a higher state of consciousness, no different from Buddha, Krishna, or other so-called spiritual masters. Some even teach that "the Christ" is an energy or spirit that has inhabited many figures throughout history.

This doctrine strips Jesus of His deity, His virgin birth, and His resurrection, the very pillars of Christian faith.

But Scripture leaves no room for confusion:

"And the Word became flesh and dwelt among us, and we beheld His glory, the glory as of the only begotten of the Father, full of grace and truth."
John 1:14 (NKJV)

"For in Him dwells all the fullness of the Godhead bodily."
Colossians 2:9 (NKJV)

"Nor is there salvation in any other, for there is no other name under heaven given among men by which we must be saved."
Acts 4:12 (NKJV)

Jesus is not one way among many; He is the only way. The New Age movement's version of Jesus is a counterfeit, one designed to make people feel spiritual without confronting sin.

The Holy Spirit

To New Agers, the Holy Spirit is not a divine person but a psychic force or "universal energy." They believe that spiritual experiences, clairvoyance, and intuition are manifestations of this "spirit."

But the Holy Spirit is not an impersonal energy. He is the third person of the Trinity—equal in essence and power with the Father and the Son.
Jesus described Him as *"the Helper"* and *"the Spirit of truth."*
John 14:26; 16:13 (NKJV)

The Holy Spirit does not awaken hidden power within us; He *is* the power within us. He convicts the world of sin, righteousness, and judgment (John 16:8) and empowers believers to live in holiness, not false mysticism.

Being "Reborn" or "Rebirth"

The Bible teaches that being born again is a spiritual transformation, a personal salvation experience through faith in Jesus Christ.

> *"Most assuredly, I say to you, unless one is born again, he cannot see the kingdom of God."* **John 3:3 (NKJV)**

To the New Age, however, "rebirth" means reincarnation, a cycle of dying and returning to earth until reaching perfection. This idea comes directly from Hinduism and is intertwined with the concept of karma, the belief that one's actions determine one's next life.

At first glance, karma may sound similar to the biblical principle of reaping and sowing. But they are not the same. Scripture teaches that "whatever a man sows, that he will also reap" (Galatians 6:7), referring to God's moral law within one lifetime, not a cycle of endless lives. The Bible declares plainly:

> *"It is appointed for men to die once, but after this the judgment."*
> **Hebrews 9:27 (NKJV)**

Reincarnation is a deception that denies both the Cross and the urgency of salvation.

Sin and Salvation

In New Age teaching, there is no such thing as sin, only "negative energy" or "lower vibration." Humanity's problem, they say, is not moral corruption but ignorance of its divine nature. Salvation, then, comes not through the shed blood of Jesus, but through self-realization and meditation.

This belief not only minimizes sin; it eliminates the need for a Savior. But Scripture declares:

> *"All have sinned and fall short of the glory of God."*
> *(Romans 3:23, NKJV)*

> *"For the wages of sin is death, but the gift of God is eternal life in Christ Jesus our Lord."* **Romans 6:23 (NKJV)**

Only through repentance and faith in Jesus Christ can a soul be made new. Any doctrine that teaches otherwise is spiritual poison.

The Real Goal

The ultimate goal of the New Age movement is not enlightenment; it is enslavement. Its purpose is to blur the line between the Creator and His creation until there is no distinction left, convincing people that the highest form of worship is to worship themselves. It teaches that man can achieve divinity through "self-discovery," that salvation is found not through repentance but through awakening to one's own supposed godhood. But this is the very doctrine of Lucifer, who declared,

"I will ascend... I will be like the Most High."
Isaiah 14:13-14 (NKJV)

This philosophy is not light; it is the oldest darkness disguised as wisdom. It steals what only Jesus Christ can give: grace, forgiveness, and eternal life. It whispers that the answer is within, when the Word declares the answer is found only in Him. New Age spirituality does not just drift away from God; it replaces Him entirely. It exalts the created over the Creator, enthrones self in the place of the Savior, and calls that blasphemy "divine awakening."

At its core, the New Age movement is nothing less than modernized Satanism, a sophisticated form of the same rebellion that cast Lucifer from Heaven. It robs people of the personal relationship with God they were made for, denies the Cross, rejects the blood of Jesus, and trades redemption for self-realization. It is the worship of self in the name of spirituality —the oldest lie, wearing new skin.

Hear my clarion call in this moment in time as you read this: this is not harmless curiosity or casual exploration, this is a dangerous ideology that must be renounced, rebuked, and removed from your life. It is not light; it is darkness disguised as wisdom. The only way to true awakening is through repentance and surrender to Jesus Christ, the Light of the World.

As Jesus said,

"No one comes to the Father except through Me."
John 14:6 (NKJV)

MUSIC, MEDIA, AND THE SPIRIT OF THE AGE

The New Age movement did not rise in isolation; it rode into the modern world through art, entertainment, and media. Satan has always used culture as one of his most effective tools for mass deception. From the Garden of Eden to the modern streaming platform, his strategy remains unchanged: disguise rebellion as revelation, and bondage as freedom.

The 1960s became the perfect stage for this global spiritual shift. Rebellion was in the air, and the world was hungry for something new, something more profound, a "higher consciousness." But rather than turning to the Bible, society turned eastward, to gurus, mystics, and occult philosophers who promised transcendence without repentance.

The Beatles and the Birth of Pop Spirituality

No single group did more to introduce Eastern mysticism and New Age ideas to Western youth than The Beatles. Their fame gave them unprecedented cultural influence—and Satan used it effectively.

When George Harrison traveled to India and became fascinated by Hinduism, the band began publicly embracing Eastern practices, such as Transcendental Meditation under the guidance of guru Maharishi Mahesh Yogi. Through their platform, yoga, mantras, reincarnation, and other mystical concepts suddenly became "trendy" and "enlightened."

This shift was more than curiosity; it marked the cultural baptism of an entire generation into New Age spirituality. Millions of fans who once sang hymns in church were now chanting Sanskrit mantras from the radio. Harrison later recorded songs like *My Sweet Lord,* which blended praise to the biblical Lord with the Hindu chant "Hare Krishna." The blending of worship between Jesus and pagan deities is one of the clearest indicators of New Age influence, syncretism disguised as peace and love.

John Lennon, deeply influenced by Theosophy, numerology, and occult symbolism, described the band's performances as spiritual experiences. Yoko Ono, a student of Eastern mysticism and performance art tied to spiritual ritual, once said that during concerts, *"The Beatles were like mediums who manifested spirits through them."* Lennon himself studied the writings of occultist Cheiro and experimented with automatic writing and psychic phenomena.

Their 1966 album Revolver included direct references to Eastern mysticism. Its final track, *"Tomorrow Never Knows,"* was inspired by *The Tibetan Book of the Dead*, a guide to navigating reincarnation and the afterlife. The lyrics, which instruct listeners to "turn off your mind, relax, and float downstream," reflected the same trance-like detachment promoted in meditation practices.

Their 1967 masterpiece, Sgt. Pepper's Lonely Hearts Club Band, was even more explicit. Its album cover featured an array of historical and spiritual figures, including famous occultist Aleister Crowley, known for his satanic mantra, *"Do what thou wilt shall be the whole of the Law."* Crowley's inclusion was not accidental; he was deliberately positioned among the band's "heroes." This public celebration of occult imagery marked a turning point—spiritual rebellion had officially become mainstream entertainment.

During their time in India, the group fully immersed themselves in the teachings of Eastern gurus, mysticism, and mantra repetition. Their journey spanned the globe, transforming the West's perception of religion and spirituality. What began as curiosity became the introduction of Hindu theology to pop culture. Soon after, an explosion of interest in yoga, transcendental meditation, and reincarnation followed, concepts that had been foreign primarily to Western minds.

Even after leaving India, the influence remained. The Beatles' later albums continued to explore mystical and New Age themes, promoting universal love, cosmic unity, and self-realization. Lennon's later song *"Imagine"* became a New Age anthem for globalism and humanism—envisioning a world without heaven, hell, or religion, but full of man-made peace. What sounded like harmony was in truth the rejection of the gospel.

John Lennon later reflected that the underlying philosophy behind The Beatles was built on personal freedom, self-rule, and the idea that people should simply follow their own desires as long as they believed they weren't harming anyone. This mindset perfectly mirrors the core message of New Age and modern occult thought: the elevation of self-will over surrender to God. It echoes the same spirit of rebellion that has shaped every generation—"live your truth," "follow your heart," and "do what feels right"—all of which directly oppose Jesus' call to deny ourselves and follow Him

"If anyone desires to come after Me, let him deny himself, and take up his cross daily, and follow Me."
Luke 9:23 (NKJV)

Through music, art, and culture, The Beatles opened a spiritual door that remains wide today. Their message of self-enlightenment, universal love, and cosmic unity laid the foundation for New Age spirituality in the West. What was once hidden in occult temples was now sung on radios across the world. It became the soundtrack of rebellion against God, wrapped in melodies that sounded like peace but carried the spirit of deception.

Rock, Rebellion, and Ritual

As The Beatles' popularity merged spiritual rebellion with pop culture, other artists began to follow their path, drawing on the spiritual influence of Aleister Crowley and reaching far beyond The Beatles. Jimmy Page, guitarist of Led Zeppelin, was another outspoken admirer of Crowley. Page collected his writings, wore his robes, and even purchased Crowley's former home, Boleskine House in Scotland, which had been used for occult rituals. He later opened an occult bookstore in London called The Equinox.

Other artists followed similar paths. The Rolling Stones released "Their Satanic Majesties Request." David Bowie openly referenced Crowley in his lyrics and once said, "Rock has always been the devil's music." The hippie movement, which preached love and peace, simultaneously normalized witchcraft, psychedelic drug use, and rebellion against biblical authority.

Even in later decades, New Age and occult imagery continued to infiltrate mainstream music. Through Madonna's Kabbalistic symbolism, Beyoncé's "I AM" deity themes, Katy Perry's occult stage performances, and countless modern artists who casually invoke "the universe," "manifestation," and "energy."

The goal has always been the same: normalize spiritual rebellion, desensitize hearts to sin, and redefine worship.

Scripture gives us a sobering reminder:

"For rebellion is as the sin of witchcraft, and stubbornness is as iniquity and idolatry." (1 Samuel 15:23, NKJV)

Modern Forms of New Age: The "Wellness" Rebrand

In our generation, the New Age no longer wears dark robes or speaks of séances; it wears yoga pants and hashtags. The same doctrines are now packaged under the labels of "wellness," "self-care," "manifesting," and "mindfulness."

- **Yoga**

Though marketed as harmless stretching, its roots are deeply spiritual. Every pose was initially designed as a form of worship to Hindu deities. True yoga's goal is union with Brahman (the Hindu concept of god), not physical fitness.

- **Manifestation and the Law of Attraction**

These teachings claim that you can create your own reality through thought and vibration. But Jesus taught us to pray,

"Your will be done," not "my will be manifested."
Matthew 6:10 (NKJV)

- **Crystals, Energy Healing, and Reiki**

These practices stem from occultism and rely on "channeling" unseen powers, often inviting demonic influence under the guise of energy balance.

• **Astrology, Angel Cards, and Tarot Readings**

Once considered fringe, these practices are now popular among young people online. But God's Word is clear:

"Do not learn the way of the Gentiles... for the customs of the peoples are futile."
Jeremiah 10:2–3 (NKJV)

Even phrases like "the universe will provide" or "trust your energy" are subtle ways of replacing God with creation. Romans 1:25 exposes this exchange plainly:

"They exchanged the truth of God for the lie, and worshiped and served the creature rather than the Creator, who is blessed forever. Amen."

Social Media and the Spread of "Soft Witchcraft"

As we exposed in the chapter on Witchcraft, platforms like TikTok, Instagram, and YouTube have become digital pulpits for New Age evangelists. Hashtags such as #manifestation, #tarot, #energyhealing, and #witchtok reach billions of views. Young audiences are being discipled by influencers who claim to offer empowerment but instead lead them into spiritual bondage.

This modern form of witchcraft is subtle; it preaches self-love instead of repentance, energy instead of the Holy Spirit, and crystals instead of the cross. Yet Jesus warned us that deception would grow before His return:

"For false christs and false prophets will rise and show great signs and wonders to deceive, if possible, even the elect."
Matthew 24:24 (NKJV)

A Call to Discernment and Holiness

The New Age movement is not a passing trend; it is the modern expression of the oldest rebellion. It whispers the same lie that ensnared Adam and Eve:

"You will be like God."
Genesis 3:5 (NKJV)

But we are not called to awaken our inner divinity; we are called to deny ourselves and follow Christ. (Matthew 16:24) The world offers "higher consciousness," but the Bible offers something greater, new life through the blood of Jesus Christ.

Paul wrote,

"For the weapons of our warfare are not carnal but mighty in God for pulling down strongholds, casting down arguments and every high thing that exalts itself against the knowledge of God."
2 Corinthians 10:4–5 (NKJV)

Now more than ever, believers must recognize that spiritual deception is not always loud or obvious. It often comes cloaked in positivity, love, and self-improvement. That's why we must be anchored in Scripture and filled with the Holy Spirit.

The Final Warning

The Bible leaves no room for compromise or neutrality:

"But the cowardly, unbelieving, abominable, murderers, sexually immoral, sorcerers, idolaters, and all liars shall have their part in the lake which burns with fire and brimstone, which is the second death."
Revelation 21:8 (NKJV)

"Nothing impure will ever enter [Heaven], nor will anyone who does what is shameful or deceitful, but only those whose names are written in the Lamb's Book of Life."
Revelation 21:27 (NKJV)

The New Age promises freedom but delivers bondage. It preaches enlightenment but leads to darkness. Yet Jesus Christ offers the real awakening, the light of salvation, and the power of truth.

"Therefore if the Son makes you free, you shall be free indeed."
John 8:36 (NKJV)

Let us be a generation that exposes the counterfeit and clings to the truth. Let us love people enough to warn them, and love God enough to stay holy in a deceived world.

"Take no part in the worthless deeds of evil and darkness; instead, expose them."
Ephesians 5:11 (NKJV)

Appendix D: Modern Expressions of Witchcraft

A Practical Reference Guide for Discernment (NKJV)

Introduction

Scripture clearly warns God's people to avoid every form of sorcery, divination, and occult mixture (Deuteronomy 18:9–14; Galatians 5:19–21). While ancient witchcraft involved rituals, idols, and open devotion to false gods, today's world disguises the very same practices under entertainment, wellness, spirituality, psychology, and self-empowerment movements.

This appendix serves as a practical reference to help believers recognize modern forms of witchcraft in culture today so they can walk in purity, discernment, and the leadership of the Holy Spirit.

I. Divination and Spiritism

Practices that seek knowledge, insight, or power from spiritual sources outside the Holy Spirit.

- Astrology, horoscopes, zodiac readings
- Tarot cards
- Oracle cards/angel cards
- Palm reading
- Psychic readings/mediumship
- Fortune-telling (online or in person)
- Automatic writing
- Spirit guides
- Channeling spiritual beings
- Séances
- Ouija boards
- Pendulum readings
- Numerology
- I Ching

- Scrying (crystal balls, mirrors)
- Occult dream interpretation systems

II. Magic, Sorcery, and Ritual Practices

Attempts to manipulate spiritual power, energy, or outcomes.

- Spell casting (love, money, protection)
- Candle magic
- White magic / dark magic
- Chaos magic
- Wiccan rituals
- Pagan ceremonies
- Enchantments, incantations, mantras
- Cursing objects or people
- Hex removal rituals
- Moon rituals (new moon / full moon)
- Crystal programming/charging
- Binding spells
- Blood rituals
- Manifestation rituals
- Burning sage (smudging)
- Sigils
- Glamour magic

III. Occult Objects, Symbols, and Tools

Items believed to carry, manipulate, or channel spiritual power.

- Crystals (used spiritually)
- Dreamcatchers
- Evil eye charms
- Pentagrams/pentacles
- Spirit boards
- Talismans, amulets, charms
- Rune stones
- Altars

- Totems
- Astrology jewelry
- Occult statues (Hecate, Kali, etc.)
- Enneagram (origin through occult automatic writing)
- Witchcraft spellbooks

IV. Eastern Mysticism and New Age Practices

Practices rooted in Hinduism, Buddhism, Taoism, or metaphysical spirituality.

- Yoga (kundalini, mantra-based, spiritual forms)
- Chakra alignment or cleansing
- Reiki
- Energy healing (chi, prana)
- Aura reading
- Astral projection
- Third-eye activation
- Past-life regression
- Karma-based spirituality
- Law of Attraction
- Twin flames
- Manifestation magic
- Sound bowls/frequency healing
- Akashic records
- Mindfulness rooted in Buddhism (emptying the mind)

V. Entertainment, Media, and Pop Culture Witchcraft

How witchcraft is normalized and glamorized through entertainment.

- Witchcraft TV shows and films (Harry Potter, Sabrina, Charmed, Hocus Pocus)
- Superhero magic (Doctor Strange, Scarlet Witch)
- Horror films involving demons or possession
- Video games with spellcasting or summoning
- Music with occult symbolism
- Stage performances involving rituals

- WitchTok /WitchTube /Manifestation influencers
- Astrology or tarot apps
- Cartoons with spells, spirit guides, or magic
- Celebrity occult performances

VI. Cultural Traditions Rooted in Superstition
Practices believed to bring luck, protection, or influence.

- Burning sage/palo santo
- Throwing salt
- Lucky charms
- Rabbit's feet
- Evil eye jewelry
- Manifestation journaling
- Vision boards (used spiritually)
- Folk magic (hoodoo, brujería, santería, voodoo)

VI-A. Common Everyday Superstitions Used in Modern Culture
Superstitions that seem harmless but are rooted in fear, folklore, or occult belief systems.

A. Luck-Based Superstitions

- Knocking on wood
- Finding a four-leaf clover
- Wishing on a shooting star
- Lucky pennies ("Find a penny, pick it up...")
- Lucky shirts, jewelry, or objects (have to wear a certain shirt so your team "wins")
- Horseshoes
- 11:11 wishes
- Lucky numbers

B. Protection Superstitions

- Throwing salt over the shoulder
- Dreamcatchers for protection

- Evil-eye bracelets or charms
- Red strings
- Protective amulets
- Knocking on wood to ward off misfortune

C. Bad Luck Superstitions

- Breaking a mirror = seven years of bad luck
- Black cats crossing your path
- Avoiding walking under ladders
- Opening umbrellas indoors
- Stepping on cracks
- Friday the 13th
- Birds flying into a house as an omen
- Eye twitching predicting events

D. Death & Spirit Superstitions

- Covering mirrors after a death
- Holding breath passing cemeteries
- Believing cardinals, butterflies, or dragonflies are the dead visiting
- Lights left on for spirits

E. Household & Daily Ritual Superstitions

- Brooms behind doors for protection
- Salt lines or herbs to block spirits
- Food offerings for the dead
- Knocking on a baby's cradle to "protect" them

F. Relationship Superstitions

- Splitting a pole = relationship trouble
- Dropping wedding rings as a bad omen
- Fertility superstitions at weddings

VII. Church-Related Witchcraft (Spiritual Mixture)
When control or manipulation replaces the Holy Spirit.

- Manipulative prophecy
- "Charismatic witchcraft" (control disguised as spirituality)
- Prayer used to manipulate
- Spiritual intimidation
- Celebrity-driven ministry
- Performance-driven worship
- False impartations
- Mixture of Jesus + New Age beliefs
- Emotional manipulation posing as anointing

VIII. Occultism in Wellness and Mental Health Trends
Practices that blend spirituality with self-help or therapeutic tools.

- Manifestation journals
- "Positive energy" techniques
- Subconscious reprogramming
- Hypnosis
- Mindfulness based on Eastern religions
- Crystal therapy
- Angel numbers
- Universe-based spirituality
- Personality systems rooted in occultism

IX. Practices That Open Doors to Spiritual Oppression
Activities that invite spiritual influence outside of God's covering.

- Cursing someone (verbally or spiritually)
- Rage, hatred, rebellion (1 Samuel 15:23)
- Unforgiveness
- Drugs altering consciousness
- Sexual sin tied to spiritual bondage

- Necromancy
- Summoning rituals
- Demon-centered entertainment
- Horror content involving spirits

X. Words and Phrases Rooted in Witchcraft, New Age, or Occultism

Common language rooted in modern spirituality and occult belief systems.

A. Energy, Vibration, and Spiritual Power Language

- Energy (as spiritual forces)
- Positive vibes/negative vibes
- High frequency/low frequency
- Aura
- Energy alignment
- Manifestation through the Universe
- Spiritual awakening
- Ascension to higher consciousness
- Channeling
- Third eye
- Universe (as God)
- Sacred space
- Soul contract
- Hold space
- Timeline jump

B. Witchcraft and Ritual Language

- Spell/hex/curse
- Enchanting/enchantment
- Intention setting
- Ritual
- Smudging
- Moon manifesting
- Sacred feminine/goddess energy
- As above, so below

- Blessed be
- Conjuring
- Cauldron

C. New Age and Eastern Mysticism Language

- Everything happens for a reason (karma concept)
- Follow your truth / live your truth
- Your higher self
- Look within for the answers
- Find the god within
- You attract what you are
- You create your own reality
- Trust the universe
- Sending good energy
- The *universe* is giving me signs

D. Identity Terms Used in Mysticism

- Empath
- Energy healer
- Lightworker
- Mystic (occult sense)
- Oracle
- Starseed
- Indigo child/crystal child
- Shaman / shamanic

E. Christian-Sounding Phrases With New Age Roots

- I'm manifesting blessings my life
- Sending positive energy in prayer
- Following spiritual signs alone over God
- God is the universe

XI. Questions for Discernment

1. Where does the power come from?
2. Does this open a door to any spirit besides the Holy Spirit?
3. Would I do this if Jesus physically walked in?
4. Does this depend on energy, the universe, or self-power?
5. Does it replace prayer, Scripture, or surrender?
If any answer is "yes" or "maybe," the believer should avoid it.

XII. Simple Renunciation Prayer

"Jesus, I renounce every form of witchcraft (call it by name, even if it's multiple items), occult practice, and spiritual mixture I have touched knowingly or unknowingly. I close every door to darkness, break every agreement, and ask You to fill every place that was opened with Your Holy Spirit. I choose You alone. Amen."

This Is Not Legalism — It Is Holiness

What you have read in these last two chapters is not a call to legalism, fear, or rule-keeping. It is a call to holiness, the joyful separation unto God that protects our hearts and preserves our intimacy with Him. Legalism says, "Do this to earn God's love." Holiness says, "I am loved, therefore I set myself apart for Him."

The purpose of exposing any form of witchcraft is not to burden believers with anxiety, but to open our eyes to the spiritual reality around us so we can walk in freedom, purity, and discernment. Holiness is not bondage; it is the pathway to liberty. Legalism attempts to control behavior; holiness transforms the heart.

Avoiding the occult is not about living in fear of darkness — it is about choosing the light, choosing the presence of Jesus, and choosing to remove anything that competes with our affection for Him. The Holy Spirit does not lead us into legalism; He leads us into truth, purity, and deeper intimacy with Christ.

May these chapters and this appendix not create condemnation, but clarity. Not fear, but freedom. Not burdens, but boldness to walk fully aligned with the One who has called you out of darkness into His marvelous light.

Chapter 11: Deliverance
The Plan of Redemption
"Therefore if the Son makes you free, you shall be free indeed."
John 8:36 (NKJV)

We've walked through the many ways Heaven speaks, the language written in the very DNA of God within us. We've uncovered how dreams, visions, discernment, prophecy, imagination, and even angelic ministry reveal the Father's heartbeat. We've also seen how the enemy seeks to twist and counterfeit every holy thing, how he distorts the language of Heaven through witchcraft, New Age deception, and false light.

Now, we come to the final and most crucial part of this entire journey: redemption.

The message of deliverance is not about demons, though they are mentioned; it's about Jesus. It's about His power to break chains, cleanse hearts, and restore what sin and Satan have stolen. Every revelation we've explored leads to this moment, the plan of salvation that restores humanity to right standing with God.

THE PLAN OF REDEMPTION: GOD'S RESCUE MISSION

From the very beginning, mankind's fall shattered the divine communion between Heaven and earth. When Adam and Eve sinned, the voice that once walked with them in the cool of the day grew distant. The fellowship between Creator and creation was fractured. Humanity exchanged glory for shame, authority for bondage, and intimacy for exile.

Sin didn't just break a rule; it broke a relationship. It silenced Heaven's language within man. But God, rich in mercy, had already set into motion a rescue plan, a plan not merely to forgive, but to **redeem**, to **restore**, and to **reconcile** His children back to Himself.

"For all have sinned and fall short of the glory of God."
Romans 3:23 (NKJV)

"For the wages of sin is death, but the gift of God is eternal life in Christ Jesus our Lord."
Romans 6:23 (NKJV)

Even from the first pages of Scripture, God revealed that blood would be the bridge between death and life. When Adam and Eve covered themselves with fig leaves, it was God who made them tunics of skin, showing that innocent blood had to be shed to cover sin. That crimson thread of redemption continued through every covenant, every altar, and every sacrifice until it reached its perfect fulfillment on the Cross.

The Cross was Heaven's plan from the foundation of the world. The Lamb was already slain in God's eternal design (Revelation 13:8). Jesus came as the Word made flesh, stepping into the story of fallen humanity to restore what sin had stolen.

"For the Son of Man has come to seek and to save that which was lost."
Luke 19:10 (NKJV)

"For He made Him who knew no sin to be sin for us, that we might become the righteousness of God in Him."
2 Corinthians 5:21 (NKJV)

Salvation is not merely an escape from hell; it is a restoration of fellowship with the Father. To be saved is to be *born again,* recreated in the image of Christ, and transferred out of the kingdom of darkness into the kingdom of light.

"He has delivered us from the power of darkness and conveyed us into the kingdom of the Son of His love."
Colossians 1:13 (NKJV)

Through the blood of Jesus, the power of every curse is broken, the power of every sin is forgiven, and every chain is shattered. The blood doesn't just cleanse our record — it reclaims ownership over what once belonged to darkness. The Cross was both a courtroom and a battleground: justice was satisfied, and victory was secured.

"Having disarmed principalities and powers, He made a public spectacle of them, triumphing over them in it."
Colossians 2:15 (NKJV)

"In Him we have redemption through His blood, the forgiveness of sins, according to the riches of His grace."
Ephesians 1:7 (NKJV)

But salvation is not the finish line; it is the starting point of transformation. Many receive Jesus as Savior yet never allow Him to become Deliverer and Lord. They are rescued from Egypt but remain wandering in the wilderness, unaware that freedom must touch not only the spirit but also the soul and body.

Deliverance is the continuation of redemption, the ongoing cleansing of the believer's life, the removal of every foothold of darkness, until Christ fully reigns in every part. It is the practical outworking of what Jesus declared finished on the Cross.

"Therefore if the Son makes you free, you shall be free indeed."
John 8:36 (NKJV)

"Work out your own salvation with fear and trembling; for it is God who works in you both to will and to do for His good pleasure."
Philippians 2:12–13 (NKJV)

Salvation brings you out of bondage; deliverance removes bondage from within you. Salvation rescues you from Egypt; deliverance takes Egypt out of you. Salvation gives you a new identity; deliverance cleanses the old residue that tries to remain. Both are acts of grace, all flow from the blood. One restores the relationship, and the other restores rulership. Through salvation, we are redeemed; through deliverance (sanctification), we are refined.

DELIVERANCE AND THE CALL TO ABIDE IN CHRIST

Before we go deeper into the freedom Jesus purchased, it must be understood that not all doctrines surrounding salvation align with Scripture. One teaching in particular has misled many believers, the idea known as *Once Saved Always Saved*. In my Spirit-led understanding of Scripture, this doctrine is unbiblical. The Bible never portrays salvation as a one-time decision that grants automatic eternal security *regardless* of how a person lives afterward. Salvation is a covenant that must be walked out in faith, obedience, holiness, and perseverance.

Salvation begins by grace, freely given, unearned, and undeserved. But the moment grace enters the life of a believer, Scripture calls them into a life of transformation. Grace is God's empowerment to overcome sin, not permission to continue in it. Grace saves us from sin's penalty but also strengthens us to resist sin's power. Paul himself asked, "Shall we continue in sin that grace may abound?" and immediately answered, "Certainly not."

"For the grace of God... teaches us to deny ungodliness and worldly lusts, and to live soberly, righteously, and godly in the present age."
Titus 2:11–12 (NKJV)

"Sin shall not have dominion over you, for you are not under law but under grace."
Romans 6:14 (NKJV)

This verse is misunderstood. It does NOT say: "Sin won't matter because you're under grace."
It says: Grace breaks sin's dominion. It empowers victory over sin, freedom from bondage, and a new lifestyle of holiness. If sin is still your master, you are not walking in grace; you are walking in the flesh.

True grace always produces change, and true faith always produces fruit. A walk that bears no fruit contradicts the very nature of salvation, because faith without works is dead. The New Testament repeatedly warns believers about the danger of drifting, departing, or falling away. Hebrews speaks of those who were once enlightened and partakers of the Holy Spirit, yet later fell away. Hebrews 10 warns that willful, unrepentant sin after receiving the truth leads to judgment, not security. Peter describes believers who escape the corruption of the world but return to it, ending worse than before. Even Paul—the apostle of grace—feared becoming disqualified if he did not discipline his own life. These are not descriptions of unbelievers; they are warnings to believers about the real possibility of departing from the faith they once embraced.

Jesus Himself refutes OSAS most clearly in John 15. Speaking directly to His disciples—men already connected to

Him—He warns that every branch that *does not remain* in Him will be cut off, wither, and be thrown into the fire. These branches were once attached. They once had life flowing through them. Yet they were removed because they stopped abiding. Abiding is not automatic; it is a continual posture of obedience, surrender, and faithfulness. Fruitlessness leads to removal. Disobedience breaks the connection. Jesus makes it unmistakably clear: life is only found in abiding in Him, and death is the result of departing from Him.

"'I am the vine, you are the branches. He who abides in Me, and I in him, bears much fruit; for without Me you can do nothing. If anyone does not abide in Me, he is cast out as a branch and is withered; and they gather them and throw them into the fire, and they are burned. If you abide in Me, and My words abide in you, you will ask what you desire, and it shall be done for you. By this My Father is glorified, that you bear much fruit; so you will be My disciples.'
John 15:5-8 (NKJV)

Throughout the New Testament, salvation is consistently tied to endurance: "He who endures to the end shall be saved." We remain reconciled *if* we continue in the faith. The crown of life is promised to those who *remain* faithful unto death. Nowhere does Scripture support the idea that a one-time confession guarantees everlasting salvation while ignoring a life of holiness.

Lukewarmness—the half-devoted life—is another danger Jesus exposes. He warns that those who live lukewarm lives will be vomited out of His mouth. Lukewarm faith is not weakness; it is rebellion clothed in Christian language. To take the Lord's name while refusing His nature is to take His name in vain. Holiness is not optional. The fear of the Lord is not legalism; it is protection. It keeps the heart clean, the conscience sharp, and the spirit anchored in truth.

Revelation delivers one of the clearest refutations of OSAS. Jesus promises that the one who overcomes will not have their name blotted out of the Book of Life. A name cannot be blotted out unless it was first written in. Clearly, salvation is not an irreversible stamp, but a covenant maintained by abiding in Christ.

Deliverance is not merely about expelling darkness but about aligning your life under the Lordship of Jesus. True freedom is sustained by abiding, obeying, enduring, and remaining faithful. It is not simply about what leaves you, it is about who leads you. When Jesus becomes both Savior and Lord, the believer walks in continual purity, power, and transformation.

CAN A CHRISTIAN HAVE A DEMON?

The short answer is yes.

Many believers resist this idea, but Scripture and spiritual reality confirm it. Satan does not spare the uninformed; he exploits them. Ignorance is not bliss; it is his entry point. When believers fail to guard their spiritual lives, the enemy gains access to areas that God intended to be holy.

We are not just physical beings; we are temples, houses meant to carry God's presence, His Spirit, and His authority. The Bible often refers to people as houses, because we are dwelling places. What resides in the house depends on what doors we open.

We Are a House with Doors

God warned Cain:

"You will be accepted if you do what is right. But if you refuse to do what is right, then watch out! Sin is crouching at the door, eager to control you. But you must subdue it and be its master."

Genesis 4:7 (NKJV)

The heart is the doorway of the soul. Just as physical doors open and close to let things in or keep things out, so do spiritual doors. Every human life has gates, and what we allow through those gates determines who has access.

Jesus confirmed this spiritual truth in Luke 11:24 (NKJV):

"When an unclean spirit goes out of a man, he goes through dry places, seeking rest; and finding none, he says, 'I will return to my house from which I came.'"

Even the enemy refers to the human body as a *house*.

Our lives are dwelling places of authority. God designed us to host His Spirit, yet when we open doors through sin, trauma, or ignorance, we allow intruders to occupy rooms that belong to Him.

The Temple Within

The structure of the Tabernacle reveals the divine pattern of humanity itself. God instructed Moses to build it with three distinct parts: the Outer Court, the Holy Place, and the Most Holy Place. The Outer Court, where daily sacrifices were offered, represents our body, the part of us visible to all. The Holy Place, filled with the light of the lampstand and the fragrance of incense, symbolizes our soul: our thoughts, emotions, and desires. The Most Holy Place, where the Ark of the Covenant rested and the glory of God dwelt, represents our spirit, the innermost place where the Holy Spirit abides. And just as any defilement in one area of the Tabernacle affected the entire sanctuary, it is with us. Every part—body, soul, and spirit—must be purified and fully surrendered to Him.

"Hear, O Israel: The Lord our God, the Lord is one! You shall love the Lord your God with all your heart, with all your soul, and with all your strength."
Deuteronomy 6:4–5 (NKJV)

We love Him with every part because every part was created for His dwelling. Even when Jesus said,

"Destroy this temple, and in three days I will raise it up,"
John 2:19 (NKJV),

He was speaking about His body, a living temple.

When Jesus Cleansed the Temple

Jesus once entered the physical temple and drove out the money changers, turning over tables and cleansing what had become defiled. That was not only a historical moment, but it was also a prophetic picture of deliverance.

If the temple that held the manifest presence of God required cleansing, then our temples, too, must be purified. Jesus still enters His temples today, our lives, to cast out what does not belong. Paul warned the Church:

"Be angry, and do not sin": do not let the sun go down on your wrath, nor give place to the devil."
Ephesians 4:26–27 (NKJV)

That phrase—*give place*—literally means to provide territory. When believers harbor sin, bitterness, fear, or compromise, they yield territory that was meant for the King.

A Christian cannot be possessed, because their spirit belongs to God. But a believer can be oppressed or inhabited in areas of the soul or body that have not yet been surrendered. Demons can only dwell where they are given legal access.

Self-Examination

Ezekiel 8 describes a striking moment when God brought the prophet to a wall in the Temple and instructed him to dig. As Ezekiel obeyed, he uncovered a hidden doorway, and behind it, secret chambers filled with carved images, idols, and practices carried out in darkness. Though the Temple outwardly appeared holy, within its walls were rooms no one talked about, places no one saw, and sins no one confronted. Then God asked the piercing question: *"Have you seen what they do in secret?"*

This passage is more than historical; it is prophetic. It reveals that even sacred places can harbor unseen corruption. The Temple was God's house, yet hidden rooms existed where darkness thrived. Likewise, a believer can be genuinely devoted to God and still have inner rooms: wounds, memories, compromises, or unhealed places, that have not yet been brought into the light. Deliverance often begins in the exact same way: by digging. It requires courage to go beyond the surface and humility to let God unveil what has been buried. The Holy Spirit does not expose these hidden chambers to condemn us, but to free us. His light never comes to embarrass; it comes for liberation.

Demons thrive in unexamined areas. They dwell in the corners we avoid; the wounds we pretend are healed, the habits we justify, and the memories we refuse to touch. They hide in the cracks of pride, resentment, fear, or rebellion, any place we leave unguarded or unsubmitted. But when we invite the Lord to search us, He becomes the divine excavator, shining His light into every hidden room. What the enemy tries to conceal, God reveals. What the enemy tries to occupy, God reclaims. When the Lord exposes a chamber, it is because He intends to cleanse it. When He uncovers darkness, it is because He is ready to command it to leave.

Deliverance is God opening the hidden doors of the heart so that His glory can fill every room. Nothing He exposes is beyond His ability to heal, cleanse, or restore. The moment His light enters, darkness loses its place.

Guarding the Gates

Our bodies have gates, entry points that can welcome the King or open to the enemy. The eyes, ears, mouth, and even imagination are spiritual doorways. What we feed through them shapes what takes root within us.

> *"Lift up your heads, O you gates;*
> *And be lifted up, you everlasting doors;*
> *And the King of glory shall come in."*
> ***Psalm 24:7 (NKJV)***

Every believer is a temple designed for the habitation of God. Like any temple, our lives have gates, spiritual entry points, that either lead to the Kingdom of Heaven or to the kingdom of darkness. These gates are not made of stone or iron but of flesh and spirit: the eyes, the ears, the mouth, the mind, and even the imagination. Through them, we invite influence. What passes through these gates determines what takes root in the heart.

> *"The lamp of the body is the eye. If therefore your eye is good, your whole body will be full of light. But if your eye is*

bad, your whole body will be full of darkness."
Matthew 6:22–23 (NKJV)

The eye gate is not merely physical sight; it is perception. What we continually behold, we eventually become. When we gaze upon what is pure, honorable, and holy, we are transformed by the same Spirit we behold. But when we fix our eyes on what defiles, darkness begins to fill the inner room of the heart.

"He who has ears to hear, let him hear!"
Luke 8:8 (NKJV)

Hearing is more than the act of listening—it is the posture of the heart that determines which voice we will obey. "So then faith comes by hearing, and hearing by the word of God." (Romans 10:17, NKJV). Faith is built by what we listen to, but deception enters when we lend our ears to lies. The enemy knows that if he can control what we hear, he can influence what we believe.

"Death and life are in the power of the tongue,
And those who love it will eat its fruit."
Proverbs 18:21 (NKJV)

The mouth is a gate of great power. What we speak creates an atmosphere around us. Words either release Heaven's authority or empower darkness. When we gossip, curse, or complain, we open the gate of agreement to the enemy. But when we speak blessing, truth, and praise, we invite the presence of God to dwell among us.

"Casting down arguments and every high thing that exalts itself against the knowledge of God, bringing every thought into captivity to the obedience of Christ."
2 Corinthians 10:5 (NKJV)

Even the imagination is a gate. It was never meant to be a playground for fear or fantasy but a sanctuary for divine vision. The imagination becomes holy when it is surrendered to the Word, when every image, idea, and memory bows before the authority of Jesus.

Every gate must be guarded, because what we permit determines what we host. You cannot continually watch impurity and expect holiness to reign. You cannot fill your ears with profanity and expect peace to abide. You cannot harbor unforgiveness and expect freedom to flourish.

The spiritual law remains unchanged: what you tolerate will eventually dominate.

> *"Sin lies at the door. And its desire is for you, but you should rule over it."*
> ***Genesis 4:7 (NKJV)***

Sin still crouches at the door, just as it did in the days of Cain, waiting for permission to enter. But the Spirit of God empowers us to rule over it.

> *"Resist the devil and he will flee from you. Draw near to God and He will draw near to you."*
> ***James 4:7–8 (NKJV)***

The key to victory is vigilance, keeping every door shut to darkness and open only to the King of Glory.

When the gates of the heart are lifted toward Heaven, the King enters in.

The same Spirit that once filled Solomon's temple now fills the believer's life.

The voice that once thundered on Mount Sinai now whispers in the surrendered heart.

Guarding your gates is not an act of fear but of devotion; it is protecting the dwelling place of God within you. And when every gate is yielded to Him, the temple becomes radiant with His presence. The King of Glory does not merely visit; He abides.

DELIVERANCE: PURGING AND GROWTH

As the Kingdom of God grows within a believer, so does the need for pruning. The greater the light, the greater the warfare. The more ground Christ claims within you, the more fiercely the enemy will attempt to reclaim it. Deliverance is not a sign of spiritual weakness; it is evidence that transformation is taking place. When God begins to refine a vessel, He exposes what does not belong so that His glory can dwell without hindrance.

Not everything a believer struggles with is a demon that needs to be cast out. Some battles are spiritual, and some are carnal. Deliverance is for casting out demons; the flesh, however, cannot be cast out; it must be crucified. You cannot rebuke what God has called you to crucify. Demons are driven out by authority in Jesus' name, but the flesh is put to death daily by denying self, taking up your cross, and walking in obedience to the Spirit. Confusion comes when we try to use deliverance to avoid discipleship. Both are needed: demons must be expelled, and the flesh must be surrendered and crucified.

"Every branch in Me that does not bear fruit He takes away; and every branch that bears fruit He prunes, that it may bear more fruit."
John 15:2 (NKJV)
"Being confident of this very thing, that He who has begun a good work in you will complete it until the day of Jesus

Christic.
Philippians 1:6 (NKJV)

Pruning is painful but necessary. It is the process by which the Gardener removes what would limit the harvest. When God prunes, He is not cutting you off; He is preparing you to carry more. Deliverance functions in the same way: it clears away the dead branches of sin, fear, pride, and compromise so that the life of Christ can flow freely through you.

Repentance, worship, and renewing of your mind are all acts of deliverance. They continually align you with Heaven's order. Each time you submit to the conviction of the Holy Spirit, another root of darkness is pulled out, and more room is made for the Spirit's fruit to grow.

"Do not be conformed to this world, but be transformed by the renewing of your mind, that you may prove what is that good and acceptable and perfect will of God."
Romans 12:2 (NKJV)
"If we confess our sins, He is faithful and just to forgive us our sins and to cleanse us from all unrighteousness."
1 John 1:9 (NKJV)

Deliverance is not something to fear; it is a gift to God's children. Jesus called it "the children's bread", meaning it belongs to those who are His.

"It is not good to take the children's bread and throw it to the little dogs."
Matthew 15:26 (NKJV)

Deliverance is part of the covenant of salvation. It is nourishment for the believer's soul, the children's bread, the sustaining work that keeps the temple clean, and the heart aligned with Heaven. Salvation (justification) removes the penalty of sin; deliverance (sanctification) removes the remnants of sin's influence. One redeems you; the other restores you. Deliverance brings the believer into wholeness and strengthens the bond of intimacy between the Redeemer and the redeemed.

Justification happens instantly at salvation, when your spirit is cleansed, forgiven, made new, and declared righteous, white as snow. But sanctification is the *ongoing* work that touches your soul and body. While salvation transforms your spirit, it does not automatically heal your mind, emotions, or habits, nor does it crucify your flesh. These areas must be renewed, restored, and brought under the Lordship of Christ. This is where deliverance becomes essential. Deliverance does not replace salvation; it *applies* salvation to the parts of you still being sanctified. It breaks the strongholds, influences, and residue that sin and bondage left behind. Justification rescues you from sin's penalty; sanctification removes sin's patterns. Your spirit is made new in a moment, but your soul is transformed over time. Together, justification and sanctification complete the work of redemption within you: one gives you a new identity, and the other removes everything that contradicts it.

> "He who has begun a good work in you will complete it until the day of Jesus Christ."
> **Philippians 1:6 (NKJV)**
> "Put off, concerning your former conduct... and be renewed in the spirit of your mind... and put on the new man..."
> **Ephesians 4:22–24 (NKJV)**
> "...pulling down strongholds... bringing every thought into captivity..."
> **2 Corinthians 10:4–5 (NKJV)**

Deliverance does not always manifest the same way. Sometimes it looks like repentance. Sometimes it comes through tears, worship, prayer, the washing of the Word, or in the form of demonic manifestations being cast out. Every act of surrender that removes the enemy's grip is deliverance. Every step of obedience that draws you nearer to Christ uproots what darkness once held. Deliverance is not confined to a dramatic moment; it is woven throughout the life of a believer who continually yields to the sanctifying work of the Holy Spirit.

"For the word of God is living and powerful, and sharper than any two-edged sword, piercing even to the division of soul and spirit... and is a discerner of the thoughts and intents of the heart."
Hebrews 4:12 (NKJV)
"Sanctify them by Your truth. Your word is truth."
John 17:17 (NKJV)

Deliverance is not always loud; sometimes it is as quiet as surrender. When you bow in worship and yield your will to the Father, you are declaring that He alone has authority. When you repent, the chains of agreement with darkness are broken. When you meditate on Scripture, the truth drives out deception. The Word of God itself becomes the weapon of deliverance: dividing soul from spirit, truth from lies, and purity from pollution.

The arrival of the Kingdom is always marked by freedom. Jesus said that casting out demons is a sign that the Kingdom of God has come. Where Jesus reigns, darkness must leave. Deliverance is not a side ministry; it is part of salvation itself.

"But if I cast out demons by the Spirit of God, surely the kingdom of God has come upon you."
Matthew 12:28 (NKJV)

Demons thrive in apathy and ignorance. They hide in complacency and feed on passivity. But when a believer hungers for wisdom and truth, every hiding place of the enemy is exposed. The Holy Spirit is the great Teacher; He not only brings revelation but gives strategy for resistance and maintenance of freedom.

"My people are destroyed for lack of knowledge."
Hosea 4:6 (NKJV)

"The entrance of Your words gives light; it gives understanding to the simple."
Psalm 119:130 (NKJV)

"Watch and pray, lest you enter into temptation. The spirit indeed is willing, but the flesh is weak."
Matthew 26:41 (NKJV)

The Spirit trains you to guard your gates, to discern what enters through your eyes, ears, and thoughts. Freedom is sustained through vigilance. Deliverance may break the chains, but discipline and discipleship keep them from returning. The same fire that sets you free must continue to refine you.

You cannot entertain darkness and expect your light to remain bright. You cannot feed your flesh and expect your spirit to flourish. You cannot live lukewarm and call it surrendered. The Apostle Paul warned,

"Do not be deceived: Evil company corrupts good habits."
1 Corinthians 15:33 (NKJV)

And again,

"Walk in the Spirit, and you shall not fulfill the lust of the flesh."
Galatians 5:16 (NKJV)

Deliverance is not merely the removal of demons; it is the enthronement of Jesus. It is the Holy King taking His rightful place in every room of your heart. He does not come to visit; He comes to reign. When He enters, He overturns every table of compromise, silences every unclean voice, and restores His house to holiness.

"Then Jesus went into the temple of God and drove out all those who bought and sold in the temple, and overturned the tables of the money changers… And He said to them, 'It is written, "My house shall be called a house of prayer."'"
Matthew 21:12–13 (NKJV)

When Jesus is enthroned within you, deliverance becomes a lifestyle, a continual purification of His temple. Every trial becomes pruning, every conviction becomes transformation, and every victory becomes another room surrendered to His Lordship.

The Kingdom is not built by those who appear perfect, but by those who allow the King to perfect them from within.

Deliverance is the ongoing miracle of sanctification, the daily bread of those who belong to Him. It is not merely an event; it is the evidence that the King of Glory has come in.

LORD AND SAVIOR

There are reasons Scripture calls Him both Lord and Savior. These are not interchangeable titles; they reveal two dimensions of His identity and two depths of our response. Most people love Jesus the Savior, but few truly surrender to Jesus the Lord.

The Savior rescues; the Lord reigns. The Savior delivers you *from* sin; the Lord governs your life *after* salvation. One offers mercy; the other requires obedience. One pulls you out of the grave; the other commands that the old man must die!

Many profess love for the Savior yet resist the Lord. They want forgiveness without repentance, comfort without consecration, and blessing without obedience. But loving God and fearing God are not the same. True love for Him produces holy fear, not the fear that runs away from His presence, but the kind that trembles ever to leave it.

"The fear of the Lord is clean, enduring forever; The judgments of the Lord are true and righteous altogether."
Psalm 19:9 (NKJV)

Notice that word, *clean*. The fear of the Lord purifies. It is not terror; it is transformation. It is the inner cleansing that keeps a believer set apart. The fear of the Lord is the spiritual agent of holiness, not legalism, but sanctification. It does not drive you from God; it keeps you *under* His covering.

Holiness is not a suggestion; it is a command.
"Be holy, for I am holy."
1 Peter 1:16 (NKJV)

To be holy means to be *set apart*, *sacred*, and *distinct*. The Hebrew word qodesh means *apartness* or *separateness*. It conveys a sense of being devoted to a sacred purpose. The Greek word hagios means *most holy thing, a saint*, something consecrated for divine use.

Holiness is not achieved by effort; it is maintained by obedience. It is the natural result of fearing the Lord and yielding to His Spirit.

"Therefore, having these promises, beloved, let us cleanse ourselves from all filthiness of the flesh and spirit, perfecting holiness in the fear of God."
2 Corinthians 7:1 (NKJV)

When God says, *"Be separate from the world,"* He means exactly that. Separation is protection, not punishment. It is the invisible wall that guards you from the trading grounds of the enemy. Every time you step outside of holiness, you step onto foreign soil. Compromises always have a cost.

This is why there are Christians who love the Lord, yet still live entangled in bondage, believers who profess faith but never pursue freedom. They love the Savior who forgives but resist the Lord who commands change. So, you see those who confess Christ but still yield to addiction, still entertain sin, still refuse to let go of what defiles the temple. It is not because they do not love Him, but because they have not yet learned to fear Him.

> *"Do you not know that to whom you present yourselves slaves to obey, you are that one's slaves whom you obey, whether of sin leading to death, or of obedience leading to righteousness?"*
>
> ***Romans 6:16 (NKJV)***

The name LORD in Hebrew, YHWH, means *the Self-Existent One, the Eternal, Jehovah*. It declares God as the sovereign, uncreated Being, the One who depends on no one yet sustains all things. In Greek, **kurios** means *master, owner, or sovereign ruler*. It refers to one who has complete authority over a person or thing, one who decides, directs, and commands.

To call Jesus "Lord" is not a title of respect; it is a declaration of ownership. It means your life is no longer your own. It means your choices, your desires, your will, and your body belong to Him.

> *"Why do you call Me 'Lord, Lord,' and not do the things which I say?"*
> **Luke 6:46 (NKJV)**

The word Savior, from the Hebrew yasha and Greek sōtēr, means *to save, deliver, rescue, or give victory*. It is the name that reveals His mercy and compassion, the Redeemer who pulls you out of destruction and restores you to life.

But once He saves you, He also calls you to submit. The Savior opens the door to the Kingdom; the Lord rules within it. Salvation is the beginning; surrender is the continuation.

To receive Him as Savior and reject Him as Lord is to live in spiritual contradiction, to want Heaven's safety without Heaven's authority. True discipleship embraces both.

> *"If anyone desires to come after Me, let him deny himself, and take up his cross daily, and follow Me."*
> **Luke 9:23 (NKJV)**

> *"For you were bought at a price; therefore glorify God in your body and in your spirit, which are God's."*
> **1 Corinthians 6:20 (NKJV)**

When you make Him Lord, holiness becomes your new nature. The fear of the Lord keeps you clean, and love for the Lord keeps you close. One guards your heart from sin; the other draws your heart into intimacy. Together they form the foundation of a life that is both pure and powerful, separate, yet full of glory.

Deliverance, then, is not just freedom from darkness; it is alignment under His Lordship. It is when Jesus is not only your Rescuer but your Ruler. When every room of your soul bows before Him, every unclean thing must go. He will not share His temple with idols.

He alone is Savior, the One who delivers. He alone is Lord, the One who reigns. And when both are embraced, the believer becomes what they were created to be: a holy vessel, set apart for the Master's use.

THE CALL TO SALVATION

If you have never surrendered your life to Jesus, true freedom begins here, with salvation. Deliverance is the fruit of redemption, but salvation is its foundation. Without Christ, there is no authority over darkness, because He alone is the One who conquered it.

Salvation is not simply repeating a prayer; it is a transfer of kingdoms. It is leaving the dominion of sin and stepping into the rulership of Christ. It is the moment when Heaven's ownership is restored over your life, spirit, soul, and body.

"If you confess with your mouth the Lord Jesus and believe in your heart that God has raised Him from the dead, you will be saved. For with the heart one believes unto righteousness, and with the mouth confession is made unto salvation."
Romans 10:9–10 (NKJV)

To be saved is to invite Jesus to be Lord, not just Savior, but Ruler of all that you are. It means to yield ownership of your life to the One who gave His for you. Salvation is not about joining a religion; it is about being restored into a relationship with the living God.

The message of the Gospel is eternal yet straightforward: Jesus Christ came to earth, lived a sinless life, died in our place, and rose again on the third day so that we could live forever with Him. He did not come to make bad people good; He came to make dead people live.

*"For God so loved the world that He gave His only begotten Son,
that whoever believes in Him should not perish but have everlasting life."*
John 3:16 (NKJV)

"Nor is there salvation in any other, for there is no other name under heaven given among men by which we must be saved."
Acts 4:12 (NKJV)

Salvation is both a gift and a covenant. It is offered freely but must be received personally. It is not earned by works or achieved by merit; it is accepted by faith. The Cross was Heaven's transaction; all that remains is your surrender.

When you believe in your heart and confess with your mouth, something supernatural happens. The blood of Jesus cleanses your sin, the Holy Spirit enters your spirit, and your name is written in the Book of Life. The chains that once held you are broken, and the power of death loses its claim.

"Therefore, if anyone is in Christ, he is a new creation; old things have passed away; behold, all things have become new."
2 Corinthians 5:17 (NKJV)

"For by grace you have been saved through faith, and that not of yourselves; it is the gift of God, not of works, lest anyone should boast."
Ephesians 2:8–9 (NKJV)

To receive salvation is to step under the covering of the Lamb and into the covenant of grace. It is the doorway to deliverance, the entrance to eternal life, and the restoration of your divine purpose. When you surrender to Jesus, you are no longer a slave to sin, you become a son or daughter of God.

"But as many as received Him, to them He gave the right to become children of God, to those who believe in His name."
John 1:12 (NKJV)

"He has delivered us from the power of darkness and conveyed us into the kingdom of the Son of His love."
Colossians 1:13 (NKJV)

Salvation is not the end of the story; it is the beginning of your transformation. The same Spirit that raised Jesus from the dead now lives within you, empowering you to live in holiness, victory, and peace.

"And you He made alive, who were dead in trespasses and sins... But God, who is rich in mercy, because of His great love with which He loved us... made us alive together with Christ."
Ephesians 2:1, 4–5 (NKJV)

To those who are weary, bound, or broken, this invitation remains:

Come.

Surrender.

Be made new.

Jesus stands at the door and knocks. Open the gate of your heart, and the King of Glory will come in.

"Behold, I stand at the door and knock. If anyone hears My voice and opens the door,
I will come in to him and dine with him, and he with Me."
Revelation 3:20 (NKJV)

LIVING FREE

Deliverance may seem final, but it is a persistent pursuit of a life lived in continual victory. It is a starting point of transformation, a doorway into deeper intimacy with God. Freedom must be maintained through relationship, obedience, and fellowship. The same Spirit who sets you free also teaches you how to stay free.

True deliverance leads to discipleship. It's not a single moment of relief; it's a lifelong pursuit of holiness. Freedom is sustained through intimacy with God, obedience to His Word, and community with other believers. Isolation invites the enemy back, but accountability keeps the door closed.

"Stand fast therefore in the liberty by which Christ has made us free, and do not be entangled again with a yoke of bondage."
Galatians 5:1 (NKJV)

"Therefore submit to God. Resist the devil and he will flee from you. Draw near to God and He will draw near to you."
James 4:7–8 (NKJV)

Deliverance begins in the heart, but it must be walked out in the mind and body. It is the process of aligning every part of your life with the rule of Christ. When darkness is expelled, the now-empty space must be filled with truth, prayer, and the Holy Spirit; otherwise, the enemy seeks to return.

"When an unclean spirit goes out of a man, he goes through dry places, seeking rest; and finding none, he says, 'I will return to my house from which I came.'"
Luke 11:24 (NKJV)

Deliverance, then, is both an event and a discipline, a decisive confrontation followed by daily surrender.

How to Walk Through Deliverance

Deliverance is the ministry of Jesus continued through His Church. It is not complicated, mystical, or reserved for the few;

it is the birthright of every believer filled with the Holy Spirit. The same authority that Jesus used to drive out darkness has been given to His people.

"And these signs will follow those who believe: In My name they will cast out demons."

Mark 16:17 (NKJV)

Deliverance operates through the authority of His name and the power of His blood. The enemy has no legal right to remain where sin has been confessed, repentance has been made, demonic authority has been broken, and the Lordship of Christ has been declared.

Below is a biblical framework for walking through deliverance:

1. **Repentance and Forgiveness: Closing the Door and Releasing the Offense**

Deliverance always begins with repentance and forgiveness. These two keys unlock Heaven's authority and close every door the enemy has used to gain access to. Repentance breaks agreement with sin; forgiveness breaks agreement with bitterness. Without these two, no lasting freedom can remain.

The very first step I always tell others to take when guiding them through deliverance is forgiveness. No matter how much we pray, rebuke, or renounce, freedom cannot take root in a heart that still clings to bitterness. Unforgiveness is one of the most common doorways the enemy uses to gain legal access to a believer's life. It chains the soul to the past and binds the heart to torment. Until forgiveness is released, deliverance will always be incomplete.

"And whenever you stand praying, if you have anything against anyone, forgive him, that your Father in heaven may

also forgive you your trespasses. But if you do not forgive, neither will your Father in heaven forgive your trespasses."
Mark 11:25–26 (NKJV)

Forgiveness opens the flow of God's mercy; unforgiveness blocks it. You cannot be delivered from what you still hold onto. When we release others from their debt, we ourselves are released from the enemy's grip.

Jesus also told a sobering parable of a servant forgiven a great debt who refused to forgive another. The result was torment:

"And his master was angry, and delivered him to the torturers until he should pay all that was due to him. So My heavenly Father also will do to you if each of you, from his heart, does not forgive his brother his trespasses."
Matthew 18:34–35 (NKJV)

The "torturers" in this passage represent demonic torment: anxiety, fear, oppression, and unrest. Unforgiveness is not harmless; it invites spiritual torment. When people come for deliverance but hold onto resentment, they remain tethered to the very thing that binds them.

Paul warned of the same principle:

"Be angry, and do not sin": do not let the sun go down on your wrath, nor give place to the devil."
Ephesians 4:26–27 (NKJV)

That phrase *give place* means "to give territory." Every time we choose to hold an offense, we surrender spiritual ground. Forgiveness closes that door.

Before beginning deliverance, I always ask the Holy Spirit to reveal anyone the person needs to forgive — sometimes even themselves. As those names come, we speak them aloud, forgive from the heart, and release every debt into the hands of God.

Forgiveness does not excuse what was done — it removes the power it still has over you. It is not saying, "What they did was right"; it is saying, "I choose freedom over bondage."

Scripture ties healing and forgiveness together:

"Therefore confess your trespasses to one another, and pray for one another, that you may be healed. The effective, fervent prayer of a righteous man avails much."

James 5:16 (NKJV)

When you forgive, the enemy loses his legal right to torment you. You can pray something like this:

"Father, I choose to forgive those who have wounded me. I release them (call each name out) from the debt they owe. I place them in Your hands and ask You to bless them. I renounce bitterness, anger, and resentment. I close every door that unforgiveness has opened, and I declare that Jesus Christ is Lord over my heart."

Forgiveness is not a weakness; it is warfare. It is the weapon that breaks the enemy's strongest chains. Repentance and forgiveness together form the first and most vital act of deliverance.

Healing begins where forgiveness is released. Freedom begins where mercy flows. But forgiveness is only the first strike—repentance is the next.

Repentance is not merely feeling sorry; it is the turning of the heart away from darkness and back toward the light of God. It is not gentle; it is a military-level reversal. It is violent to the flesh and hostile to hell. Sin is the legal doorway the enemy uses to enter, but repentance slams it shut. It is a transfer of allegiance, like fleeing a tyrant and submitting to a rightful

King. When you confess your sin and come into the light, the covenant blood of Jesus answers every accusation and breaks every legal claim.

> *"Repent therefore and be converted, that your sins may be blotted out, so that times of refreshing may come from the presence of the Lord."*
> **Acts 3:19 (NKJV)**

Confess specific sins aloud before the Lord. Speak truth where the enemy once had agreement. Ask Him to forgive you, wash you clean, and restore your fellowship with Him. Repentance doesn't just remove guilt; it restores intimacy. It invites the Holy Spirit back into areas that sin once occupied.

Where repentance breaks the agreement with sin, forgiveness removes the enemy's right to torment through offense and bitterness. Forgiveness is the next essential act of deliverance, the cleansing of the heart.

Father, in the name of Jesus, I come before You with a surrendered heart. I confess my sin before You, and I bring every hidden thing into the light. I repent for every action, thought, desire, and agreement that has opposed Your will. I turn away from darkness, and I turn fully toward You. I renounce every sin that has opened doors to the enemy. I renounce every lie I believed, every compromise I tolerated, and every pattern that pulled me away from Your truth. I repent of every sin known or unknown. I choose Your truth over every lie. By the power of Your blood, I ask You to cleanse me: spirit, soul, and body. Let Your blood speak on my behalf and silence every accusation of the enemy. Wash me, purify me, and restore me. Renew my mind. Heal my emotions. Transform my desires. Strengthen my will to obey You. I yield every part of myself to

Your Lordship. Today, I choose life. I choose holiness. I choose Your ways over my own. I close every door I opened to the enemy, and I open my heart fully to You. Jesus, rule and reign in every part of me. I declare that I belong to Jesus Christ alone, washed by His blood, filled with His Spirit, and set apart for His glory. Amen.

2. **Renunciation: Breaking Agreement**

Once repentance and forgiveness have taken place, the next step in deliverance is renouncing, formally breaking every agreement with darkness. Before you begin, ask the Holy Spirit to reveal what needs to be renounced. He will gently bring to mind the specific sins, lies, relationships, or past involvements that opened doors to the enemy. What the Spirit exposes, He intends to remove. Deliverance is never about guessing; it is about partnering with His light to uncover hidden things.

The word *renounce* means to reject, disown, or verbally cancel. Every sin, lie, or false identity we have accepted becomes an agreement in the spiritual realm. When we renounce, we are legally dissolving the enemy's right to operate in that area of our lives.

Deliverance is not just emotional release; it is a legal transaction in the Spirit. The moment you renounce what is false and confess what is true, the blood of Jesus enforces Heaven's verdict against the kingdom of darkness.

"Let the redeemed of the Lord say so,
Whom He has redeemed from the hand of the enemy."
Psalm 107:2 (NKJV)

This is why verbal confession is so important. The tongue carries the power of agreement. What once permitted darkness can be revoked with your words. Renouncing is not begging God to move; it is enforcing the victory of the Cross.

Jesus modeled this principle in His ministry. Before physical healing or restoration took place, He often first broke the enemy's legal access. In Luke 13, He encountered a woman who a spirit of infirmity had bound for eighteen years.

"But when Jesus saw her, He called her to Him and said to her, 'Woman, you are loosed from your infirmity.' And He laid His hands on her, and immediately she was made straight, and glorified God."
Luke 13:12–13 (NKJV)

Notice the divine order: Jesus first declared her *loosed*, He revoked the enemy's legal hold, then healing manifested. He explained what had taken place:

"So ought not this woman, being a daughter of Abraham, whom Satan has bound—think of it—for eighteen years, be loosed from this bond on the Sabbath?"
Luke 13:16 (NKJV)

Jesus revealed two vital truths: first, that Satan had bound her through a legal right, and second, that her covenant identity as a daughter of Abraham overruled that bondage. Once the claim was broken, healing flowed naturally.

In the same way, when believers renounce sin, lies, and demonic influence, they are tearing up every spiritual contract that once gave the enemy permission to dwell. Renouncing withdraws his claim and removes his foothold.

You can pray something like this:

"In the name of Jesus Christ, I renounce every lie, habit, and unclean influence that has claimed authority in my life. I cancel every agreement I have made knowingly or unknowingly with darkness *(ask the Holy Spirit to expose areas; use the list from the previous 2 chapters if needed).* I break every curse, every soul tie, and every false identity. I declare that I belong to Jesus Christ alone. My body is the temple of the Holy Spirit, and every part of me is now under His rule."

When you renounce, you are standing in the authority of the Cross. You are declaring the verdict of Calvary: "It is finished." The blood of Jesus cancels every accusation, breaks every claim, and silences every voice of condemnation.

Renouncing is not shouting at demons; it is standing in your legal right as a redeemed child of God. The power is not in your volume, but in your position. You are seated with Christ in heavenly places, and when you declare His truth, all of Hell must obey.

3. Remove: Commanding Freedom

Once sin is confessed and agreements are broken, the next step is to command the enemy to leave in the authority of Jesus' name. Deliverance is not a request; it is a command. It is not done through emotion or striving, but through authority; the authority that was purchased by the blood of the Lamb and delegated to every believer who walks in His name.

When you were saved, you were not only forgiven, but you were also seated with Christ in heavenly places. From that seat of victory, you speak as one who represents the King. You are not begging the enemy to leave; you are enforcing the legal judgment that was rendered at Calvary.

> *"Behold, I give you the authority to trample on serpents and scorpions, and over all the power of the enemy, and nothing shall by any means hurt you."*
> **Luke 10:19 (NKJV)**

Authority is positional. It is not based on how you feel but on where you stand. You stand in Christ, clothed in His righteousness, covered by His blood, and backed by the power of His throne. When you speak His name, the entire kingdom of darkness must yield.

"Therefore submit to God. Resist the devil and he will flee from you."
James 4:7 (NKJV)

Notice that Scripture does not say, "He might flee;" it says, "He will flee." Resistance is not passive; it is active. To "resist" means to stand your ground, to oppose, to enforce the Word of God.

Deliverance operates through both submission and command. You first submit to God, aligning your life under His Lordship, and then you **resist** the enemy by commanding him to release every area that he has occupied.

When you speak, speak with faith. The authority is not in your tone; it's in your covenant. You carry the same Spirit that raised Jesus from the dead (Romans 8:11). The name of Jesus is not a formula; it is a throne. It represents the highest government in Heaven and Earth. Every demonic spirit must obey when the name of Jesus is declared from the mouth of a surrendered believer.

"And these signs will follow those who believe: In My name they will cast out demons; they will speak with new tongues."
Mark 16:17 (NKJV)

"For the weapons of our warfare are not carnal but mighty in God for pulling down strongholds."
2 Corinthians 10:4 (NKJV)

When commanding freedom, there is no need to fear or strive. Deliverance is not a power struggle; it's a truth encounter. The moment the enemy is exposed, and the Word of God is declared, his power is broken. The darkness must yield to the light.

You can pray something like this:

"In the name of Jesus Christ, I command every unclean spirit, every stronghold, and every influence of darkness to leave me now. I break your power by the blood of Jesus and command you to loose my mind, my body, and my soul. I am redeemed, I am cleansed, and I belong to Jesus Christ alone. Every spirit that is not of the Holy Spirit must go now, in the mighty name of Jesus."

The Holy Spirit may lead you to address specific areas: eyes, ears, words, mind, emotions. As each one is named and renounced, command everything the Holy Spirit is showing you to leave. Speak boldly, knowing that you are not fighting for victory; you are fighting *from* victory.

Deliverance is not a moment of chaos; it is the government of Heaven being enforced. The believer who walks in purity, humility, and submission to the Word will walk in sustained freedom. The same Jesus who spoke to the storm and said, *"Peace, be still,"* now speaks through you.

Command freedom in His name, and peace will come. Because where the Spirit of the Lord is, there is liberty.

> *"Now the Lord is the Spirit; and where the Spirit of the Lord is, there is liberty."*
> ***2 Corinthians 3:17 (NKJV)***

You can pray:

"In the name of Jesus Christ, I command every unclean spirit that has tormented my life to go now. You no longer have authority over me. The blood of Jesus covers me, filled with His Spirit, and sealed for His glory."

"I renounce every unclean image, every defiling thing, every moment of lust, envy, comparison, or darkness I looked upon. In the name of Jesus, I break agreement with anything that entered through my eyes and claimed access to my mind or emotions. I command every demonic unclean spirit that entered my life through this gate to leave my body now in the name of Jesus. I shut the eye gate to the enemy, and I declare it belongs to Jesus Christ alone."

"I renounce every word of darkness that entered my gates through my ears. I silence every demonic whisper and ungodly influence in Jesus' name. I command every demonic unclean spirit that entered my life through this gate to leave my body now in the name of Jesus. I close the ear gate to the enemy, and I open it only to Your Word and Your Spirit."

"I renounce the power of every idle or ungodly word I have spoken. In Jesus' name, I cancel their effect and break their assignments. I dedicate my mouth to the Lord Jesus Christ. Holy Spirit, fill my mouth with truth, praise, blessing, and life. I command every demonic unclean spirit that entered my life through this gate to leave my body now in the name of Jesus. I declare my tongue belongs to the Kingdom of God."

Deliverance is not about shouting at demons; it is about standing in the victory of Christ and enforcing what He already won.

4. **Replace: Filling the House**

When the enemy leaves, fill the space immediately with worship, thanksgiving, and the Word. Never leave a spiritual room empty. Jesus warned that when a spirit departs and finds the house "empty, swept, and put in order," it tries to return with seven others worse than itself (Matthew 12:43–45).

Deliverance is not complete until the empty places are filled. When darkness is cast out, it creates space, and the light of God's presence must occupy that space. Freedom is never maintained by willpower alone; it is sustained by infilling.

Jesus warned of this principle in Matthew 12:

"When an unclean spirit goes out of a man, he goes through dry places, seeking rest, and finds none. Then he says, 'I will return to my house from which I came.' And when he comes, he finds it empty, swept, and put in order. Then he goes and takes with him seven other spirits more wicked than himself, and they enter and dwell there; and the last state of that man is worse than the first."

Matthew 12:43–45 (NKJV)

Deliverance clears the temple for the Holy Spirit to fill it. If you drive out what is unclean but do not invite the Holy Spirit to dwell in that space, the enemy will seek to return. Freedom is not just about eviction, it's about occupation. The Spirit of God must become the permanent resident of every room in your heart.

When you are filled with His Word and His presence, the enemy cannot re-enter. The darkness that once occupied your mind, emotions, or body is replaced by light, truth, and holiness.

"Your word I have hidden in my heart, That I might not sin against You."

Psalm 119:11 (NKJV)

"Do you not know that you are the temple of God and that the Spirit of God dwells in you?"

1 Corinthians 3:16 (NKJV)

To "fill the house" means to cultivate new habits and holy rhythms that keep your spirit strong.

- **Worship** fills the atmosphere of your home with the presence of God.
- **Prayer** keeps the gates of your life open to Heaven's influence.
- **Scripture** renews your mind and builds truth into your foundation.
- **Community** surrounds you with accountability and encouragement.

Freedom is maintained through fellowship with the Holy Spirit. He will train you to discern His voice, resist temptation, and guard the doors of your heart.

"Walk in the Spirit, and you shall not fulfill the lust of the flesh."
Galatians 5:16 (NKJV)

"If you then, being evil, know how to give good gifts to your children,
how much more will your heavenly Father give the Holy Spirit to those who ask Him!"
Luke 11:13 (NKJV)

Invite the Holy Spirit to fill every part of you: your thoughts, emotions, imagination, and desires. Speak it out:

"Holy Spirit, I welcome You into every room of my body, soul, mind (whatever area of your body the Holy Spirit had you remove demonic authority). Fill me with Your presence, Your power, and Your peace. Where darkness once ruled, let Your light shine. Where fear lived, let faith rise.
Where sin took root, plant Your Word that I may bear fruit for Your glory."

Freedom is not sustained by perfection but by presence. The more filled you are, the less room there is for the enemy. This is the reason daily fellowship matters. Reading the Word, worshiping in your home, praying in the Spirit, and walking in obedience; all these practices keep the fire burning and the temple filled.

When you replace what was removed, you move from deliverance into dominion. You are no longer just set free; you are now a vessel of divine authority and habitation for the King.

"Do not be drunk with wine, in which is dissipation; but be filled with the Spirit."

Ephesians 5:18 (NKJV)

"The light shines in the darkness, and the darkness did not comprehend it."

John 1:5 (NKJV)

The Holy Spirit is the seal of your freedom. He does not simply visit; He indwells. When He fills you, every lie loses its power, every habit loses its hold, and the light of His glory dispels every shadow.

Freedom maintained through His presence becomes unshakable, because what is filled cannot be overtaken.

5. **Remain: Walking in Obedience**

Deliverance is not the end of the journey; it is the beginning of a new walk. Freedom is sustained through obedience. The same Jesus who cast out demons also said, *"Follow Me."* True deliverance is not only about what leaves you; it is about who leads you.

Every act of obedience reinforces your freedom. Every compromise threatens it. The Kingdom of God operates by submission to His Word, and lasting victory comes when you walk in continual surrender.

"Therefore submit to God. Resist the devil and he will flee from you.

Draw near to God and He will draw near to you."
James 4:7–8 (NKJV)

Obedience keeps the doors shut to the enemy. It aligns your life under Heaven's covering and ensures that the freedom Jesus purchased is protected by faithfulness. The Holy Spirit will guide you daily, what to keep, what to remove, what to guard, and what to pursue. To remain free, you must remain yielded.

Freedom is never passive; it is maintained through watchfulness. You cannot walk with God and flirt with darkness. Deliverance requires discernment to recognize anything that would reintroduce the bondage you've been freed from.

"Watch and pray, lest you enter into temptation. The spirit indeed is willing, but the flesh is weak."
Matthew 26:41 (NKJV)

To "remain" is to live as a disciple. A disciple doesn't just visit the presence of God—they abide in it. Jesus said:

"If you abide in My word, you are My disciples indeed. And you shall know the truth, and the truth shall make you free."
John 8:31–32 (NKJV)

Freedom grows deeper the longer you stay close to the truth. Obedience is what keeps the fire burning, keeps the house clean, and keeps the heart soft.

No Gray Areas

There are no neutral zones in the spirit. Heaven and hell both operate by access and agreement. Every word, thought, and action either aligns with life or with death.

In Eden, there were two options: obedience or rebellion.
In Noah's Ark, two positions: inside or outside.
In Revelation, two temperatures: hot or cold.

God does not dwell in the middle ground of compromise. If we are not fully surrendered to Him, we have already yielded ground elsewhere.

"I know your works, that you are neither cold nor hot. I could wish you were cold or hot. So then, because you are lukewarm, and neither cold nor hot, I will vomit you out of My mouth."
Revelation 3:15–16 (NKJV)

If you have never invited the Lord to cleanse every area of your life, there are likely areas that need freedom. That is not a condemnation; it is an invitation. Deliverance is not punishment; it is restoration.

When you choose obedience, you choose life. When you choose holiness, you align with Heaven's rhythm. The believer who walks in reverent fear of the Lord cannot be easily shaken.

"Choose for yourselves this day whom you will serve... But as for me and my house, we will serve the Lord."
Joshua 24:15 (NKJV)

"Do not be conformed to this world, but be transformed by the renewing of your mind."
Romans 12:2 (NKJV)

There are no gray areas in the Kingdom. You are either pursuing light or tolerating darkness. You are either advancing the Kingdom or yielding ground to the enemy. Every choice is a seed that grows into either fruit or bondage.

To remain free, walk in the fear of the Lord. The fear of the Lord is clean; it keeps you pure, the conscience sharp, and the spirit alert.

> *"The fear of the Lord is clean, enduring forever;*
> *The judgments of the Lord are true and righteous altogether."*
> **Psalm 19:9 (NKJV)**

Deliverance is sustained through a lifestyle of holiness, not because God is controlling, but because His holiness is protection. It shields you from deception, compromise, and contamination. Holiness is Heaven's atmosphere made visible in your life.

Obedience is not bondage; it is safety. Separation is not restriction; it is preservation. God calls His people to be set apart because freedom cannot thrive in compromise.

> *"Come out from among them and be separate, says the Lord.*
> *Do not touch what is unclean, and I will receive you."*
> **2 Corinthians 6:17 (NKJV)**

To remain free, you must stay close to Jesus, the Deliverer Himself. Daily fellowship with Him through prayer, worship, and the Word keeps your spiritual gates fortified. Freedom fades where fellowship is neglected.

Deliverance begins with repentance, but it is sustained by relationship. Freedom begins with faith, but it endures through obedience.

The longer you walk with Him, the more His nature becomes your own. You will think like Him, speak like Him, love like Him, and live like Him.

> *"If you love Me, keep My commandments."*
> **John 14:15 (NKJV)**

Deliverance is not just an event; it is a covenant. To remain in freedom is to stay in Christ. The same power that sets you free will sustain you if you keep walking in His ways.

So, stand firmly. Guard your gates. Live holy. Walk in obedience. Because when Jesus reigns in every part of your life, freedom becomes permanent.

FINAL WORD: THE REDEEMED SHALL WALK FREE

Deliverance is the crescendo of redemption; the moment Heaven's language restores harmony to every part of your being. Salvation brings justification, but deliverance continues the work of sanctification. Justification declares you righteous before God; sanctification makes you live righteously with God. One happens in a moment; the other unfolds over a lifetime. The blood of Jesus justifies, and His Lordship sanctifies. Together, they complete the full circle of redemption.

Deliverance is where the voice of God silences the lies of the enemy, where the blood of Jesus cleanses every defilement, and where the Holy Spirit takes His rightful place within His temple. What began with separation in Eden ends with restoration at the Cross.

Freedom is not the absence of warfare; it is the presence of victory. It is not a fleeting feeling; it is a covenant sealed by the blood of the Lamb. Every chain broken, every lie exposed, every fear silenced, all point back to one truth: **Jesus still saves, heals, and delivers.**

The same Spirit who hovered over the waters in Genesis now dwells within you. The same power that rolled away the stone now lives to raise you from every grave of darkness. The same voice that said *"Let there be light"* now speaks through you, commanding light to pierce every shadow.

You were not created to live bound; you were created to carry glory. You are the dwelling place of God, the house of prayer, the vessel of His presence. The Deliverer lives within you, and His Kingdom flows through you.

> *"The Spirit of the Lord God is upon Me,*
> *Because the Lord has anointed Me*
> *To preach good tidings to the poor;*
> *He has sent Me to heal the brokenhearted,*
> *To proclaim liberty to the captives,*
> *And the opening of the prison to those who are bound."*
> **Isaiah 61:1 (NKJV)**

Walk in that liberty. Guard what He has given. Let your life become a testimony that Jesus Christ is still the same yesterday, today, and forever.

For whom the Son sets free, **is free indeed.**

> *"Therefore if the Son makes you free, you shall be free indeed."*
> **John 8:36 (NKJV)**

Part IV
Walking It Out
Reflection · Application · Transformation

The voice of God was never meant to be studied alone— it is meant to be lived.

This final section provides practical steps to apply the revelation found throughout the book. Through guided questions, reflection, and study, believers are invited to walk out what they've learned: to hear clearly, discern wisely, live purely, and overcome completely.
It is not only a conclusion but a beginning, a call to daily communion and spiritual maturity.

- Chapter 12:   Study Guide

Chapter 12: Study
& Reflection Guide
For Personal Growth and Group Discussion

This study and reflection guide was created to help readers go deeper into the truths revealed throughout this book. Whether you are walking through it in a small group, teaching a class, or studying privately with the Lord, take time to sit in prayer before each section.

Allow the Holy Spirit to highlight what He wants to reveal. Let this not be a checklist of questions, but an invitation into encounter. Write down what you sense God saying. Revisit these pages as you grow. The goal is not to rush through, but to reflect, apply, and be transformed.

Chapter 1 — Dreams & Visions
Scripture Focus: *Acts 2:17–18; Job 33:14–16; Numbers 12:6; Matthew 2:12–13; Daniel 2:19; Genesis 40:8*

1. How do the Scriptures above collectively demonstrate that dreams and visions are not random phenomena but intentional communication from God? Consider what this reveals about His character, His nearness, and His desire to guide His people.
2. Reflect on a dream or recurring theme that has stayed with you. What emotions, warnings, or invitations did it stir? In what ways might God have been revealing something deeper beneath the surface?
3. Job 33 teaches that God speaks in dreams to "open the ears of men." What distractions, fears, or habits in your life may have made you less attentive to His voice while awake, prompting Him to speak at night?
4. Dreams can expose hidden motives, fears, or spiritual battles. Has God ever shown you something in a dream that you disregarded but now recognize as important?

What do you sense the Holy Spirit highlighting about that dream today?
5. Using 1 John 4:1 as a filter, what practical steps can you take to test the origin of your dreams and avoid emotional, fleshly, or deceptive interpretation?
6. How can journaling, prayer, and Scripture help you steward dreams with spiritual maturity rather than superstition or over-analysis?
7. Consider Joseph, Daniel, and the Magi. What patterns do you see in how they responded to dreams? How can their responses shape your own posture of obedience?
8. Are there any warning dreams you ignored that now deserve prayerful reconsideration? What might repentance, course correction, or renewed attentiveness look like?
9. God sometimes redirects our steps through dreams (Matthew 2:12). What area of your life currently needs divine direction, and how can you invite God to speak clearly, even through dreams?
10. How can you remain sensitive to "night visions" in a culture filled with noise, distraction, and spiritual dullness? What practical rhythms will you put in place?

Chapter 2 — Discernment

Scripture Focus: *Hebrews 5:14; 1 Kings 3:9; Philippians 1:9–10; 1 John 4:1; Proverbs 2:3–5; Isaiah 11:2–3*

1. Hebrews 5:14 describes discernment as the mark of maturity. In what areas of your life do you see spiritual immaturity, and how might those areas be affecting your ability to discern truth from deception?
2. Recall a moment when the Holy Spirit gave you a gentle warning or internal check. How did you respond at the time, and what do you now understand that you didn't then?
3. Solomon asked for an "understanding heart." What motivates your desire for discernment: purity, fear,

pride, or love? How might the Holy Spirit be inviting you into a deeper purification of motives?
4. Philippians 1:9-10 teaches that love and discernment work together. How can genuine love sharpen rather than cloud your discernment? Who in your life requires both tenderness and clarity from you right now?
5. Modern culture often cloaks deception in language that sounds compassionate or progressive. Where have you personally seen truth blurred or compromised? How did it affect your spirit?
6. Discernment is not suspicion. Where have you confused fear or past hurt with spiritual insight? What would it look like to surrender that to the Holy Spirit?
7. What practices (Scripture study, prayer, quietness, wise counsel) can you establish to train your spiritual senses to recognize God's voice more quickly and confidently?
8. Reflect on Proverbs 2:3–5. How intentionally do you "seek discernment as treasure"? What must shift in your daily life to pursue it wholeheartedly?
9. Discernment also helps us recognize the hand of God, not just the schemes of the enemy. What blessings or opportunities have you hesitated to embrace because you didn't recognize God in them?
10. What relationships, media influences, or environments may be dulling your discernment, and what boundaries is the Holy Spirit prompting you to set?

Chapter 3 — Signs & Wonders
Scripture Focus: *Mark 16:17–18; Acts 4:29–31; John 4:48; Exodus 14:13–31; Hebrews 2:4; Psalm 77:14*
1. When you review these passages, what consistent purposes of signs and wonders do you see? How do they point to God rather than to people?
2. Jesus rebuked those who demanded a sign. In your own walk, have you ever desired the miracle more than the Miracle Worker? What did that reveal about your heart?

3. Why do humility and purity safeguard believers who witness or desire to operate in the supernatural? How can you cultivate both?
4. Recall a miracle you have witnessed or heard of that deeply impacted you. How did it glorify Christ and strengthen your faith?
5. Sometimes the greatest wonders are quiet or unseen. What signs of God's presence have you overlooked because they did not fit your expectations?
6. What fears or misconceptions have hindered you from stepping out in faith to pray for healing, deliverance, or breakthrough?
7. In Acts 4, boldness and miracles were tied together. How does fear of man hinder the flow of the supernatural in your life?
8. What is the danger of sensationalism, seeking experiences for emotional excitement rather than spiritual edification?
9. How can you develop a posture of expectancy that honors God's sovereignty but refuses unbelief?
10. In what ways might God be calling you to believe for the impossible in your own life, family, or ministry right now?

Chapter 4 — Supernatural Senses
Scripture Focus: *2 Corinthians 4:18; Hebrews 11:1; John 10:27; Ephesians 1:17–18; Psalm 119:18; Revelation 3:22*
1. What does it practically mean to "see the unseen"? How do your spiritual senses help you interpret reality differently from your natural senses?
2. Which spiritual sense (seeing, hearing, feeling, knowing, etc.) has God awakened most in you? How have you noticed this in your prayer or worship life?
3. What habits, sins, distractions, or emotional patterns tend to dull your spiritual perception? What steps can you take to remove them?

4. The Holy Spirit sanctifies imagination, intuition, and perception. Where does your imagination need cleansing or reorienting, so it aligns with God rather than fear or fantasy?
5. How can you guard your senses from counterfeit spiritual experiences or emotional impulses masquerading as revelation?
6. What practices help keep your spiritual senses sharp: fasting, quietness, Scripture meditation, worship, or community?
7. In what ways does awareness of the unseen realm change the way you pray for your family, church, or community?
8. Have you ever dismissed something the Holy Spirit was showing you because it didn't make sense naturally? How can you grow in trust?
9. How can you better distinguish between the Holy Spirit's voice and your own thoughts or emotions?
10. What specific area in your life currently requires you to see with "eyes of eternity" rather than through temporary circumstances?

Chapter 5 — The Prophetic
Scripture Focus: *1 Corinthians 14:1–3; Amos 3:7; John 16:13; Romans 12:6; Joel 2:28; Revelation 19:10*

1. According to Scripture, what is the primary purpose of prophecy, and how can you ensure your desire for the prophetic aligns with God's heart rather than personal ambition?
2. How does the gift of prophecy differ from the office of a prophet, and why is understanding this distinction crucial for avoiding error or pride?
3. Reflect on a prophetic word you gave or received. How has time, Scripture, or fruit confirmed or corrected your understanding of it?

4. How do humility, accountability, and submission to spiritual authority protect prophetic ministry from deception or misuse?
5. What should your response be when a prophetic word does not unfold in the expected way? How can this deepen your dependence on God rather than discourage you?
6. How can prophecy build intimacy with Jesus rather than draw attention to the vessel delivering the word?
7. What fears or insecurities hinder you from stepping out in prophetic obedience?
8. How do you discern whether what you are sensing is a revelation from the Holy Spirit or a projection of your own thoughts or desires?
9. What relational or emotional wounds might distort how you hear God's voice, and how can the Holy Spirit heal those places?
10. How can you cultivate a lifestyle that is sensitive to the Holy Spirit's whisper throughout the day?

Chapter 6 — Imagination

Scripture Focus: *2 Corinthians 10:5; Romans 12:2; 2 Corinthians 5:7; Philippians 4:8; Ephesians 3:20; Psalm 19:14*

1. How does imagination serve as a spiritual faculty when surrendered to the Holy Spirit? How have you seen your imagination either strengthen your faith or feed your fears?
2. What patterns or thought cycles in your mind need to be taken captive according to 2 Corinthians 10:5?
3. Where have you allowed imagination to drift into anxiety, fantasy, or distraction? What might repentance look like in this area?
4. How does walking by faith require a sanctified imagination that sees beyond temporary circumstances to eternal truth?

5. What daily habits (Scripture meditation, gratitude, worship) help renew your thought life according to Romans 12:2?
6. In prayer or worship, how does your imagination help you behold the Lord? What parts of this experience need refinement or deeper surrender?
7. What influences (media, relationships, environments) shape your imagination in unhealthy ways, and what boundaries is God asking you to set?
8. How can you partner with the Holy Spirit to cultivate divine creativity and revelation through your imagination?
9. Are there dreams or visions God gave you in the past that you laid down due to discouragement or unbelief?
10. What practical steps can you take to guard your imagination from deception, comparison, or worldly influences?

Chapter 7 — Angels: The Lord of Hosts and His Ministering Spirits

Scripture Focus: *Psalm 91:11; Hebrews 1:14; 2 Kings 6:17; Revelation 5:11–12; Psalm 103:20; Daniel 10*

1. What do the Scriptures above reveal about the nature, hierarchy, and responsibilities of angels? How does this broaden your understanding of the unseen realm?
2. Why is acknowledging angelic ministry important, yet seeking or glorifying angels dangerous?
3. Reflect on a time when you sensed divine protection or intervention. How might angels have been involved, according to Psalm 91:11?
4. In 2 Kings 6, Elisha prayed for his servant's eyes to be opened. What spiritual battles surround you that you may be unaware of?
5. What characteristics of angels, obedience, reverence, and swiftness, challenge you in your own walk with God?

6. In Daniel 10, spiritual resistance delayed angelic movement. What does this reveal about persistence in prayer?
7. How can awareness of angelic presence cultivate greater awe of God's sovereignty and authority?
8. What misconceptions about angels have you carried, and how does Scripture correct them?
9. What role do angels play in spiritual warfare, and how does understanding this affect how you pray?
10. How can you remain Christ-centered while being aware of the heavenly help assigned to you?

Chapter 8 — The Bride: The Call to Holiness and the Fear of the Lord

Scripture Focus: *Ephesians 5:25–27; Revelation 19:7–8; Proverbs 9:10; Matthew 25:1–13; 1 Peter 1:15–16; Isaiah 66:2*

1. What does it mean to be the Bride of Christ in your daily walk, not just in theological understanding?
2. How does holiness prepare you for deeper intimacy with Jesus, and what areas of compromise is the Holy Spirit calling you to surrender?
3. What are common ways modern Christianity reshapes Jesus into a version that accommodates human comfort rather than calling for repentance?
4. Reflect on what it truly means to take the Lord's Name in truth, not in vain. How does this deepen your understanding of covenant?
5. How does the fear of the Lord liberate you from fear of man? Identify specific situations where fear of man has influenced your decisions.
6. What spiritual disciplines help cultivate reverence and purity in a culture consumed with self?
7. In the parable of the ten virgins, what does it mean to keep your lamp filled with oil? Where do you sense your flame needs tending?

8. What does Jesus desire His Bride to look like, according to Ephesians 5:27? How does this challenge your current spiritual condition?
9. How does the fear of the Lord increase wisdom and discernment in your decisions?
10. What practical steps can you take to walk in purity of heart, speech, and conduct this week?

Chapter 9 — Witchcraft in Culture
Scripture Focus: *Galatians 5:19–21; Deuteronomy 18:10–12; 1 Samuel 15:23; 2 Corinthians 11:14; Acts 8:9–24; Isaiah 8:19*

1. How have you seen witchcraft and occult imagery become normalized in entertainment, social media, and culture? What impact has this had on spiritual sensitivity?
2. What subtle forms of witchcraft, control, manipulation, and rebellion are most likely to appear in Christian environments? Have any shown up in your own life?
3. Reflect on how rebellion is described as "the sin of witchcraft." Where might you need repentance or deeper surrender to God's order?
4. Why is it dangerous to mix occult practices, even unknowingly, with Christian faith?
5. How can discernment help you detect spiritual counterfeits that appear harmless or even "positive"?
6. Describe a moment when the Holy Spirit convicted you about something you once saw as harmless. What changed your perspective?
7. What does repentance look like for those who have dabbled in, exposed themselves to, or come into agreement with occult practices?
8. How can you cultivate a lifestyle that resists deception and stands firm in biblical truth?
9. What voices, influences, or content do you need to remove from your life to maintain purity of spirit?

10. How can you intercede for others who are entangled in spiritual deception?

Chapter 10 — The New Age Deception
Scripture Focus: *Genesis 3:4–5; 2 Corinthians 11:3–4; Colossians 2:8; Isaiah 42:8; Romans 1:25; Jeremiah 23:16–17*

1. What similarities exist between the serpent's lie in Eden and the core teachings of New Age philosophy? How does this reveal Satan's unchanging strategy?
2. Why is self-worship at the center of New Age belief, and how does it distort the biblical truth of being God's creation rather than our own god?
3. What New Age practices or ideas have subtly slipped into Christian culture, often disguised as "spiritual growth" or "enlightenment"?
4. How can you lovingly confront New Age deception without pride, fear, or harshness?
5. Which Scriptures most clearly expose the false promise of becoming "your highest self"? Reflect deeply on how these verses anchor you in truth.
6. What vulnerable areas in your life might make New Age ideas appealing—trauma, desire for control, self-esteem wounds, or hunger for experiences?
7. How does deep surrender to Jesus protect you from seeking supernatural encounters outside of God's boundaries?
8. What relationships, influences, or environments might be blurring truth and deception in your life?
9. How can you guard your mind from philosophies that appear wise or positive but oppose the Word of God?
10. What steps can you take to help others who are unknowingly participating in New Age practices?

Chapter 11 — Deliverance and Freedom in Christ

Scripture Focus: *Luke 4:18; John 8:36; Ephesians 6:10–12; James 4:7; Mark 1:23–27; 2 Corinthians 10:3–5*
1. Why is deliverance still necessary for believers today, and how does Jesus' ministry model its importance?
2. What is the difference between oppression, bondage, and possession? Reflect on how the enemy commonly gains access through wounds, agreements, or sin.
3. How does repentance shut the doors the enemy has used? What areas of your life need deeper repentance or renunciation?
4. What role does renewing the mind play in maintaining freedom after deliverance? Identify specific thought patterns the Holy Spirit wants to transform.
5. What fears or misunderstandings have shaped your view of deliverance, and how does Scripture correct them?
6. How can churches operate in deliverance with compassion, humility, and biblical order instead of fear or sensationalism?
7. What spiritual disciplines (fasting, prayer, Scripture, accountability) help guard the freedom Christ has provided?
8. Reflect on a stronghold that used to bind you. How did Jesus break it, and what can you learn from that victory?
9. What lies has the enemy spoken over your identity, and how can truth confront and dismantle them?
10. How is the Holy Spirit teaching you to walk daily in authority, purity, and submission to God?

Final Reflection
1. Which specific truth from this book exposed the greatest area of spiritual vulnerability in your life? How will you intentionally guard that area moving forward?
2. Reflect on the ways the enemy attempted to distort, distract, or deceive you before you learned these truths.

How will you recognize those patterns more quickly now?
3. In what ways has the Holy Spirit matured you through the topics of dreams, visions, discernment, and the supernatural?
4. What part of your thinking has been renewed, and what part still needs ongoing transformation according to Romans 12:2?
5. What disciplines will you put in place to keep your spiritual senses sharp, humble, and submitted?
6. Which counterfeit or deception from our culture did the Holy Spirit most clearly expose to you, and how will you respond?
7. How has your understanding of spiritual warfare changed, and how will that impact how you pray and live?
8. What is one bold step of obedience the Lord is asking you to take as a result of this study?
9. Who in your life needs the truths you've discovered, and how will you steward your influence to help them?
10. Looking ahead, what is the Holy Spirit calling you to pursue, release, or refine in order to walk in deeper intimacy with Jesus?

Walking It Out

The language of God is not confined to pages or moments; it is alive, speaking still, woven into creation, written upon your heart,
and echoing through every breath of those who walk with Him.

As you've journeyed through these chapters,
you've explored the many ways Heaven communicates
and the subtle ways the counterfeit tries to imitate it.
But now comes the most sacred part of the journey—living it.

Carry what you have learned into your daily communion with Him.
Listen for His whisper in the stillness.

Look for His fingerprints in the ordinary.
Speak His truth with purity and boldness.
  The same Spirit who hovered over the waters now rests upon you.
The same voice that called light out of darkness
still calls your name and sends you forth to carry His language into the world.
  May your life become a living sentence in the story of God—
one written by His Spirit, read by all who encounter you,
and spoken with the vocabulary of Heaven.

Final Prayer
  Father,
Thank You for speaking, for revealing, and for drawing us closer to Your heart.
From the beginning, You have desired a relationship with Your creation,
and through Jesus Christ, You restored the conversation between Heaven and earth.
  Teach us to walk as those who carry Your language within.
Let every thought, every word, and every act of our lives.
echo the purity of Your truth and the power of Your presence.
  Open our spiritual senses to discern Your voice clearly—
to see as You see, to hear as You speak,
and to move as Your Spirit leads.
  Guard our hearts from deception and distraction.
Give us courage to expose false light and stand firmly in Your truth.
Let Your Word be the rhythm of our hearts and the language on our lips.
  We surrender our voices to You, Lord.
May our lives declare Your glory,
and may the earth be filled with the sound of Heaven once again.

In the mighty name of Jesus, Amen.

"The grace of our Lord Jesus Christ be with you all. Amen."
Revelation 22:21 (NKJV)

Fellow Saints

Be sanctified, called out, set apart, walking Jacob's ladders, signed, sealed, and delivered, carrying the full, explosive power of your inheritance.

Live for God who formed you in beauty and let your life become His full reward.

Let every breath, action, and thought carry the language of God, Heaven's voice released through a redeemed vessel.

Sounding the alarm—
With a heart submitted,
Your sister in Christ,

Crystal Thomas

Sources & Works Consulted

Alter, Joseph S. Yoga in Modern India: The Body Between Science and Philosophy. Princeton University Press, 2004.

Avalon, Arthur (Sir John Woodroffe). The Serpent Power: The Secrets of Tantric and Shaktic Yoga. Dover Publications, 1974.

Badman, Keith. The Beatles: Off the Record. Omnibus Press, 2008.

Bailey, Alice A. A Treatise on Cosmic Fire. Lucis Publishing Company, 1925.

Bailey, Alice A. A Treatise on White Magic. Lucis Publishing Company, 1934.

Bailey, Alice A. The Externalisation of the Hierarchy. Lucis Publishing Company, 1957.

Bailey, Alice A. The Reappearance of the Christ. Lucis Publishing Company, 1948.

Besant, Annie. Esoteric Christianity. The Theosophical Publishing Society, 1901.

Beyoncé. I Am... Sasha Fierce. Columbia Records, 2008.

Blavatsky, Helena P. Isis Unveiled. J.W. Bouton, 1877.

Blavatsky, Helena P. Lucifer: A Theosophical Magazine. Theosophical Publishing Society, 1887–1897.

Blavatsky, Helena P. The Secret Doctrine. Theosophical Publishing Company, 1888.

Booth, Martin. A Magick Life: The Biography of Aleister Crowley. St. Martin's Press, 2001.

Bowie, David. Interview with Cameron Crowe. Rolling Stone, 12 Feb. 1976.

Brown, Peter. "The Occult Symbolism of Sgt. Pepper." Rolling Stone, 1967.

Cheiro. Cheiro's Book of Numbers. Foulsham, 1926.

Claire Gecewicz. "'New Age' Beliefs Common Among Both Religious And Nonreligious Americans." Pew Research Center, 2018.

Crowley, Aleister. Magick in Theory and Practice. Castle Books, 1929.

Crowley, Aleister. The Book of the Law (Liber AL vel Legis). Ordo Templi Orientis, 1904.

Doniger, Wendy. *The Hindus: An Alternative History.* Penguin Press, 2009.

Edelstein, Emma J., and Ludwig Edelstein. Asclepius: A Collection and Interpretation of the Testimonies. Johns Hopkins University Press, 1998.

Eliade, Mircea. The Myth of the Eternal Return. Princeton University Press, 1954.

Eliade, Mircea. Yoga: Immortality and Freedom. Princeton University Press, 1958.

Ellwood, Robert S. Introducing Religion: From Inside and Outside. Pearson, 2008.

Enoch, 1. The Book Of Enoch. Public Domain Ancient Jewish Text. Referenced For Historical Background Only; Not Considered Scripture.

Feuerstein, Georg. The Yoga Tradition. Hohm Press, 1998.

Feuerstein, Georg. The Yoga Tradition: Its History, Literature, Philosophy, And Practice. Prescott, Hohm Press, 2001.

Ferguson, Marilyn. The Aquarian Conspiracy. J.P. Tarcher, 1980.

Frazer, James George. The Golden Bough. Oxford University Press, 1998.

Govinda, Lama Anagarika. *The Tibetan Book of the Dead.* Oxford University Press, 2000.

Godwin, Joscelyn. The Theosophical Enlightenment. SUNY Press, 1994.

Hanegraaff, Wouter J. New Age Religion and Western Culture. SUNY Press, 1998.

Harrison, George. I Me Mine. Chronicle Books, 2002.

Heelas, Paul. The New Age Movement. Blackwell, 1996.

Hiroshi Doi. Modern Reiki Method for Healing. Iyashino Gakkai, 1998.

Johnson, K. Paul. The Masters Revealed. SUNY Press, 1994.

King, Ursula. Christian Mystics. Simon & Schuster, 1998.

Klostermaier, Klaus K. A Survey of Hinduism. SUNY Press, 1994.

LaVey, Anton Szandor. The Satanic Bible. Avon Books, 1969.

Lavey, Anton Quoted In Blanche Barton, The Church Of Satan (Los Angeles: Hell's Kitchen Productions, 1990), 107.

Lewis, James R., ed. The Encyclopedic Sourcebook of New Age Religions. Prometheus Books, 2003.

Melton, J. Gordon. New Age Encyclopedia. Gale Research, 1990.

Miles, Barry. Many Years From Now. Henry Holt, 1997.

Nir, Y., & Tononi, G. (2010). *Dreaming and the brain: From phenomenology to neurophysiology.* Trends in Cognitive Sciences, 14(2), 88-100. Retrieved from PMC.

Nutton, Vivian. Ancient Medicine. Routledge, 2004.

Ono, Yoko. Interview by David Sheff. Playboy Magazine, 1981.

Page, Jimmy. Jimmy Page by Jimmy Page. Genesis Publications, 2010.

Partridge, Christopher. New Religions: A Guide. Oxford University Press, 2004.
Pasi, Marco. Aleister Crowley and the Temptation of Politics. Acumen, 2014.
Rahula, Walpola. What the Buddha Taught. Grove Press, 1974.
Singleton, Mark. Yoga Body. Oxford University Press, 2010.
Stein, Diane. Essential Reiki. Crossing Press, 1995.
Strong, James. Strong's Exhaustive Concordance of the Bible. Thomas Nelson, 1890.
Sutcliffe, Phil. "Jimmy Page's Occult World." Guitar World Magazine, 1995.
The Rolling Stones. Their Satanic Majesties Request. London Records, 1967.
Turner, Steve. The Gospel According to the Beatles. Westminster John Knox Press, 2006.
Vivekananda, Swami. Raja Yoga. The Vedanta Society, 1896.
Walsh, Michael. The Devil's Music. Eerdmans, 2015.
Washington, Peter. Madame Blavatsky's Baboon: A History of the Mystics, Mediums, and Misfits Who Brought Spiritualism to America. Schocken Books, 1995.
Weiner, Matthew. "Madonna and the Kabbalah Revival." Time Magazine, 2004.
White, David Gordon. Kiss of the Yogini. University of Chicago Press, 2003.
Yogananda, Paramahansa. Autobiography of a Yogi. Self-Realization Fellowship, 1946.

About the Author

Crystal Thomas is a teacher, equipper, and deliverer devoted to awakening the Body of Christ to the voice of God and the realities of His Kingdom. As a messenger of divine truth and a prophetic voice, she carries a mantle of boldness. Her assignment is to release truth that pierces, purifies, and ultimately restores the heart of God's people.

Crystal is unwavering in her commitment to proclaim profound and transformative truths that ignite spiritual awakening within the Bride of Christ. With steadfast resolve, she exposes and dismantles demonic strongholds, exalts the holy name of Yahweh, and calls God's people back to their true identity—measured by the eternal plumbline of His Word.

Her mission is to inspire a passionate response to the clarion call of purity, holiness, deliverance, and a rekindled devotion to our eternal First Love. She longs to see the Church rise as a sanctified Bride, called, redeemed, delivered, and walking the pathways of Heaven as heirs to the Kingdom.

Forged through years of trials, refinement, and intimacy with the Lord, Crystal's anointing has produced a depth of insight that pours out like new wine. She ministers with humility, anchored in a reverent fear of the Lord, and is wholeheartedly committed to equipping believers to understand and walk in the sacred language of God. Her life message is simple yet profound: every believer can live in supernatural communion with the One who created them.

Crystal serves her growing community through writing, teaching, and online ministry at **crystalthomasministry.com**. Her heartbeat is to see God's people strengthened, delivered, and fully awake, embodying their divine identity as sons and daughters of the Most High.